MANCHESTER CITY F.C. MILLENNIUM SQUAD

KEVIN KEEGAN FLYING THE FLAG FOR MANCHESTER CITY

Book enquiries and orders
to

THE MANAGERESS, BLACKWELLS
THE PRECINCT CENTRE
OXFORD ROAD
MANCHESTER
M13 9RW

Tel: 0161 274 3331
Fax: 0161 274 3228
Email: manchester@blackwellsbookshops.co.uk

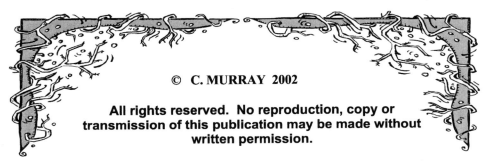

ISBN 0-9520520-9-1 (Paperback)

British Library Cataloguing in
Publication Data
Murray C.
Attitude Blue

DEDICATION

To Grandson Joel Murray who insisted I re-write and re-launch this book for him and his dedicated City fans.

CHRIS MURRAY PUBLICATIONS
16 Liskeard Drive
Bramhall
Stockport
Cheshire SK7 2JA
England
Tel: 0161 439 8252

CONTENTS

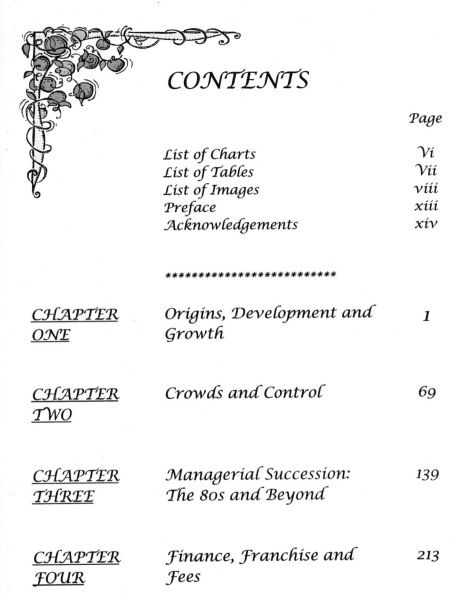

LIST OF CHARTS

LIST OF TABLES

LIST OF IMAGES*

* Acknowledgements with each caption

Chapter Two

Chapter Three

Chapter Four

PREFACE

The comments furnished by the previous Chairmen of the Club, Peter Swales and Francis Lee for an earlier edition of the book are still relevant to the current one and may be provided as follows:

"The problems that any football club encounters on a daily basis are usually adequately dealt with by staff in the normal course of their duties, however, we at Manchester City recognise that there are occasions when an outside party such as Doctor Chris Murray, formerly of Manchester University's School of Education may look at a particular aspect of the club's functioning in a detached and informative way. He has had considerable experience in researching crowd behaviour at Maine Road and other grounds since the mid 70's and I have pleasure in introducing this book to you. We look forward to facing the 1990's with spectators in an 'all seated' stadium and trust we will continue to provide entertainment and value to what Chris Murray calls the focused crowd. I commend the book to you."

PETER SWALES
Late Chairman

"I am particularly pleased that this book, while being suitable for the general reader, has an educational focus. Our society is increasingly laying emphasis on the importance of schooling and qualifications and these pages should provide students with an informative and accessible guide, especially in the Social Sciences. In the hands of a trained teacher good use can be made of much of the material in many areas of the curriculum.

Enjoy reading Attitude Blue...."

FRANCIS LEE
Past Chairman

ACKNOWLEDGMENTS

I would like to thank and acknowledge the help afforded to me by personnel, at various levels of Manchester City FC. Their contribution is clear in terms of the comments and views expressed in largely unedited form, which appear in the following pages. The Greater Manchester Police and The Professional Footballer's Association have been very open and supportive in agreeing to their members being interviewed and by showing a generalised interest in my work. My indebtedness to the Economic and Social Research Council (formerly SSRC) and Sports Council, (now Sport England) who initiated the research in the late 1970's, is long standing. Manchester University Research Committee helped support the project at an early stage.

My thanks to City's architects, Howard & Seddon, need to be put on record as does my appreciation of the images and information supplied to me by Sir Robert McAlpine Ltd, their Maine Road builders. More recently, Arup and Arup Associates and Laing Construction has offered me every facility with regard to documenting the impending move of Manchester City from Maine Road to the City of Manchester Staduim and this has been ably supplemented by the press office and responsible offices and elected officials of Manchester City Council. In terms of book production and word processing, I am indebted to Prontaprint of Stockport and Jackie of REISS Independent of Wilmslow, who desktop published the work and suggested many innovative ways of portraying my basic typographical forms to make them more interesting. Others who supplied images and textual comment, apart from Arup and Arup Associates, are the Manchester Evening News and Manchester City's Official Magazine and City Life: Manchester Central Library 'Local Studies' section and Greater Manchester Public Records Office.

To all the above, many thanks. However, it needs to be said at the outset, in order to minimise any risk of misunderstanding regarding

the status of this book, it is not a publication of Manchester University where I taught and researched from 1972-2000 as Director of Youth Studies nor is it currently required reading for a particular course run by them; rather it is an independently produced work by myself as author and researcher: as such the book is not to be confused or associated with any official Manchester City club merchandise. No personality, management or representative of the club has at any time been involved in the approval of its content.

Finally, as with the companion volume to this book, 'Manchester United at the Millennium', my indebtedness to the football fan has a degree of poignancy in that this case study of a soccer organisation can only partially portray the rich complexity of 'everyday football life' today and as it was in years gone by; its inadequacies in this regard are fully acknowledged and remain with the author.

Chris Murray

CHAPTER ONE ⚮

ORIGINS, DEVELOPMENT AND GROWTH

What! Manchester City as a cricket club? Yes, strange as it may sound, that's how it all began! Interested? Then read on. Cast your mind back to the closing quarter of the 19th Century as Manchester flexed its industrial muscle and spawned heavy industry with the associated terraced houses and factories which determined the lifestyle of so many of its citizens. Clowes Street in West Gorton, only a couple of miles from the City Centre, was home to St Mark's Church which attempted to alleviate the appalling living conditions of its parishioners by organising social activities which would in some way compensate for the bleakness of industrial life in what is now defined as 'the inner city'. One such activity was a cricket team for the men, initiated in 1879, which, with them playing football in the off-season, became the seedcorn from which Manchester City FC and then PLC grew. Known as St Mark's (West Gorton), it was nurtured by one William Beastow who was a company secretary at the local iron works, situated virtually one hundred yards from St Mark's and who saw the virtue in attracting players from his workforce. The men had to be hardy, because their first pitch was a croft adjacent to the ironworks which lacked amenities of any kind. The first reported game was a 2-1 loss, no cynical remarks please!, against a Baptist Church from Macclesfield on 13th November 1880 with the final game being against Stalybridge Clarence on the 15th March 1981, the clubs one and only victory that season! Thus, though the club was forged locally, football being intertwined with the spiritual and industrial fibres of men's existence at that time, it also involved travel, even during the first season, to what were then such faraway places at Stalybridge and Macclesfield. Faraway places but easily reached by rail with stations at Gorton and Ardwick, which were within easy walking distance of the players homes or, if they felt so disposed, travel by tram to the station which ran along Clowes St. In some respects, such places were more easily accessed then, than in the Millennium!

From November 1881, the club began to outgrow its humble beginning and over the next seven years played under the name of West Gorton (St Mark's), showing a weakening affiliation with the church, by it being placed in parenthesis, and then Gorton AFC. A number of grounds were used before the club moved to Bennett St, Hyde Rd in 1887 where it stayed until finding a new home in Maine Road in 1923. Gary James, in his seminal encyclopaedic history of the club, 'Manchester the Greatest City' (1997, Polar) – a book which we will return to from time to time – comments about this early period:

> **"... although only four match reports exist for the 1984/85 season, the Annual Dinner was reported in the Gorton Advertiser and provides an interesting insight into the success of the team during that first season. Virtually all the names mentioned in that article had links with the clubs' earliest formation at St Mark's and .... Interestingly, the senior committee men and driving force behind the club were James Moores and William Beastow. Moores was the senior churchwarden at St Mark's and a member of the Union Iron Works Board of Directors, while Beastow also maintained influential positions at both organisations. Both the welfare of the community and the leisure pursuits available were important in helping to establish a satisfied workforce.**
>
> **Beastow himself had tried to provide identity for the Gorton Team in October 1884, by presenting them with a complete set of black jerseys emblazoned with a white cross.* The cross was significant as it signalled the St Mark's connection was still there, while at the same time, the name Gorton emphasised that the side aimed to represent the whole of the district."**

The land at Ardwick originally belonged to the Manchester, Sheffield and Lincolnshire Railway Company and was rented for £10 to cover seven months of the year. By the summer of 1987, the ground was ready and the club adopted the name of the district in

* A photographic impression of this Gorton side in the new kit referred to above, is provided at the conclusion of this chapter.

which it was now located and became Ardwick AFC; situated under half a mile from its original home at St Mark's.*

Reference is made to City's HQ being the Hyde Road Hotel at this time, with the first ever meeting being held there during which a member of an influential local brewing family, Stephen Chesters-Thompson was installed as Honorary President of the club. An association which was to become mutually beneficial, with Chester's brewery deriving revenues from the increased custom at the Hyde Road Hotel on match days and, in the fullness of time, from the 'refreshment points' within the ground which catered largely for a beer drinking middle class and proletariat; the bowler and cloth hat brigades. The notice of the inaugural meeting is shown in Chart 1, typed in the form in which it originally appeared.

The ground was ready for the opening fixture scheduled for the 10th September 1887 against Salford AFC but anticlimax ensued with Salford failing to turn up; the 'grand opening' was a non-event! The first game was in fact played the following week but crowd trouble marred early season performances with a 1-0 defeat by Edenfield, on 26th November 1887, being accompanied by the visitors 'being stoned off the field', (James, Gorton Reporter). However, with the support of Chesters Brewery, a grandstand was built capable of holding 1,000 spectators and the ground began to sport pay boxes – the forerunners of turnstiles, thus producing 'gate money'.

The attraction of professional players to the club and ambitions to be regarded as Manchester's Premier Club, was reflected in the club's entry to the FA Cup competition for the first time in the season 1890/91. The following decade was a benchmark one for the club's development with attendances increasing beyond the 5,000 mark. Though still not able to gain access to the League system, Ardwick did manage to gain acceptance to the next best alternative, the Alliance, alongside Newton Heath (Manchester United); the beginning of the 'derby' rivalry between the two clubs thus began, with the first such match occurring in the 1891/92 season.

* A map of the City as at the present day with a sketch plan of the Hyde Road ground in Ardwick as it was in the 1890's aligned to it, is included at the end of this chapter.

ARDWICK

ASSOCIATION FOOTBALL CLUB

HYDE ROAD HOTEL

ARDWICK, August 23rd, 1887

Sir

Having formed a Club under the above title and secured a Ground situate between the L.N.W. Railway and Galloways' Works, in Bennett Street, Hyde Road, we have decided to hold a M eeting in connection with the same at the above Hotel on Tuesday next, the 30th inst., at 8p.m. prompt.

The bearer of this Circular will be glad to give you all particulars you may require respecting the prospects of the Club.

Hoping you will give this your favourable consideration.

We are, Sir,

Yours respectfully,

W. CHEW. Hon Sec.
J. H. WARD Pro Temp.

N.B. Your attendance at the Meeting will be greatly esteemed.

In 1892/93, the League system was modified with sixteen clubs forming a First Division and twelve in a Second; the Ardwick club gaining admittance to the latter with Newton Heath being voted straight into the First Division. During this time, some stability was provided for the club with Chesters Brewery taking over the lease of the ground from them and then sub-letting it back for football. Accompanying this change, was a change in name with Manchester City Football Club Ltd becoming a registered company with that name, on 16th April 1894. Expansion and diversification continued and transfers became the order of the day. A star Welsh player called Meredith, made his second appearance in a derby game against Newton Heath, who had been relegated from the First Division, on November 3rd 1994 only for City to be defeated 5-2 before a crowd of 14,000 in what was billed in the local paper, 'The Championship of Cottonopolis'.

In the following season, a crowd of 20,000 watched the Derby with consequent increase in revenue and interest; the biggest attendance being 30,000 for a Good Friday (1896) fixture against Liverpool in a Division Two championship decider. James reports:

"... by this point, City supporters were famous for creating a carnival-like atmosphere at big games.... Regularly during the 1890's the supporters played bugles and drums when the Blues attacked and would occasionally wear fancy dress.... This carnival spirit helped lift many a game for the blues and the noise and fervour all added to the experience of being a Blue. Without this atmosphere, even on the brightest of days, Hyde Road must have provided a very real picture of gloomy, dreary industrial Manchester; a tightly packed ground surrounded by terraced streets, factories and railway viaducts. 'Typical Manchester' many would say but then it has always been the people, and in particular the City supporters, who have brightened this part of the industrial city."

City's increased revenue from the growing crowds was used, in part, to build dressing rooms in a joint venture with Chesters Brewery. This culminated in 1897 with a Grand Stand syndicate being formed to raise funds to erect a new covered stand. The result being the purchase of a stand from the Fulham Pageant for

£1,500, it's transportation to Manchester and its re-erection as the main stand at Hyde Road. Manchester City had arrived; transformed from a scratch, church cricket team to a major league soccer company, with its own grandstand, in just short of two decades and not above a half mile between both events, though separated in time by some twenty years. Paralleling this development, came further changes in the league structure with the 1898/99 season being the first to see automatic promotion and relegation with the test matches (play-offs) between the top and bottom clubs of the two Divisions, being discontinued.

While Newton Heath (Manchester United) often appeared superior to Manchester City when they met on the field of play, it must be remembered for the record, that during the decade from the season 1894/95 to that of 1904/05, City was Manchester's Premier club both in terms of home attendance and senior league football; in the eleven seasons, they played in the First Division five times (1899/00, 1900/01, 1901/02, 1903/04 and 1904/05), whereas Newton Heath played their football in the Second Division during the whole of this period; a reversal of the position in the late 1990's some one hundred years later. During this period Manchester City reached new heights winning the FA Cup in 1904* and beginning 'end of season' tours in Europe, which were to further their reputation internationally.

Continued success led to a re-appraisal of the Hyde Road venue. Perhaps we can reflect the thinking of the times by quoting at length from James:

> **"Although everything was bright on the pitch, there were a few concerns off it. There was a belief that Hyde Road was not good enough for First Division football. No matter what the club did to improve the facilities, it would always be a cramped ground. Access was restricted to two sides and the shape of the enclosure made the erection of huge stands almost impossible. Because of potential problems with the large crowds City expected in the First Division, the club**

A photograph of the Cup winning side of 1904 is placed at the end of this chapter.

management looked at what was available further down Hyde Road at Belle Vue.

Belle Vue was a huge pleasure gardens and entertainment centre. Like City, it offered Mancunians a release from the daily grind – and was hugely popular. Alongside the pleasure gardens was the Belle Vue Athletics track, which had played host to the floodlit friendly between Ardwick and Newton Heath in 1889. This ground offered potential. Already it was a popular sporting venue, was relatively close to City's Hyde Road ground and was only yards away from the St Mark's church hall where City were founded. It had perfect access, was capable of holding between forty and fifty thousand and seemed to offer everything that Hyde Road did not. However, for some unknown reason it was decided to stay at Hyde Road and erect the Fulham Pageant stand. Perhaps Chesters were keen to keep their investment in Ardwick. The Belle Vue venue may not have offered the brewery as many money making opportunities, or maybe everyone associated with the club, simply felt Hyde Road was home and that it should be given at least one more season. After all, both the club and brewery knew the ground rental could not increase for another four years, thanks to the agreement struck the previous year, and that Hyde Road had become an established football ground.

Whatever the reason, City decided to refurbish Hyde Road ready for top flight soccer. They wanted to be a real credit to Manchester and although Newton Heath had featured in the First Division in 1892 to 1894, City were proud of the fact they were the first of the two Manchester sides to reach Division One on merit. All they needed to do now was prove how a successful Manchester side could benefit football."

Such proof was directly demonstrable in 1900, the dawn of the 20th Century, with the 1887 stand replaced by a new one which could accommodate 4,000 fans under cover, better turnstiles and office accommodation, plus Russian and Turkish baths for the players. The scene was set for the visit of England's political and aristocratic leaders. Future Prime Minister and local MP, A.J.

Balfour,* visited Hyde Road in September 1900 to witness City's 2-0 victory over Stoke – well to be completely accurate, not quite, as he left at half-time! With regard to the photograph referred to in the footnote, the reader will note the mix of classes in the main stand; the bowler and cloth cap being the irrefutable insignia of the middle and working classes: Chesters refreshment bar is also prominently featured. During the same year, Edward VII visited Hyde Road. Manchester had certainly been put on the political map by the prominence of its then, premier football team. It is little wonder that given this national prominence, the club decided in 1910 to improve the ground still further and erected multi-span covered stands providing shelter for a near capacity of 35,000 spectators. A further royal visit by King George V in 1920, to witness City's 2-1 victory over Liverpool and seven months later when the main stand was destroyed by fire, indicated the prominence of the club in the nation's life.

The consequences of the fire and the continual problem of access and egress from the ground along the Bennett St frontage for thousands of spectators on home match days, eventually led to a move. The move was not to Belle Vue, which seemed 'natural' as we have discussed previously – the site of eight acres was deemed too small and the available lease of fifty years too short – but to a purpose built stadium on a sixteen acre site in Moss Side; a tip and clay pit surrounded by terraced houses, but approachable on all sides by the most efficient form of transport then available, the tram car. A form of transport being recently reintroduced to Manchester some one hundred years later! A public notice in the Manchester Evening News, giving a plan of the site, describes its accessibility in the following terms:

"Although the site is on the Withington side of the Moss Side border line, it is, from the point of view of accessibility, most conveniently situated. The Greenheys terminus of the

* *His photograph with City Chairman, John Chapman is included at the end of this chapter.*

Manchester tramways is at the corner of the next street on the North Westerly side – Lloyd St – 200 yards away from the plot. Wilmslow Rd, whereby Rusholme, Fallowfield, Palatine Road and Chorlton circular route cars pass to and from the city, is near to the Easterly side of the plot.

The circular route trams from Cheetham Hill via Belle Vue, Dickenson Rd and Great Western Street, pass the Northerly side along the latter named street 300 yards away and on the return journey, via Moss Lane East, the distance is 400 yards from the nearest point.

The tramways committee are at present contemplating opening up another route along Claremont Road, thereby getting a connection with Alexandra Park and Brook's Bar on the Westerly side.

The tramways depot and terminus of the Princess Road route, where cars ran alternatively to Piccadilly and Albert Square, is situate on Princess Road about 600 yards to the West".

The land was purchased for £5,500 and plans laid for a stadium to accommodate 120,000 spectators being developed in two phases; Phase 1, to be ready for the start of the 1923/24 season, was to be a grandstand seating some 15,000 spectators with terracing for 55,000. Phase 2 would extend the terracing and see the erection of a circular 'C' shaped roof over them to join up with the grandstand, thereby increasing the capacity to 120,000 with ingress and egress on all four sides: a forecourt would allow the masses to congregate outside the ground on match days. These plans were eventually scaled down to provide for a stadium, which would accommodate between 80,000 and 90,000 people with the only covered area being the grandstand. It duly opened on August 25th, 1923 with the inaugural match being against Sheffield United with City winning 2-1 before a then record crowd of 56,993. Photographs of the stadium in its pristine state and development stages are included with the pictorial illustrations at the end of this chapter, as is one of Max Woosman, the City Captain introducing the players to the Lord Mayor of Manchester prior to kick-off. Max lived and worked locally and was one of the last 'true blue' amateurs of the period.

So the new stadium was ready for the start of the 1923/24 season. Its impact on the lives of Mancunians at the time, is described in a Manchester Guardian editorial for August 24th 1923, the Friday before the following days' match; the paper speculates in the prose of the time:

"The opening of the new ground of the Manchester City Football Club at Rusholme on Saturday, is an event of varying impact to different people. How it bulks in the mind of the man who thinks Mr Max Woosnam matters more in Europe at the moment than M. Poincere (French Premier) – the faithful 'follower of City' – can only be faintly apprehended. To him, weighing it up in a front room in Openshawe, (inner city area), the event must stand on the same plane of significance as the wedding to the bride or a visit from an archbishop to a curate.

At the other end of the scale, it will mean for West Didsbury (opulent suburb), a few quickly forgotten headlines in the papers. Then there are the folk in between – the good people of Longsight who are going to miss big factions of twenty or thirty thousand people charging by their doors to Hyde Road every Saturday, and the equally good folk of Rusholme, who are going to be presented with that gratuitous spectacle every week. What regret there may be in one case and what satisfaction in the other, who can tell?

The change is not a matter of indifference to some others – the tramway authorities and the police. There may be fifty thousand people waiting to get to that oval of concrete in Maine Road, Rusholme on Saturday and within the memory of man, fifty thousand people have never been wanted to go in bulk to Rusholme. There is, at all events a sufficient network of streets about the ground, to provide adequate conduits for such a multitude, but the chief problem is how to transport them to Rusholme. The tramway authorities intend to be on the right side in one respect. They are going to run twice as many cars as they usually do for a football match – that is 150 as against 80 or 90. What the authorities cannot gauge is the extent to which the various routes will be used and therefore all Saturday's arrangements must be largely experimental. The quickest route is through Greeheys, but there is only a single track that way. Wilmslow Rd and Princess Rd are the best alternative routes from town. The fullest provisions are being made for, through car services from all points wide of the city proper and in course of time, it is hoped to construct an ancillary route along Morton St to Great Western St and to provide sidings at Platt Lane.

Mr Magnall, the secretary of Manchester City Football Club, considers it an advantage rather than otherwise that there is no train terminus immediately outside the ground. It prevents any bombarding of the gates in mass and brings a crowd on gradually, in numbers more easily coped with. Both in exits and turnstiles, the new ground, says Mr Magnall, is much better equipped for dealing with great crowds than the old".

So much for the impact of relocating professional football on an urban environment, but what about the perceptions of those attending? What was it like participating in City match days at that time? We can draw on two sources to answer these questions. The first is an anonymous reporter for the Manchester Guardian, who wrote up the first match, but largely dwelled on stadium impact rather than the match per se. The second, is that of Sidney Rose, the club's Life-President, who attended his first match at Maine Road in 1929 and recalls the experience in an interview for Manchester City's official magazine in August 1999. To take the Guardian report first (August 23rd, 1927 p.7), under the heading 'Manchester City's new home – a symbol of size and power', the reader is conveyed to the scene in the following terms:

"By one o'clock on Saturday, the football march to Manchester City's ground was in full swing. To a cricket match, unless it be a very important one or holds the prospect of an exciting finish, men walk easily and with an air of leisure, but to a football match, they march like an army with a set purpose in their minds and the torment of the excitement to come already moving them. By one way or another, 60,000 of them went to the new ground on Saturday and watched a fast and lively game. This ground is the last word in the provision of comfort and security for (and against) the explosive force of the great crowds that follow the League teams.

There is something almost barbaric in the impression which, when it is full, it makes on the observer. As one comes on it suddenly from Claremont Rd, a great rounded embankment towers up in front and over it at one side looms the highly arched roof of a stand whose dim recesses cannot be discerned at all except from the ground level. Only the fresh green paint on the front of it, picked out with gold, detracts from the broad impression of size and power giving a rather incongruous air of neatness and modernity.

Looking out from this stand, whose roof is happily so far removed that the air blows freely through, the spectator faces an enormous stretch of terracing which at the highest point has close on 110 tiers of steps; on the flanks it falls gently away to a somewhat lower level behind the goals. With between twenty and thirty thousand people filling this great slope, there is to be seen a continuous sea of faces broken only by two great concrete pits in the centre and two tunnels at the end into which the many-headed monster is to disappear when the game is done. With the crowd actually there, with nothing to be seen but its heads and these pits and the containing wall, also of concrete which bars it from the field of play, one cannot doubt that it is indeed the monster Hydra for whom the architect has made sumptuous but fearless provision. "Come in", he says, "come in and take your ease, but here, inside these barriers, you stay and by these pits and tunnels, quietly and quickly, you depart". This scheme, in its simplicity and great scale, suggests power and force in the way that a pyramid does, or a Babylonian tower and there could scarcely be a better scheme to represent the passionate concentration of fifty or eighty thousand men and women on the fortunes of the field below. The grandioso effect is amusingly diminished by the small concrete enclosures, which are established at the base of either end of the great slopes. On a sunken seat in each sit two policemen and two first-aid men, their upper halves showing quaintly across the field, like little marionettes or toy soldiers guarding some pre-historic keep.

But it would puzzle the most fanciful to find much of Manchester about the ground. At Old Trafford, the follower of 'United' stands within sight and sound of the life and energy of the Ship Canal and Trafford Park. The former 'City' pitch, like that of Newton Heath in the old days, lay in the heart of industrial Manchester in its darkest form. At Maine Road you may look around and see two spires in the distance, a tower and a tall chimney and for the rest, the roofs of a few score houses filling the skyline where the great terrace drops away. You might be in Clungerford or Clun except for the internal evidence upon the ground. The grandstand by itself is an elaborate mechanism only to be afforded by the rich town club. For long after the match was over, curious crowds explored its many staircases by which the holders of all sorts of tickets are conducted without fail or confusion to their various seats. The topmost section sits aloof and remote at an incredible distance from the field. Like a squall falling suddenly from the hills, its clapping came at times in sudden gusts from far away.

The game was good League football, played on the happiest green turf as hardly and well as though the game had never stopped in April. There were few really young men on either side but in athletics, the day for youth and grace seems to have gone for the time. In cricket and football, experience and stamina count for as much and football runs to weight and 'build' and heavy shoulders. There can never have been so many half-bald heads in the two games as there are now and the veterans hold their own. The only sign of the beginning of the season was that the players were not quite so melodramatic as they will be when the crowd's blood is up, though when a corner is to be taken there seems always to be six captains on one side and half a dozen on the other and the extravagance with which a team throws itself on the colleague who has happened to score a goal would bring a blush to the cheek of the average schoolboy, that admirable standard of reserve.

Sidney Rose begins his account:

"On Friday 29th March 1929, Good Friday, I was taken by an old family friend and stalwart City supporter to see my first full match at Maine Road. Our old friends and rivals, Bolton Wanderers, who had beaten us the FA Cup final of 1926, were our opponents that day. We joined the excited but orderly crowds walking down Claremont Road, all similarly attired in the customary flat caps, mufflers and macs.

There was a smattering of blue and white scarves on the lucky few who could afford them. All the boys were in short pants. There were very few cars but a multitude of bikes. The exuberant crowd often spilled into the centre of the road. City and Bolton fans mingled indiscriminately. There was some good natured chivvying, but no aggro.

We passed the many signs offering to mind bicycles for a penny. There was the same sense of mounting tension that we all still feel today as kick-off time approaches. We turned off Claremont Road at Yew Street and crossed the St Edward's School playground to the turnstiles set in the high wall at the back of the Kippax. It cost me 6d. (2½p) to get in.

We made our way across a stretch of rough ground to the tunnel in the stand which was situated directly opposite the centre line and I was pushed through to the front until I was just behind the low whitewashed wall, where I had a wonderfully wide view at pitch level. The open terraces of the Kippax rose behind me to what seemed a frightening height. It was twenty five minutes to kick-off and the Manchester City Police Band in their dark blue uniforms faced the main stand playing its repertoire of military marches and popular tunes of the day, including 'Sonny Boy' from The Singing Fool, Al Jolson's first 'talkie' picture which was showing at the New Oxford Cinema.

The main stand covered the four central blocks only, but this was one of the most modern grounds in the country. It rivalled the newly built Wembley itself. We used the latest methods of communication with the crowd. Two men in white coats carried a long placard round the touchline with team changes, while another little group in opposite corners of the ground (to the right of the stand and the left of the Kippax) put the finishing touches to the placement of letters A to W on the black slates, next to which are the numbers 0-0 ready for the half-time and full-time scores.

The main score board was situated at the back of the mound now occupied by the North Stand. A few youths in white coats sold bags of sweets. With ten minutes to go, the band marched off with a final flourish. The stand seats were now full and I saw the empty seats in the directors' box beginning to fill with those august bowler-hatted dignitaries who directed the fortunes of the club.

They gazed benignly down on the crowd with justifiable pride. They commanded unquestioned respect from all and sundry, the public, the players and everyone in their employ.

By now, there were just seven minutes to go and a mighty roar from the 45,000 crowd greeted the City team in their spotlessly clean light blue shirts and floppy white shorts, the blue and white socks bulging with enormous shin pads. They ran on the pitch with confident arrogance and kicked the heavy leather ball about with deceptive ease.

Bolton received marginally less acclaim but obviously had brought good support. We looked for our captain, Sam Cowan, our new stars Freddy Tilson and Eric Brook, signed together the previous season and our old war-horse Johnson, the leading scorer. We settled down to watch the match reassured by their presence.

The captains shook hands, we lost the toss and changed ends and the ball was placed on the spot. It had to be adjusted because the March wind was almost gale force. The whistle blew to an almighty roar of anticipation and we were off. From the word go, it was all City.

After a few brief skirmishes, the ball was cleared in a flowing movement from Barber to Cowan, he nodded it on down to the centre to Tilson who dummied the centre-half and put the ball out to the right wing a long way in front of Ernie Toseland who hared after it to the corner flag, crossed it to the far post where Tommy Johnson calmly slotted it past the Bolton 'keeper. There were ten minutes on the clock; by half-time City led 3-0.

Each goal was greeted with great celebration by the crowd, but only handshakes on the pitch. Partisanship by the referee was rewarded by loud booing, but there was no obscene chanting or abuse. Good play by Bolton was encouraged by loud cheers from their supporters and by appreciative applause from the City fans. There was a ten minute respite at half-time during which hot drinks and butties could be obtained, but I do not recall the sale of alcohol.

The second half was a little slower in pace than the first, but within five minutes of the re-start, Bobby Marshall added a superb individual effort using the wind to lob the goalkeeper. On 80 minutes, Johnson completed his hat-trick after a bout of inter-passing with Tilson. Almost immediately Bolton broke away, and arguably their most famous player, Ted Vizard, scored a consolation goal with a brilliant diving header.

The final whistle was greeted with a roar, which resounded around the whole of Moss Side, Rusholme and Fallowfield. 5-1. What a match! If I was only an armchair supporter before, I was now well and truly hooked.

With all City supporters of the last three generations, I have scaled the heights and plumbed the depths, known the joy and suffered the sadness, cheered every goal and groaned at every miss. Through it all, my thanks, thoughts and memories go out to all those many players and old friends I

have shared them with. My thoughts and memories remain undimmed by the passage of 70 years".

Shortly after its opening, the stadium was to witness the return of the 49 year old Welsh wizard, Billy Meredith, who we have previously referred to. In February 1926, he played his first league game at Maine Road which meant that during his career he had played home games at Hyde Road, Maine Road and for Manchester United at Clayton and Old Trafford; a feat unmatched by anybody else. Shortly after, he featured in City's goalless FA Cup draw with Cardiff before a record crowd of 76,166, only to be exceeded by the 84,569 who attended the FA Cup 6th round with Stoke City in March 1934. Having mentioned a legendary player who graced the field for both the United and City teams, perhaps we can focus on what it meant to be a footballer in the pre-war era, by presenting the actual terms and conditions for Sam Cookson, when he signed for City in the month of May 1924*:

CHART 2: A CITY PLAYER'S CONTRACT - 1924

"1   The Player hereby agrees to play in an efficient manner and to the best of his ability for the Club.

2   The Player shall attend the Club's ground or any other place decided upon by the Club for the purposes of or in connection with his training as a Player pursuant to the instructions of the Secretary, Manager or Trainer of the Club or of such other person or persons as the Club may appoint.

3   The Player shall do everything necessary to get and keep himself in the best possible condition so as to render the most efficient service to the Club and will carry out all the training and other instructions of the Club through its representative officials.

Today, all professionals receive a standard contract via The Professional Footballers' Association which can carry specific clauses agreed with the player.

4. The player shall observe and be subject to all the Rules, Regulations and Bye-laws of The Football Association and any other Association, League or Combination of which the Club shall be a member. And this Agreement shall be subject to any action which shall be taken by The Football Association under their Rules for the suspension or termination shall be decided upon the payment of wages shall likewise be suspended or terminated as the case may be.

5. The Player shall not engage in any business or live in any place which the Directors (or Committee) of the Club may deem unsuitable.

6. If the Player shall prove palpably inefficient or shall be guilty of serious misconduct or breach of the disciplinary Rules of the Club, the Club may, on giving 14 days' notice to the said Player or the Club may, on giving 28 days' notice to the said Player on any reasonable grounds terminate this Agreement and dispense with the services of the Player (without prejudice to the Club's right for transfer fees) in pursuance of the Rules of all such Associations, Leagues and Combinations of which the Club may be a member. Such notice or notices shall be in writing and shall specify the reason for the same being given and shall also set forth the rights to appeal to which the player is entitled under the Rules of The Football Association.

7. This Agreement and the terms and conditions thereof shall be as to its suspension and termination subject to the Rules of The Football Association and to any action which may be taken by the Council of The Football Association or any deputed Committee and in any proceedings by the Player against the Club it shall be a sufficient and complete defence and answer by and on the part of the Club that such suspension or termination hereof is due to the action of The Football Association or any Sub-Committee thereof to whom the power may be delegated.

CHART 2: (Cont)

8. In consideration of the observance by the said Player of the terms, provisions and conditions of this Agreement, the said *James Ernest Magnall* on behalf of the Club hereby agrees that the said Club shall pay to the said Player the sum of *£6/-/-* per week from *9th May 1924 to 23rd August 1924* and *£8/-/-* per week from *23rd August 1924 to 2nd May 1925*.

9. This Agreement shall cease and determine on *2nd May 1925* unless the same shall have been previously determined in accordance with the provision hereinbefore set forth.

If at any time during the period of this Agreement the wages herein agree to be paid shall be in excess of the wages permitted to be paid by the Club to the player in accordance with the Rules of the Football League, the wages to be paid to the Player shall be the amount the Club is entitled to pay by League Rules in force from time to time and this Agreement shall be read and construed as if it were varied accordingly."

It will be seen from the contract, that the contract was of limited duration, one year, and that weekly wages were to be less during the non-playing period. There is no mention of agents or image rights! To a certain extent, the players in this era were not the direct descendants of 'the lads' from the Iron Works and St Mark's, being unable to trace their antecedents locally. Indeed, professional players were brought from Scotland and other 'faraway' places. However, the local tradition lived on in such players as Tommy Johnson, who is featured by Gary James as one of the 'Maine Men'. Such 'locals' are contrasted with the 'cosmopolitans' of Manchester United and drawing on this text, we learn that Johnson played 354 times for City in both the League and FA Cup scoring a total of 166 goals; approximately one every other game. He was the most prolific club goal scorer of the 1920's and holds the club record of most goals in a season, 38 goals in 39 games during the 1928/29 season. He was born on 19th August 1901, joined City in February 1919 and played first as an inside left and then as a centre forward. He won every honour available including full international caps and his persona and unassuming lifestyle, may be glimpsed from James' transcription of an interview with veteran City fan, Harry Hughes, who lived near Johnson in Gorton:

"Johnson was idolised by the supporters. Harry Hughes, who lived near Johnson in Gorton remembers that although he was often seen in the Gorton area, he wasn't one for talking about his football: 'He lived in Park Avenue, the first house on the right near Sunny Brow Park. I used to see him quite regularly pushing a pram and, if they'd be playing on the Saturday, he'd be pushing the pram in the morning all around the neighbourhood. You'd all go 'Hello Tom' and he'd nod his head and you'd then tell everyone Tom speaks to you, y'know. Anyway, he was very dignified and always wore a big brimmed trilby – it quickly became very fashionable then! And he always walked with a very deliberate stride, pushing the pram. There was a billiard hall on Hyde Road and he used to go in there and get involved with the wrong set – bookies and the like – but it never really affected him. Never dishonest or anything like that. But they were a real rum lot these 'Smiths' I think they were called. Every time he went into the billiard hall, they'd give him the best table out of the 30 odd there and we used to go in after work just to watch. Learn a few shots and that.

Then he'd go in the Plough Hotel on Hyde Road which I also patronised at times. But unlike me, he never had to buy his own beer. All the toadies would buy it, they'd ask him what he was having and he always replied 'I'll have a draught Bass – a pint'. It was the best and most expensive beer in the house! They would ask him his prediction for the City game and he always said 'I think we'll lose!' that was his stock answer as if to say, 'shut up, I don't want to talk about football'.

I never ever mentioned football to him. I'd speak with him occasionally. Usually I'd chat with him at the bank – I was always drawing out, he was always paying in!' "

Johnson was eventually sold to Everton for £6,000, which shocked and angered many City supporters who had lost their star goal scorer and who had local roots and passed among them on a daily basis. Such local identification was fairly typical of the stars of yesteryear, whose off-field leisure pursuits reflected the tenor of the times, where children would attend the cinema matinees for less than 1p (2d./3d.) and perhaps come across such established City stars as Johnson, or somewhat later on, Sam Barkas, captain of both his club and England. Barkas was a left-back who joined City on 20th April 1934 for a fee of £5,000. This was the year City won the Cup, appearing in the Final for the third consecutive time. In their Cup run, they were drawn at home to Stoke City in the Quarter Finals and as stated previously, the game drew the ground record attendance of 84,569; indeed the record for any club fixture either then or since. With such an enormous throng, there were inevitably crowd and safety problems and the club were required by the police to close the gates some twenty minutes before the game was due to begin; this was the first time that this had happened since the ground had been opened. City won 1-0, went on to beat Aston Villa in the Semi Final and conquered Portsmouth 2-1 to win the Cup wearing their first change strip of maroon, before 93,258 fans at Wembley. Photographs, illustrating details of that great day and the teams' triumphant return to Manchester, contrasting markedly with the dismal 'non-reception' of 1904, are provided at this chapter's close.

Having won the Cup for the second time, City went on to win the League in 1937 but were demoted to the Second Division before the war years threw professional soccer, as a spectator sport, into disarray. City's difficulty was compounded just before the war because as they were demoted, Manchester United were promoted; both clubs serving a role reversal at the start of the 1938/39 season. A watershed which would lead to the eventual supremacy of Manchester United as the City of Manchester's top club, with City continually striving to re-enact its previous successes. This reversal in fortune was brought about in no small measure by luck, accident and charitable intent. How so? Well, with the onset of War in September 1939, the League programme was cancelled and all professional players contracts suspended. Only with the termination of hostilities in 1945 could professional soccer resume as a mass spectator sport and City had to start in the Second

Division for the 1946/47 season. United were, however, without a ground because their stadium at Old Trafford had been bombed on 22nd March 1941* and City acting out of sympathy, offered United the use of Maine Road for an annual rent of £5,000, plus a share of gate receipts. In return, City's reserve squad, now left without a venue, were provided with the use of United's training ground at the Cliff, Salford. United were managed at this time by Matt Busby who, as we have seen, appeared in City's victorious 1934 Cup winning team. The consequence of the shift in ground, division and managership – Wilf Wild resigned in 1946, followed by Sam Cowan's resignation in 1947 – in terms of Manchester City's future development is succinctly expressed by James:

> **"This was a significant period in the history of Manchester football as City, throughout the pre-war era, had been Manchester's best supported and popular club ... (After the War), with United in the First Division playing at Maine Road many of City's traditional supporters returning from the war, chose to watch both clubs. Those who found it difficult to pay for a game every week drifted towards fixtures with the biggest stars – obviously United games in Division One.**
>
> **For many Blues, the fact United were now playing good football and challenging for the League, as they did in 1946-47, was good news. City fans had always seen them as the poor relations – remember the Reds had been close to relegation to the Third Division and near extinction during the 30's and were genuinely pleased for the club. Many saw success for United as being good for the whole City; especially as a former Blue (Matt Busby) was helping to restore pride to the club. There was only friendly rivalry between the two outfits.**
>
> **With hindsight, United's stay at Maine Road was bad news for the Blues. Remember City had broken many attendance records pre-war. It was now United who gained the upper hand and were quickly becoming the better supported club**

* See 'Manchester United at the Millennium' for a pictorial image of the damage.

... winning the FA Cup in 1948 and finishing runners-up to Arsenal in the League gave the Reds an edge. The United vs. Arsenal game on 17th January 1948 was the first post-war league crowd above 80,000. City's best crowd during the 1947/48 season was 78,000 who attended a goalless derby match in September. Apart from that, the best City league crowd was a little over 56,000. Even the normally popular City vs. Arsenal fixture could only attract 20,782.

A comparison made in 'The Pride of Manchester' derby book highlighted how United were averaging almost 55,000 for their first nineteen home games of the season, while City were a little short of 42,000 – still impressive but significantly less than United's for the first time in history.

For the Reds, the stay at Maine Road had been a financial bonanza. A Manchester Evening News article in 1949 highlighted the huge increase in United's takings while playing at the higher capacity Maine Road. It revealed that United were poised to announce an aggregate profit over the three Maine Road league seasons of £75,000 – easily an all time record... in December 1948 perhaps aware of the effect United were having on City gates, the Blues gave their rivals notice to quit. Later that season at Maine Road, United attracted 82,711 for the visit of Bradford Park Avenue, then 81,565 for Yeovil. Still not the record for the stadium but a sure fire warning to the City management that the days of the total Blue's dominance were over. Manchester City were now the ones who needed a lift!"

The 1950's saw episodes of relegation, experimentation and consolidation as City strived to maintain the support it had enjoyed pre-war. Such episodes were punctuated by successful runs in the FA Cup, which brought back huge crowds such as Liverpool's fifth-round visit in the 1955/56 season, which was attended by over 70,000 fans and Everton for the sixth-round attracting 76,129 culminating in the winning of the FA Cup in 1956. During the same year, Manchester United won the League with the Manchester Evening News bringing out a special edition in that year, to celebrate the City's double triumph, under the headline 'King Soccer City of Britain'. Such euphoria was to be blighted by the

Munich tragedy of 6th February 1958 in which Manchester United lost the cream of its playing squad in an aircraft crash. City continued to attract large crowds with the ground being modified to accommodate 50,000 under shelter, with the Kippax Stand being roofed during the 1957 close season. The 'popular side' still being the uncovered scoreboard end which is now the North Stand.

The early 1960's saw a fall in attendance mirrored by the teams' poor performance with the club again being relegated at the close of the 1962/63 season; salt was rubbed in the wound by Manchester United winning the FA Cup in 1962 and improving their ground for the 1966 World Cup. The 'Reds' had replaced the 'Blues' as Manchester's Premier Club. Indeed by the close of the 1964/65 season, the lowest attendance ever recorded at Maine Road was notched up for a league match; 8,015 against Swindon Town. Fans demonstrated in the forecourt and stoned the boardroom windows and compared their situation with that of Manchester United who finished as League Champions, FA Cup semi-finalists and Inter-City Fairs Cup semi-finalists. However, rejuvenation and reorientation came about with the appointment of Joe Mercer and Malcolm Allison as the management team in the mid-1960's; change was desperately needed. James remarks:

"The two men arrived at City when the club was in its worst ever state. Even the decimation of the 1904 Cup winning side and subsequent struggles did not leave the Blues as low as in 1965. In fact, even the poor position of the club in 1996 when Frank Clark was appointed as City Manager cannot be prepared with the immediate per-Mercer period. Clark's City were in a lower position in the League, however the loyalty of City's supporters ensured that the club remained a strong one, whereas in 1965 support had diminished and caused the new men serious concerns".

Promotion from the Second Division and a successful Cup run saw the crowds return with 63,034, seeing City play Everton in the Quarter Final of the FA Cup. City returned to the First Division in 1966, the year England won the World Cup; furthermore, they beat Manchester United at Old Trafford in March 1968, 3-1, signalling that they had regained their corporate composure and respect. In the words of a spectator poem:

> **"In the years to come they would tell the story,**
> **of the night City regained their glory.**
> **For now out of the shadows they had come,**
> **a vital game they'd fought and won!"**

City finished champions of the 1967/68 League, two points ahead of United and went on to win the FA Cup in 1969 against Leicester City, thus, establishing themselves once again as an elite club. However, boardroom takeover challenges and the sacking, then reinstatement of Malcolm Allison, led to problems of team morale which were translated into poor playing performances on the pitch to last, by and large, for the next quarter of a century.

It is appropriate to leave our historical narrative at this point and don tape recorder and microphone to relate to the reader experiences of 'match day' at Manchester City, from a totally different perspective to that so far employed; the focus being on the crowd, rather than the players and the author's research mode shifting from desktop analysis to actual 'in situ' interviews and observations.

The Crowd: Troublesome times in the 70s

The 'Crowd' has always had a fascination for the scholar, the media and the layman. Millions of words have been used to describe its characteristics, emotions, motivations and actions but is it possible to refer to the crowd as an 'it'? Is the crowd nothing more than an assemblage of individuals or does it have a 'mind' of its own? In particular what of crowds that are focused around particular activities and how do these impact on local consciousness? Can we describe the familiar in terms which are readily understood but which in fact show, paradoxically, that the familiar is in fact unfamiliar? By this I mean that there is often a simplified way of thinking about crowd situations which may have little correspondence to their reality. We will attempt to provide answers to these questions mindful that such answers can be at best partial given the intractable nature of our data. In this regard, the reader should be made aware that a match day is, in fact, a convenient shorthand for describing the operating set of a leisure organisation which, as we have seen, is continually structuring and restructuring itself to achieve particular goals – both literally and metaphorically!

We can initially carry the reader into and around City's stadium, by drawing on observations made by the author while acting as a consultant for a government sponsored survey on public disorder and sporting events in the late 70's. In order to familiarise you, the reader, with how these observations were conducted we may first of all describe the typical way in which the author conducted interviews and recorded relationships on match days. Throughout this account the author will be referred to as 'the observer', partly for literary convenience but also to emphasise that the descriptions contained herein are made, as far as possible, in a factual way. The various participants in the Saturday spectacle are given free reign to express the meaningfulness of their experience in their own, largely unedited terms.

The typical way in which the observer worked was to attend a given fixture on a similar basis to Police Officers detailed to police that event without, of course, donning the uniform! Crowd duty police officers were expected to attend a briefing by a senior officer, some one and a half hours before kick-off, usually scheduled for a Saturday afternoon at 3.00pm, and those on traffic duty, some two hours before. Generally speaking attendance at the pre-match briefing was followed by interviews with police officers stationed in the ground, stewards and fans. Over a typical four to five hour observation period on a match day, a routine became established of recording what was happening within a mile or two of the ground to that of recording the sequence of events which unfolded within the stadium. In terms of the latter and prior to kick-off, the observer attempted to move between different parts of the ground from terraces to seats, from toilets to turnstiles, from snack counters to well appointed bars and boxes and from programme sellers to studiously minded stewards. During the actual course of the game, such movement was limited by the press of humanity and consequently the observer took up a position at a known 'flash-point' or area of the stadium where there had been repeated crowd turbulence or actual violence. This was not out of a desire to obtain some perverse pleasure from such scenes but rather arose from the consultant's brief to examine the crowd dynamics associated with disorderly behaviour. Recordings of conversations, events, scuffles, fights and full-scale battles, as well as the usual coinage of match day exchanges between fans, were made by means of a lapel microphone attached to a portable tape-recorder. No attempt was made to conceal the microphone from participants; when questioned the observer explained to the enquirer that he was interested in 'crowd behaviour' and was tape recording the opinions and views of some of those present in an attempt to gain greater understanding of 'match days'.

Having familiarised the reader with the observer's 'modus operandi' of recording crowd dynamics, let us turn to the results of this work by looking at the arrangements for crowd control and spectator behaviour at Maine Road at that time. In conducting this instructive and fascinating work, a neutral stance was adopted as far as possible, and this could often cause some initial consternation and concern from fans who were used to thinking in dichotomous terms: us and them. This was particularly apparent in the perplexed looks given to the author when he moved between segregation areas.

Policing

Let us first of all examine police arrangements for receiving and marshalling the crowd. Such arrangements had, in the seventies, become an inseparable part of crowd dynamics with the police, somewhat unwittingly becoming major actors in the Saturday afternoon drama. Crowd configurations in the 70's and even today, cannot be understood without an awareness and sensitive surveillance of their role. A role which, throughout the 90's and into the Millennium, is changing dramatically with the rise of active stewarding and electronic means of surveillance. This modern multi-technology contrasts vividly with the MOP (Mobile Observation Platform), which was presented to the club by the author in the late 70's in order to assist fans and police in the accurate identification of troublemakers at the segregation point in the Kippax terracing and which is shown at the conclusion of this chapter in photographic form.

We may remark that the police officer on duty at a major sporting event such as a soccer match is a vital part of a large scale exercise designed to ensure the safety of spectators and which is largely invisible to the public at large. The typical paying spectator, eager to get to the match and return home safely from it without undue delay is to a degree, unaware of the careful and elaborate planning which is necessary to ensure that he and his thousands of fellow supporters can realise these expectations. To provide the reader with some awareness of the form of briefing used for police officers at Maine Road, he or she may accompany the author, in the imaginary sense of course, as we report for 'duty' at 1.00pm on a particular Saturday match day in the early 70's. This particular pre-match briefing takes place in a garage adjacent to a police station some half a mile from the ground and is the assembly point for a large number of officers.

There is an air of excitement and considerable noise as the men find the sergeant who is responsible for their particular group as named on a duplicated operational order. It is immediately apparent that the police officers are drawn from all divisions in the Greater Manchester area on a voluntary overtime basis; hence it is necessary for each sergeant to ensure that the members of his group are familiar with the areas or sections of the ground which they are to police. Thus the sergeant will brief a constable with regard to his duties at a particular location, check on any equipment he might need, for example coat for directing traffic or a traffic key that will suspend the operation of traffic lights and allow him to control them manually, and then ask the constable to confirm his ground seat number. This latter point refers to the seat allocated to him on the periphery of the pitch which he will occupy, after finishing his duties outside the ground, some fifteen minutes after the game has started. He is reminded to leave the ground fifteen minutes before the end of the game to resume his 'point', that is, locational responsibilities for traffic and crowd control outside the stadium.

In addition to instructions about traffic duty, various men are put on what is termed 'damage patrols'. They work in pairs, again under a sergeant and are briefed to prevent damage, theft or disorderly conduct by groups of supporters on their way to and from the match. These men are quite mobile without specific locational responsibilities and can be called on to police the ground's immediate surroundings should there be a particular need for their services; depending on the number of visiting spectators involved, they may also act as an escorting 'cavalry' for such supporters. Once the match has started these men are held in reserve and assemble inside the ground at particular points. However, like their colleagues on traffic duty, they are instructed to report to certain locations after the match, chosen on the basis of previous experience as areas where there is likely to be crowd disturbances. They may also make themselves available after the game as escorts for visiting supporters on their way to railway termini and coaches should this be necessary.

The hubbub in the garage begins to subside as an inspector calls the officers to order. He checks with each sergeant, standing at the head of his men behind a notice bearing the number of his group, on the disposition of constables as outlined in the operational order. Adjustments are made as necessary to cover absent officers or unforeseen contingencies. A superintendent then takes over from the inspector and, after reminding the officers that any people apprehended are to be taken to a prison van situated at one end of the ground's exits so that their names and addresses can be recorded and verified, briefs the men as follows:

> **"I've told you before and I mean it. You don't leave your points or your patrols until quarter of an hour after the kick-off. That means you'll be getting inside the ground after 3.25pm and when you get inside the ground you'll report straight to your position because you might be needed immediately. I repeat, go straight to your position. At the end of the game you'll be on your patrols and your points fifteen minutes before the end of the match.**
>
> **I don't know if the television's there today, but those of you who will be working around the touch line make sure that you act as police officers and don't stand around talking and chewing gum. If there's a goal or an unpopular decision get to your feet and face the crowd. Before the half-time whistle, stand on your feet and face the crowd; this is to stop anyone from coming across the wall and running onto the pitch.**

> It has been brought to my attention that on one or two
> occasions coaches have been allowed to park on the Kippax*
> car park. If that's the case, if anybody's on duty there and a
> coach comes along and tries to park, you must send them to
> the authorised coach parking areas. These areas are
> adequately controlled by police officers who will take care of
> the supporters on them. Does everybody know what they are
> doing? Anybody got any questions?"

The comments of the superintendent thus reinforce what the
inspector has told the sergeants and the sergeants have told their
men. In addition any special circumstances associated with a
match can be readily brought to the attention of all the men on
duty that day.

The purpose of this briefing is to make clear to the men on duty
their specific locations and responsibilities, which will span a
period of some five hours. The need for this arrangement is readily
apparent for, as we have already noted, the officers are drawn from
all divisions in the Greater Manchester area and have varying
experience of duty at football matches in general and Manchester
City's ground in particular.

An officer remarks:

> "We get men from Oldham and Bolton; we get them from
> Stockport, we get them from Leigh Division; we call them in
> from all over and, of course, this is overtime for these
> fellows."

With the briefing completed the men are dismissed and the mobile
patrols, cars and motorcycles tour the area in the vicinity of the
ground to assist with traffic control and to identify likely causes of
congestion. To illustrate this latter point, a mobile car patrol, which
the observer had joined, noted that roadworks were about to begin
at a major road junction near the car park reserved for visiting
spectators situated some two miles from the ground. This caused
some concerns because it was thought that the traffic flow both

* Large unsurfaced car park behind the main terraced stand known as
the Kippax.

into and away from the ground would be seriously disrupted. Discussions were held between the police officers and the site foreman and it was decided that the matter should be referred to Divisional HQ who would then have to make a decision as to the appropriate action to take. The source of the officers' anxiety lay in the fact that they were unaware road works were scheduled to begin on this particular match day and consequently had little time to deal with the situation when they came across it, one hour before the match was due to start. The importance of adequate communications with the local authority Direct Works Department is thus emphasised because traffic congestion outside the ground arising from such unforeseen circumstances, particularly after the game, can hinder the police from attending to any problems of crowd behaviour which might occur.

This unexpected restriction on police mobility is specific but also arises from 'irresponsible parking' in the vicinity of the ground. As we have seen in terms of relocation from Ardwick to Moss Side, Maine Road is situated in the midst of narrow streets and terraced housing and as such is not untypical of many other major football league grounds which were spawned by the industrial revolution. This will be readily apparent from the photographs at the end of this chapter. An officer on traffic duty comments:

> **"There's signs all over the place for motorists. It's just impossible. You've got to leave it to their common sense. You know they're supposed to be responsible people, not to put it (the car) in a place where they can cause an obstruction. I mean this is common sense isn't it? Surely if someone comes along and parks it bang in the middle of an entry (passageway), then obviously it's causing an obstruction isn't it? But they say "Well there's no sign there, why are you 'doing me' (issuing a ticket) for obstruction?" "**

On this particular match day, the patrol accompanied by the observer, booked thirty seven cars for obstruction. As kick-off time approaches the observer still travelling with the mobile patrol, notices a motorist, unable to find a space for his car, 'abandon' rather than park it on a pavement in a street facing the ground. The car door is left unlocked and the man, middle-aged and well dressed, sprints for the turnstiles as the crowd roars in response to the players coming on to the pitch. It is difficult in the printed word to convey the look of utter despondency on the man's face as he is stopped in mid-flight by a police officer who escorts him back to his car and requests him to move it. It is clear that 'common sense' is often suspended on match days, even by usually law-abiding citizens, as the emotional fervour to get to the match overrides inhibitions built up since childhood: in this case, safety concerns and securing possessions.

As we enter the Stadium, it is readily apparent that the game has a magnetic attraction with formal arrangements for spectators being overturned by informal ones. Participation in a group bonded by membership of a formal sports organisation such as Manchester City allows for a different type of 'game' to be played on the terraces compared with that on the field of play. We will describe the nature of this particular 'game' in subsequent pages both in terms of the interaction between fans and the views they hold of each other. However, suffice to mention here that the 'car abandoning incident' above is related to individual rather than group behaviour. The common sense view of this type of behaviour is one of "attitude". In brief the individuals "personality" is described by police as undergoing a change. According to this view, even the tranquil and placid are transformed into boisterous and emotionally charged individuals depending on what happens during the duration of the match. CCTV pictures coupled with observation provides ample evidence of what heightened emotionality does to an individual. This match day "personality" is, in part, situationally determined with the phrase 'acting out of character' being used to describe such situational variation in actions. Anxiety, elation, hope and despair are written on the faces of supporters as the drama on the field unfolds before them. This is not to deny that there are relatively enduring traits which help us to predict behaviour but rather that 'state' and 'trait' interact in a very complex way to determine both group and individual actions. It is this interplay of individual and group behaviour we now illustrate by describing patterns of interaction of group dynamics as they unfold, during the 70's, in two big fixtures; City v Liverpool and City v Everton. The 'modus operandi' was as described previously with the author taking up a position at the segregation barrier shown in the photograph at the end of this chapter. Switching between home and away fan enclosures provided an interesting perspective.

A separate briefing, to that already described, is conducted for police officers who have been assigned to duty inside the ground. This follows a similar pattern to that already reported for outside personnel but is conducted in the club's gymnasium under the main stand. The briefing is for a match which is something of a local derby in that the visiting team is Liverpool. After the usual liaison between sergeants and constables, the superintendent draws attention to the fact that there will be a near capacity crowd and that the visiting supporters will bring with them teams of 'dippers' or pickpockets. He indicates that the toilets are the areas where the pickpockets will operate and suggests that the policemen inside the ground should co-operate in all aspects of policing to combat this. This point is stressed because some of the men are on regular duty whereas others are new to the situation. The superintendent also warns his officers to be on the look out for visiting fans carrying metal discs with serrated edges, (holds one up by way of demonstration), which when spun into the crowd can cause serious injury*. After this sombre warning the men disperse to various parts of the ground which have been assigned to them.

The observer emerges from the players' tunnel under the main stand into the brightly lit arena into a stadium which is fully seated at both 'ends' and on one side. The standing area being confined to one stand, referred to as the Kippax, which we have mentioned earlier and which is depicted at the end of the chapter. This runs along the remaining side of the ground facing the tunnel. Egress from the Kippax is from the back of the terracing through openings in corrugated metal sheeting which leads to flights of concrete steps running down earth or ash embankments. An open surfaced area some twenty yards wide separates these embankments from a perimeter wall which is punctuated by turnstile gates. A fixed fence broken by a gate, runs obliquely across this surfaced area to separate 'home' and 'visiting' spectators before they reach the

* These particularly nasty 'weapons' mimicked those shown on the TV martial arts programmes at the time in which Buddhist monks skimmed metal stars into wooden targets. They were approximately the size of a 50p piece.

steps leading up to the terraces. Thus at this point of entry the crowd becomes divided or segmented along lines of 'partisanship'.*

During the game a police officer directs the observer's attention to a particular section of this terracing and indicates that this is the area of the ground where crowd problems are likely to occur. The area in question is, in fact, a segregation point with visiting fans being allocated a section of terracing behind a fixed iron railing. A temporary barrier has been erected in front of this railing to 'distance' the home supporters from the visitors. The terracing on the visitor's side continues into the corner of the ground where it abuts a stand providing accommodation for seated spectators; the Platt Lane stand. A steel mesh curtain covers the opening on the side of this seated stand. The presence of this curtain is explained by a police officer in the following terms:

> **"You see, when we get a lot of visiting supporters they fill that corner up, you know, when there's a big match. The local supporters are next door in the seats, and, of course, the visitors used to throw stones and bottles in didn't they? So the curtain stopped that; they can't do that now."**

Turning our attention once again to the Kippax, the segregation point of a fixed and movable fence is helpful from a police point of view in that it localises the disorder inside the ground as most of the 'trouble' is associated with rival groups of supporters. A police officer, with some fifteen years experience of duty at the ground recalls:

> **"I remember a time when you could walk from one end of the stand (Kippax) to the other. There were no barriers. Now they've put the barriers in so that the crowd is divided into sections. As far as we're concerned this is much easier to control. The lads, (fellow officers), can go in there and take out the trouble makers."**

* *Initially temporary barriers were used to segregate supporters once they had passed through the turnstiles. However these were easily 'turned over' and were later superseded by the fixed fence.*

However, segregating fans sideways on' in steep sections of terracing rather than at opposite ends of the ground, as at other stadia, can create special problems. We may illustrate by referring to observations conducted at the particular match in question. At the start of the game an officer who performs regular duty at the segregation point indicated that the crowd here are mainly young home fans who pack against the barriers so that they can be near the visitors' enclosure. He comments:

> **"I would imagine that they didn't expect this sort of density of crowd at this particular point. When they designed the stand there was no indication that this was going to be a very, very dense area. In consequence, I don't think there are enough barriers to stop the tiers of fans crashing down and crushing somebody."**

This comment refers to the 'wave' effect engendered by spectators at the back of the terracing pushing forward. The officer is in a good position to observe this for he is situated some half way down the terracing and uses the raised wall above an exit tunnel as an observation point. The observer on accepting the invitation contained in the following quotation, can endorse the points made:

> **"This sort of thing, the 'wave' effect with few barriers to break it up, is terrifying. Just get up here and have a look; it frightens me, it really does. A lot of kids, the innocent ones who just come to watch the game, think if they go to the front, the wall above the exit, that's the best place to be and then this lot comes down on top of them. Also if any of those in the wave fall, they've no chance; the others will be over the top of them."**

The nearness of opposing fans, sideways on, separated by the fences, also lends itself to missile throwing. In the darkened areas under the stand the officers on duty occupy the gangway at the back of the terraces and man the 'no-man's land' which runs down the terracing between rival factions; in such circumstances it is extremely difficult to spot the missile throwers. A missile thrower may activate his immediate neighbours in the crowd to jump up and down in a bobbing motion, often with respect to events on the pitch, and during the resulting turbulence throw the missile with a low overhand action, virtually impossible to spot. The observer, positioned in the buffer zone between the rival fan groups, noted two bottles thrown into the home fans' section by the visitors. During half-time, an officer drew the observer's attention to an unusual missile; this was a football stocking with a heavy wooden ball, the size of a tennis ball, in the foot end with a knot tied round the 'ankle' section to secure it in place. He explains:

> **"It came out of the Liverpool crowd. Went into the City crowd and caught someone. They were going to throw it back when one of the lads (officer) spotted it."**

Such missiles can cause serious damage to a person but when thrown in large numbers into a densely packed section of the crowd can result in what may be termed 'crowd displacement', that is supporters moving away from the scene of an incident or missile to seek safety elsewhere with consequent overcrowding in other sections of the ground, leading to injuries not directly associated with the objects in question. The difficulty in spotting missile throwers, or those engaged in disorderly behaviour, arises from the limited area of terracing which can be observed from the back gangway or from the same level of terracing as that occupied by the spectators along the segregation fences. The officer who uses the wall above the exit as his observation platform points this up in the following remarks:

> **"To pull people out of a crowd where there's been trouble is very difficult. You've only a small area to work in that you can actually observe. If you've got some high point to get on to, it's surprising the difference it makes. They've done it on motorways; motorway police now have ramps to sit on in their cars and it must be a good thing."**

Observing the fans who congregate at the segregation point we note that spitting between enclosures and the flicking of lighted cigarettes into the opposition's 'camp' is fairly routine practice; however, it tends to be accentuated when, as at the match in question, there are a large number of visiting supporters. The police, who are stationed down the terracing in the buffer zone between fixed fences and temporary barriers, bear the brunt of this exchange. The officer previously quoted recalls a similar situation at a match earlier in the season:

> "I don't recall who City were playing but we had one about as busy as this earlier on. They got to spitting at one another; they were also throwing bottles at them but mainly spitting. We ended up having to hose down when we'd finished. It was shocking to have to go home and have to wipe it off …. They spit at one another but, of course, we get it."

Some mid-way into the first half of the game we observe two officers moving into the home fans' section. One of them extracts a young City fan from the crowd with some difficulty. An edited summary of subsequent conversations with this officer, conducted during the half-time interval, may be given as follows:

> "I could see something going on so I followed him (fellow officer) in. One of the kids in the crowd kicked me on the leg and he thought I was going past him and that I wasn't going to take any notice of this. (A crowd surge began as the officers fought their way into the closely packed area). However I connected so naturally I had him out. I wasn't even going for the lad, I was going past him so he tried to take a kick at me. I think he was 16. After, in the prison van, he admitted what he had done."

Over the period of this and subsequent observations, it became clear to the observer that in the immediate vicinity of the segregation point, a different though related 'game' to that taking place on the field of play was in progress. The young home fans are attracted to this point well before the match starts and as the density of spectators increases they are in a quite unsuitable position to see the match once it begins. Their attention is focused on the visitors' enclosure with each new arrival adding to the excitement and heightening the baiting and chanting which begins to build up. Thus for an hour or so before the match, the home fans are in a state of 'anticipatory excitement', with increasing levels of arousal being notched up, which is related to the number and age of visiting supporters; older visitors are a disappointment. During this drama, muscle and sinew are strained as home fans give their total attention to the Liverpool crowd; packed in an emotionally and physically tight mass they strain, like hunting dogs on the leash, ready to attack if given the opportunity. Mixing these crowds together is out of the question in such circumstances. Taking up this point, it is of interest to note that three men, in their late thirties and standing in the visitors' enclosure were asked to move to the home fans' section for they were identified as City fans. They moved reluctantly, one of them saying:

"We used to stand here for twenty years; why should we move because of those yobs down there (pointing to young home fans at the barrier) who know nothing about football."

The officer makes the following point about these fans:

They've come here to get a good view of the game and they were alright; no trouble. But if we let them stay this time they would expect to come back here again. You can't give them (the fans) any leeway at all. If you're going to segregate it's got to be <u>pure</u> segregation."

Thus relaxing the 'segregation rule' to let different groups of home spectators use the visitors' section, is seen as 'asking for trouble' even though their territorial claims, both physical and psychological, may go back many years.

At the start of the game, interest shifts to the field of play but observation suggests that this is only a partial interest with match incidents being commented on and relayed, as it were, by home fans to the visitors' enclosure to bait and provoke. For those home fans who have chosen a position next to the barrier and are unable to see the game, the incidents are sensed rather than observed. Thus City scored a goal and immediately cat-calls and derogatory shouts were directed towards the Liverpool fans; these choruses are "collective" and reach deafening proportions. City fans dance up and down, glare at the visiting fans and sing "We're going to win the league". This persists for some time with the City fans being seemingly oblivious to the fact that the game has restarted. Indeed the goal presents an opportunity for a heightened interest in the visitors with the home fans missing few opportunities to stress **their** ascendancy which has just been achieved on the field of play.

When a Liverpool fan criticises a pass made by a member of his own team by shouting, "Rubbish, absolute rubbish". This is greeted with cheers by the home fans followed by the rhetorical chant, "what's the score?" This is followed immediately by a chant, "We're only warming up, we're only warming up", accompanied by rhythmical hand clapping; the noise of which reverberates off the corrugated roof of the stand.

A noticeable feature of the City fans' behaviour, both throughout the pre-match and match period is the establishment of their superiority over the rival supporters. Thus when the Liverpool fans attempt to chant in support of their own team, "Come on you Reds", their teams' colours, it is *incorporated* by the home fans who blend in with the chant but substitute their own colour. An *oppositional* chant is generated when the visiting fans chant the name of their own team; the pattern is as follows:

"Liverpool (immediate collective expletive from home fans); Liverpool (expletive); Liverpool (expletive, expletive, expletive, expletive)."

Thus by incorporation and opposition, the visitors are put in their place; they are degraded. Such a process has the effect of 'drawing out' the opposing fans and it is of interest to note that the first chant of the Liverpool fans is greeted by an *immediate* collective rejoinder suggesting that the home fans are well rehearsed in such successful degradation ceremonies.

Towards the end of this particular match, the observer took up a position adjacent to the top of the steps at the back of the stand leading down towards the exits allocated to the home supporters. At this point, some ten minutes before the final whistle and the score still 1-0 in City's favour, the fringe of the crowd at the back of the terracing 'ebbs' and 'flows'. Groups of young supporters, 18 years of age and younger, half-heartedly attempt to leave the ground. They are anchored by the expectation of another goal or the speculation that some noteworthy incident might take place. Though it is bitterly cold, the young fans in their tee-shirts and bomber jackets appear immune to the weather. Small groups do break away, however their destination is not home but the exit allocated to the visiting supporters. These groups begin to form into larger aggregates outside the exits leading to the car parks but are broken up and moved on by prompt mounted police action.

The 'ebbing' and 'flowing' of the crowd continues, governed largely by a monitoring of reactions to what is happening on the field of play, for the youngsters are quite unable to see the game. With the match about to end, a great roar goes up from the crowd; Liverpool have equalised through an 'own goal'. At this point as if in response to a command, a large body of young fans certainly in excess of two hundred, 'emerge' from the back of the Kippax stand and stream at high speed down the concrete stairway towards the exit gates only slightly impeded by older spectators leaving other sections of the terracing. Like an avalanche accumulating volume, they pick up additional numbers as they begin moving through the car park outside the ground towards the visitors' exits. From the vantage point of the observer high upon a ledge behind the stand, the advancing crowd, now several hundred strong, resembles a great tidal wave gathering momentum as it rushes shore-wards; in this case, the 'shore' being the location of visiting spectators. However, this advance is checked by mounted police and the crowd surges back. This wavelike motion of the crowd, surging and retreating continues for several minutes until the main body of spectators leaving the ground in an orderly fashion assimilates it by sheer weight of numbers. As the crowd begins to disperse groups of youngsters, some seven or eight in number, are still to be observed in the vicinity of the car park and there are occasional 'flashes of violence' like sparks from the glowing embers of a dying fire. To illustrate, a young man aged about 35, smartly dressed in a leather coat is attacked by a group of youths about 17 years of age and seven in number who drive him to the ground. He struggles to his feet and in a somewhat dazed condition move towards them – the youngsters run off. The incident lasts less than a minute. A police officer joins the observer and comments:

"It was quiet until that goal was scored; it only takes one or two to run and they all go together."

As the observer leaves his 'perch' and makes his way along the back of the stand three youths aged about 18 approach and draw the attention of the officer to another youth at the back of the terracing. In a state of agitation they say he is a Liverpool supporter and has a knife. A subsequent search revealed that the youth, though in a fact a Liverpool supporter, was unarmed. He explains:

> **"I jumped up when Liverpool scored and they (the three youths) said, "what are you doing in this section?" and I said "What do you mean, what am I doing in this section?" and that was it."**

Conversation with the three youths revealed that they felt affronted by a visiting supporter being in **their** section of the terracing and having identified or 'clocked' him, had decided to wait until the end of the match before 'moving in'. When they confronted him he had threatened them by saying he had a knife and this had temporarily saved him from being attacked. The appearance of the police officer enabled the youths, by reporting him, to check whether in fact the visitor was armed. The gist of their subsequent conversation with the observer was that if the search was negative and the individual allowed to go 'free', then they would wait for him outside the ground assured, inadvertently by the police officer, that their target was an easy one as he did not possess a weapon. A low degree of cunning, frequently and brazenly employed by the hard core trouble makers.

The general police view about this being 'a quiet match' appeared to be in line with that expressed by a St John's Ambulance Officer:

> **"Well it's been quiet. We've sent two to hospital, one with an eye injury and one with a nasty gash across the top of the eye-lid. We've had a couple with head injuries that needed stitching."**

A quiet match too for the 50,000 or so supporters who had attended the City v. Liverpool game and were no doubt unaware of the other 'game' which had taken place in a section of the Kippax stand that had only been kept within 'bounds' by the careful pre-match planning of club officials and what may be termed 'positive policing' under less than ideal circumstances. The 'game' we have referred to previously, refers to systems of interaction where the term 'atmosphere' takes on a new meaning when interpreted within this context. We will continue to chart the development of this 'atmosphere' at the City v. Everton game later in the same season.

City v Everton

With regard to this match a large number of visiting fans from Liverpool who support Everton are expected and consequently police officers have to be deployed in large numbers.

An officer comments:

> "Depends what shift we're on, you know, we don't have regular points. You see I'm on nights now so this afternoon (City v Everton) is overtime; next week I'm on two 'til ten so I can't work the football match, things like that."

Another officer comments:

> "Well this is extra duty. I volunteer but it's hard when you're on 'lates'. Got to bed about 8.00 this morning, up again about 12.00 dashing about to have something to eat, on duty again at 1.00pm. Off again at 6.00pm, snatch a few hours sleep then back on duty again."

However certain officers because of the nature of their duties are available on a regular basis. These officers are usually posted to sections of the ground where the more rowdy elements of the crowd congregate. This familiarity with the particular location and with members of the crowd is seen as being helpful in both preventing the occurrence of disorderly behaviour and in following up any problems which might arise.

A senior police officer comments:

> "These officers occupy the same position week in, week out; they're practically on Christian name terms with most of the people in the crowd. Now that degree of familiarity is helpful because they know instantly when something is wrong and they can get in (into the crowd). Of course, it's a big help if anything has gone wrong. They're a big help because they can identify faces and people and names and all sorts of things."

It would be a mistake to assume that the opportunity to watch a football match is the major motivating force for police associated with undertaking duties at these matches. All officers spoken to mentioned 'money' as being the major reason for volunteering for match duty and a considerable number are, in fact, disinterested in the game in that they were often unable to indicate the score when asked. According to a senior officer, this is how it should be:

> **"The policemen are on this ground to do a job. In their section it's up to them to stop the trouble before it starts. That's what they're there for. The policemen aren't there, as some of them think, to watch the match. Their job is to ensure the safety of the crowd; that means control. It's up to the sergeants and inspectors to ensure that they're doing the job they're supposed to do."**

The reference to 'stopping the trouble before it starts' may be puzzling to the reader but refers to the timing of police intervention which, in turn, is related to an anticipation of likely trouble based either on observation or information received. Similarly the question of crowd safety is seen as being necessarily associated with 'control' for this word tends to be used by serving officers in a wide sense to take in features of the physical environment which might be regarded as hazardous. In this connection we may remark that persistence is sometimes required from the police officer. Thus, with respect to deficient lighting under the Kippax stand, an officer explains:

> **"I phoned up but appear to have had no success. The last time I wanted anything doing I put a report in about it. That was about the barriers. They were at one time just linked end-to-end and were moving about; so I put that on paper and it was attended to immediately. The lights, I'll probably have to do the same for those."**

Let us illustrate in more detail what we mean by the phrase 'positive policing' by referring to further observations of fan behaviour made at this particular match. We note that the home supporters begin to group around the temporary barriers in the Kippax as soon as the gates are opened at 1.45pm. Collective chanting begins at 2.00pm and the full transcription of the tape may be given in an unedited form to provide the reader with an insight into fan interaction prior to the game; observing such interaction as it were through the eyes of the observer.

'The singing from the home side began at 2 o'clock. Groups of City fans gather against the barrier peering into the visiting fans' enclosure. There are only a few visiting spectators in evidence at this time and they are very quiet. As the number of visitors builds up, quite a few of them face the home fans and make various lewd gestures. Encouraged, the visitors break into a chant. This causes a great deal of excitement on the home side of the barrier. More home fans are drawn towards the barrier and respond with their chants. The crush is considerable and the emotional temperature rises as the visiting fans, though moving back somewhat from the fixed fence in response to the home fans' movement, respond with their own chants.

It's clear that the Evertonians are a spirited group, somewhat fortified by drink, and unlike the Liverpool fans previously referred to, fairly young; the majority being say 16-19 years of age.'

(Observer now moves position to the visitors' section and looks into the home area, much to the perplexity of home fans!)

'Youngsters crushed against the barrier eager faced, looking into our (Everton) section. Quite a number are only 13 or 14 years of age. It is impossible for them to see the pitch but this is irrelevant for at this stage, attention is fixed not on the pitch but on the visitors' enclosure. The visitors around me wave their scarves at the home supporters and begin to bait them across the barriers. The City fans respond with the following chant:

'We'll see you all, we'll see you all outside, see you all outside, see you all outside, we'll see you all, we'll see you all outside, see you all outside, see you all outside.........'

Undaunted, though greatly outnumbered, the visitors respond by chanting the name of the home teams' great rivals, Manchester United. This pushes the emotional temperature up another notch and the home fans chant:

'City aggro, oh, oh; City aggro, oh, oh',

The chants reach deafening proportions and resound throughout the stand. The crush builds up even more on the home side behind the temporary barrier. There is a crash and one of the barriers gives way (a wooden prop supporting the barrier against the fixed fence has snapped). The home fans are driven against the fixed fence by the pressure from behind and are held back only with great difficulty by the police.

Considerable effort is required to mobilise enough forces to push the home supporters back and to restore some kind of line along the barrier. There is considerable movement and anxiety amongst the home fans. One youngster is carried over the barrier with an injured leg. As he leaves the stadium, he gives a 'V' sign to the opposing supporters but seems glad to be out of it; the visiting fans jeer at him as he is carried out.

A wave motion begins and a tier of the crowd comes crashing down, forwards as well as sideways; people move in unison and there is a crushing movement at the front. A considerable frenzy seems to have arisen among the home supporters brought about by the visitors' boldness. For five or ten minutes, the police have to struggle hard to maintain control. I ask a young home supporter, who is crushed up against the side of the barrier and wedged in tightly at the front, why he comes to this part of the ground. With a grin between clenched teeth and fighting for breath he responds,

"More atmosphere here!'"

The last comment is characteristic of the replies received from young spectators in this section of the ground; they congregate in the vicinity of the barrier seeking excitement, not from the game which is to be played out on the pitch below, but from the action associated with asserting *their* mastery over the opposition. Interestingly, the 'hard cases' tend to position themselves further away from the barrier.

In the words of an officer:

> **"The knowledgeable ones can immerse themselves in the crowd, push, throw objects and so on, they leave it to the youngsters round the edges to be snatched. They're relatively immune in that situation."**

They are 'relatively immune' because, as previously pointed out, the officers are hampered in terms of both sighting such hardened offenders and gaining access to them. It was this problem which gave rise to the idea of a mobile platform, made from scaffolding tubes, on which a policeman could stand, thus improving his line of vision to which we previously referred. The end result being to 'dilute' the troublemakers.

Before the match starts, a fight breaks out in the visitors' section at the back of the terracing. Some spectators cascade down the stairs in an attempt to move away from the scene whereas others surge towards it. The crowd situation in the immediate area is thus momentarily unstable. Police officers quickly move in and bundle two youths, about 18 years of age, one with a bloodied face, down the stairs at the back of the Kippax towards the prison van. Equilibrium is restored, or nearly so, for three youths, obviously drunk, about 18 years of age, teeter from terrace to terrace in the visitors' section. Two of the three have their arms around each other and other fans give them a wide-berth as their behaviour is quite conspicuous. They gaze blank eyed at the home supporters across the barrier and make lewd gestures and obscene remarks. Their movements are very unsteady and they crash into a group of their fellow supporters. At this point two police officers take the young men by the shoulders and quietly remove them. There is little resistance and they are led down the exit stairs into the prison van so that their names and dates of birth can be recorded. They are then told to leave the ground. This certainly seems to have a sobering effect; quite confused as to why they're outside the ground rather than in it, they wander off, two of them still linking arms, across the now deserted Kippax car park. A point worth stressing is that these youth were the only 'drunks' observed and as much, were readily identified. Excessive drinking did not seem to be a particularly important determinant of the visiting fans' behaviour; it appeared rather to have an indirect influence by providing, with respect to our colleagues in Holland, a certain amount of 'Dutch courage', enabling them to respond in a spirited way to the home supporters' baiting and chanting.

Immediately prior to the kick-off the observer noted some forty to fifty supporters enter the visitors section and move down the terracing to its mid-point where they dispersed into the crowd. These supporters were, bar one, not wearing favours and it is clear from their accent and comments that they were City fans. A police officer has noted that 'infiltration' and mentioned the fact to his sergeant in the following terms:

> **"There's a bunch of forty or fifty City supporters in here, but I can't pick them out."**

The sergeant takes immediate action calling for extra men on his radio; when these reinforcements arrive, they are directed to disperse among the visiting supporters and are made aware of the home supporters' presence. This quick preventive action pays off, for during the game, the visiting team score first and at this point some of the infiltrators turn on the visitors and in the words of the sergeant:

> **"If the lads hadn't been there, there'd have been all hell let loose."**

The game proceeds and the home side scores an equalising goal. In response to this there is great jubilation on both sides of the barrier for a sizeable number of infiltrators are still in the visitors' enclosure. Like their brothers on the other side of the fence, they dance up and down in twos and threes, their faces transfixed for the moment, exhilarated by the goal **they** have just scored. Such exhilaration does not, of course, go unnoticed and they are escorted by the redeployed police officers up the terraces and led back to their section of terracing. They go without fuss; there is even a quiet dignity in their exit; 'honour' has been satisfied. A very quiet, impressive and effective police operation which is taken on a routine basis to ensure crowd safety. After the game there is no ebbing and flowing at the back of the stand as previously noticed at the City v. Liverpool match. Rather, small groups of youths, seven to eight in number, congregate in the passageways and attempt to re-enter the ground through the visitor's exit.

The mounted police are in the streets for that is where, as reported on an officer's radio, 'the trouble is'. This view is confirmed in a subsequent interview with a resident living in a street adjacent to the ground:

> **"We got it mostly about half an hour before the match finished. They were all youngsters between about 15 and 18; there were two or three hundred here.**
>
> **They got up here and the police charged them and tried to break them up with the horses and that. Then they started throwing milk bottles that were left on the doorsteps, milk bottles and stones and all sorts. Mind you, a lot of it is who's playing here."**

This quotation draws attention to the fact that the ready availability of missiles both inside and outside the ground makes it extremely difficult to police the crowds; searching at the turnstiles is a pointless task. Police morale is affected; an officer shows the observer two large stones similar to those found in the car park and comments:

> **"Took these off a ... (name of club) supporter. What's the point? (in response to a question about searching). They can fill their pockets with stones anytime. There are two skips of builder's rubble actually inside the ground over there (pointing). That lot could be used as missiles if things go badly wrong. Very poor arrangements. We're on a loser on this one; need another mesh fence (in the vicinity of the segregation point)."**

The reference to the skips was not verified but the comments indicate the difficulty, given the nature of the immediate physical environment of the ground, of handling this particular aspect of disorderly behaviour. With regard to the 'mesh fence', a chain-linked curtain installed between the seats in the Platt Lane stand and the corner of the Kippax, which we described earlier, the officer goes on to say (reinforcing the earlier quotation):

"Stops anybody getting hit and so stops them having a go back. Makes our job easier. Stops everything, the bottles, bricks, hot meat pies (these may be purchased inside the ground and have been used as 'missiles'), the lot."

This of course, assumes that the temporary barrier will be made permanent and 'sideways on segregation' will become an established feature of Maine Road; the chain-link fence would then be suspended from the roof of the grandstand at the segregation point. However, furthermore, darker events have overtaken this prediction. As we shall see from the following chapter, recommendations arising from the Hillsborough disaster in 1989 necessitated more radical solutions with plans for an 'all-seater' Kippax being scheduled for 1994 to turn Maine Road into an 'all-seater' stadium by that date.

Roles and relationships

We may now put the material presented in this opening chapter into a more general context, while at some time challenging and helping the reader to develop a deeper understanding of the crowd in terms of roles, relationships and leadership. Such a perspective needs to be coloured by the historical perspective which has already been provided.

We began this chapter by posing a number of rhetorical questions about the nature of crowds. In part, we can now provide answers. The crowd can be described as being large and unstructured and yet the people standing in the crowd are somehow held together by a bond. As long ago as 1896, Le bon suggested that this bond is attributed to " ... *the suggestibility of the individual and the almost hypnotic effect which people 'en masse' may have on one another.*" It has also been pointed out that there is a need to be able to distinguish between a mob and an audience. In one minute, a perfectly peaceful audience can be transformed because of one incident, into a panicking crowd or mob. While recognising the complexity of the phenomena, we are observing, observational data can be used to provide insight into, what may be termed 'group dynamics' focusing on cohesion and values. As we see if we turn to the 'Glossary' of terms appended to this book, groups are very hard to define; some commentators stipulate that for a group to exist, all of its members must relate to one another in an observable and significant way; other social scientists remark that it is simply a set of people, all with a common goal. What is apparent, is that all definitions share one characteristic and that is the need for cohesion or a 'cement' to holds members together and to keep them separate from other groups. Thus, members of the group all share, because of their norms and interconnected individual roles, a common goal that is they are an 'in group'. In this sense group cohesion has many effects and one of these is that of *collective* rather than *individual* behaviour often leading to what has been termed the process of 'de-individuation'.* We have seen many illustrations of this in the field work previously described whereby individual personality is submerged and surrendered to a collective one in terms of both attitude and behaviour.

This behavioural aspect of the crowd may be thought to come from two sources, the first is imitation, the second is the physical environment. During a match, mass imitation may occur which is contagious in character; the feelings or behaviour of one person spreading to others. There are many examples of this in our observational work with young fans catching the spirit of excitement and becoming more attentive to the behaviour of peers thus becoming more inclined to engage in devious forms of action. Emotional contagion occurs when the feelings of the crowd are unified, individuals abandon the social norms that usually constrain their behaviour and so their actions are motivated by their emotions. This is more likely to occur in situations like a football match because the participants, in particular locations, share the same attitudes and beliefs as the others around them. This is the process by which members of the crowd mutually stimulate and reinforce one another's responses until they reach, in the words of

* A process described in some detail in a companion volume to this, (Murray 2001, Manchester United at the Millennium).

a popular novel, 'fever pitch'. This view can be supported by the words of the first appointed Safety Officer at Manchester City (not the current appointee:)

> **" ..... there are some absolute hooligans and I mean demented people out there to cause trouble, but in addition, the often meek and mild person outside the ground changes into some kind of animal when he hits the terraces. This is an arena where emotions run very high... "**

In particular, football terraces can transform partisans into barbarians; on becoming a member of the crowd, a person may behave like a beast and commit acts that he would never have done had he been alone. Some people who see others behaving abnormally are able to convince themselves that they can commit similar acts without guilt or remorse. In terms of the second factor physical proximity, group cohesion is predetermined because of the dynamics of the group being geographically constrained by ground layout. In this regard, some fans feel that the presence of seats can ruin the 'atmosphere'. They argue that when they are standing shoulder to shoulder, they have a feeling of solidarity and are bonded as a group. In this sense, they conform to a psychological rather than legalistic framework of norms and resist any attempts to weaken affiliations that give meaning and substance to their lives. To be exposed to external danger increases this feeling of solidarity and the threat from visiting fans provides them with an opportunity to put down 'inhuman' or 'out group' rivals hence emasculating them. They thus 'defeat' their opponent's team vicariously if not on the pitch.

As the previously quoted Safety Officer at Manchester City points out, it is the:

> **"... loyalty to the club that plays an enormous part in how they (the crowd) will react to an incident on the field; a bad foul for example can increase pandemonia on the terraces if that foul is against their most favourite player ..."**

This problem increases if the home team loses because some of the supporters feel that they must regain the 'respectability' of their club by seeking revenge against the visiting supporters; they win in their own way. Such a stance enhances group cohesion bonding the fans together against the 'out group', because they all have the same intentions and beliefs. In the words of an academic commentator*:

> **"In the heat generated by the crowd, the fusion of individuals into a common sentiment or spirit blurs differences of personality and social status, blunts the intellectual facilities and propels the enthusiastic and credulous mass into patterns of behaviour that are sometimes heroic, but, rather more than often, destructive and anarchic."**

While empathising with this academic view, it should be pointed out that in general our observations lead us to the view that it is somewhat misleading to think of football crowds as 'unorganised herds', 'irrational mobs' or 'anarchic aggregates'. The amount of planning and administration arrangements to ensure crowd safety is, as we have seen, considerable. In addition, an actual match may be preceded by a considerable amount of publicity via the local media, particularly for a game which will attract a large number of visiting fans, such as Liverpool or Everton and consequently an expectation of excitement is generated especially among the young spectators. Let us return to our research data to illustrate this:

Young fan: **"You know, if it was a big day coming up everyone tends to get excited, like with Liverpool. Well, they come down at the end of this month and they've had 7,500 tickets sent to them. Like all City fans will know that by now. They'll be thinking how many's coming down. They'll probably be waiting for them or something. Getting ready. It's a big match as well."**

Observer: **"A big match? What's at stake?"**

(Lamb, H. and Myers, D. G. 1978, Group induced polarisation of attitudes and behaviour in Berkowitz, L. (Ed.) Advances in Experimental Social Psychology: Vol II, New York Academic Press)

Young fan: "Nothing at stake but it's more points towards a league title with Liverpool being second and City being fourth."

Thus a club with a good away following is known and prepared for, in a psychological sense, by the young home fans well in advance of the match; the relative position of the two teams in the league adding extra excitement to the occasion. For this particular home fan, the projected large number of visitors for this game posed something of a dilemma for him in terms if his likely behaviour on match day. He wished to stay out of trouble yet maintain his sense of club loyalty.

Young fan: "I've thought about it, all the fans coming down. I've been thinking what to do, like whether to wear a scarf; I didn't wear a scarf for the visit of Manchester United. You're sometimes safer without a scarf and we can take the visitors accent off, pretend to be one of them, but they can't (take off the local accent). So a City fan might go up to someone and ask the time, if they speak like that (in a 'foreign' accent), they'll get battered."

Home fans also remember how they were treated at particular clubs when they 'played' away from home. This shared memory may go back quite a long time with retribution for ill treatments being deferred until the clubs supporters visit the home ground. In this respect, a number of City fans commented on the treatment received at the hands of a Midlands club supporters, inadvertently drawing attention to the difficulty of policing this ground which is terraced at one end and on one side:

Young fan: "When we were at Birmingham, there was a lot of trouble. The police just pushed all the City fans into their (home team) end. It started off a lot of fighting. So the City fans all ran 'cause there was loads of them (home supporters), but I stayed near these men and women 'cause I felt safer there. Saw one of us getting battered, ugh!"

This treatment, seen as resulting from 'bad segregation' or the 'poor escort' of visitors from travel termini to grounds leads to a system of retribution.

Young fan: **"The City fans have got it in for Birmingham now. They really battered the City fans. We don't play them 'til next year but about two weeks before they'll be thinking of it. The ones that went to Birmingham and got battered; they'll be thinking of it and tell their mates. When they come down they'll get their own back."**

This form of shared memory also extends to actual incidents on the field of play and is reinforced by replays of previous encounters between the clubs on local TV prior to a match. Over the week there is a gradual and progressive build up in the local papers and the two television services, with the TV programmes being transmitted at peak viewing time.

A police officer with experience of dealing with the media comments:

"On Friday evening in this part of the world, Granada put their sport item on at peak viewing shortly after the evening meal. This deals purely and simply with the local teams and who they are playing; highlights certain players and incidents and so on and this pressure, this build up, goes on and people are never allowed to forget their football team from one Saturday to the next."

A Manchester City fan illustrates the point in the following terms:

"Well last year we played …. away and it was a bit of a niggling match and one of our team got sent off. Sent off for nothing; he was fouled by L.J. (one of opposing team) but got sent off. So when they came down here this season, as soon as they (visiting team) came out of the tunnel there were boos all round the ground. You see, they (home fans) had remembered (sending off previous season). Every time L.J. got the ball it was just whistles and boos. Then suddenly L.J. scores, it was a cracking goal and all, and the City fans are

booing him. Then we equalised, but then L.J. scored again and that drove them (home fans) crazy. But they didn't bring any supporters with them."

The concluding remark in this quotation draws attention to the fact that the visiting supporters would have been the recipients of the home fans' aggression had they been present in sufficiently large numbers to constitute a viable target.

Though the situations of personal ill treatment and perceived player 'victimisation' are different in both cases, the young fans' 'honour' is at stake. Such affronts to one's honour may, in fact, be satisfied by the home victory over the opposition; conversely a defeat merely adds to the insult. Even without the force of collective memory, a defeat by itself may lead to frustration which spills over into retaliation against the representatives of the victorious side.

Young fan: **"Well, if we get beat, the fans go away dejected and the others (visitors) are happy. I feel bad but just go home. You know, I don't do nothing about is 'cause I can't. But other fans go (attack) for the away fans just to get something out of it 'cause City got beat. You know, we can always say we battered ... (visiting club), you know something like that even though we got beat."**

Thus some fans 'have got to get something out of it'; success has to be achieved on the terraces or 'outside' if not on the field of play. A City fan who has been involved in a number of incidents, suggests that such action is in fact a token or measure of 'good support' for the club. When asked why he sometimes waits outside the visitors' exit at the ground, he comments:

"It's just if your team get beat. <u>Good supporters</u> don't like their team getting beat so we wait for the other supporters to come out and give it to them. Show them who's boss."

Moral inversion with a vengeance! The great majority of home fans, of course, suffer a 'personal loss' when their team is defeated but do not translate this into co-ordinated violent action against visiting supporters which is then justified on moral grounds. Given this inversion of moral values, it is little wonder that crowd control and ground improvement with respect to this are far from straightforward matters and need to be continually reviewed and attended to. Thus police arrangements, their recruitment and disposition, ground lay out, the collective force of shared memories, incidents on the field of play and the psychological importance of the match all contribute to that complex interplay of fused relationships we call 'the crowd' on match days in the UK. More specifically, in the context of Manchester City, the transmission of values which define being 'a *Blue*' has been strengthened by the cycles of success and failure which have been charted in the historical sketch with which we began this chapter and which can go some way to describing what it means to be a City fan; a psychologically significant status or perhaps, more accurately, a way of life! We will continue to describe and chart this phenomenon in the following chapters. Suffice to say here that it cannot be fully understood without describing the background factors which show how inter-generational transmission of values and 'history' combine to communicate the constellation of beliefs, attitudes and values which describe what it means to be a Manchester City supporter; in brief, to communicate, instil and reinforce an 'Attitude Blue'.

GORTON FC, CIRCA 1984/85 SEASON DISPLAYING THEIR NEW STRIP

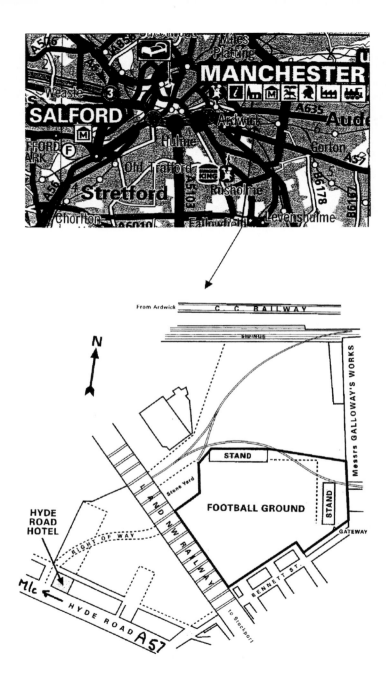

LOCATIONAL PLAN OF CITY'S HYDE ROAD GROUND

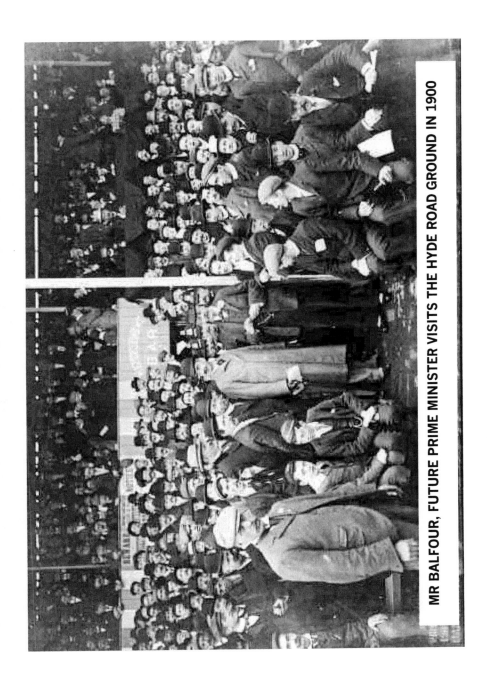

MR BALFOUR, FUTURE PRIME MINISTER VISITS THE HYDE ROAD GROUND IN 1900

CITY'S FA CUP WINNING TEAM: 1904

CONSTRUCTION OF THE MAINE ROAD GRANDSTAND BY McALPINE'S, CIRCA 1922

MAINE ROAD 1923 FINISHED AND READY FOR THE FIRST GAME

THE FIRST GAME AT MAINE ROAD, 1923. PHIL WOOSNAM, CLUB CAPTAIN INTRODUCES THE LORD MAYOR TO THE PLAYERS

CITY IN THE 1934 CUP FINAL. SAM COWAN LEADS OUT HIS TEAM. ERIC BROOK, FRANK SWIFT AND MATT BUSBY FOLLOW

CROWDS IN CROSS STREET, MANCHESTER IN 1934 GREETING FA CUP WINNERS CITY

KIPPAX TERRACING IN THE 1970's: SEGREGATION POINT: VISITORS BEYOND THE FIXED FENCE

REAR OF THE KIPPAX IN THE 1970's: SEGREGATION FROM TURNSTILE TO TERRACE

MOBILE OBSERVATION PLATFORM 1970's: BACK OF KIPPAX

CHAPTER TWO

CROWDS AND CONTROL

Introduction

Bearing in mind the concluding discussion featured in the last chapter, it is reasonable to say that on the whole, the soccer crowd is a peaceful rather than a violent one and tends to be characterised by social cohesion rather than disintegration. It is certainly far removed from 'the mob' described by Le Bon in relation to the French Revolution of 1848 and can indeed often be creative as well as destructive. There is a reasonable degree of consensus among academic commentators as to what constitutes a 'crowd' and we may begin this chapter as we did the previous one, by considering definitions; thus framing our presentation of material within an analytical framework. The following two definitions will suffice:

> **"A large, but temporary gathering of people with a common interest or focus".**
> *(Reber, A.S. Penguin Dictionary of Psychology, 1985)*

> **"Behaviour in which large numbers of people who are in the same place at the same time behave in a uniform manner which is volatile, appears relatively unorganised, is characterised by strong emotion and is often in violation of social norms".**
> *(Manstead, A. and Hewstone, M. The Blackwell Encyclopaedia of Human Psychology, 1995)*

While there is a temptation to enlarge on these definitions here, we will resist it for an analysis and explanation of crowd behaviour at soccer matches is offered in the companion volume to this, 'Manchester United at the Millennium'. Consequently, there is no need to repeat this exercise. Sufficient to say that the work of Waddington and others, provides a useful way thinking about crowd

* *Waddington, D. et al, The Crowd in Contemporary Britain, Gaskill and Benowicz, 1989*

behaviour. Their approach may be outlined in summary form in the following chart with examples being given in relation to soccer situations:

CHART 3: THE CROWD ACCORDING TO WADDINGTON et al.

LEVEL 1 **Structural**	Wider social structures which govern whole groups of individuals, for example, fans attending Premier League games having to sit rather than stand as a result of post-Hillsborough legislation.
LEVEL 2 **Political/Ideological**	A sector of society may have a political or ideological position, for example, the recruitment of young soccer fans to the National Front; the protest against increased admission charges at football grounds; the distancing of the 'terraced fan' from the multi-national soccer club.
LEVEL 3 **Cultural**	Reflects shared ideals and ideas within groups, for example, what constitutes being a fan, in short, 'Attitude Blue'.
LEVEL 4 **Contextual**	The sequence of events which might be described in short-hand as 'Match Day'; involving police, stewards and fans.
LEVEL 5 **Spatial**	The environment which constrains the crowd. Stadia, grandstands, exits, entrances and so on; the symbolism of the arena.
LEVEL 6 **Interactional**	Relationships between the various groups which make up the crowd, for example, police and spectators.

Let us continue this chapter by taking the last point first as our focus while bearing in mind all levels are interrelated.

A question of crowd safety

It would be erroneous to assume that the cost of policing and ground improvements at Manchester City are a 'once and for all' expenditure and that match day can proceed unencumbered by the demands of a safety conscious society. An interview with a club official indicates how Manchester City had to adapt in the 80's and early 90's to meet the safety and leisure time expectations of their supporters. The following extract from the interview reveals the drain on club finances arising from the need to take on board continuing legislation and to stay abreast of new developments in the 'football industry', such as the introduction of the Premier League in 1992 and, prior to that, government legislation with regard to the Hillsborough Disaster in 1989:

Observer: **"What efforts has the club made to ensure the safety and comfort of supporters at Maine Road in the 90's and prior to that?"**

Respondent: **"Since the mid 70's we have constructed a new roof on the main stand. This major improvement was carried out in 1982; that is, before various government reports recommending modifications to soccer stadia. The club has always been very positive about this and indeed, after long consultation with the local authority, safety advisory council and the football trust devised an overall plan for the stadium."**

The reference to the Main Stand's new roof draws attention to how ground improvements can fall foul of insufficient revenue arising from the need to attract first class players to sustain success on the field of play. In this case, Peter Swales, the then Chairman, announced during the summer of 1981 after City's appearance in the Cup Final that Maine Road would be re-developed at a cost of around £6M over a five year period ending in time for the start of the 1986/87 season. The plan was to replace the Main Stand and Kippax roofs with modern "corrugated" ones and with the Platt Lane end of the ground re-fashioned to mirror the North Stand. The changes were seen as increasing the stadium's capacity from 52,600 to 54,000 and incorporated the provision of 36 private boxes to be suspended from the Main Stand roof, a new TV-gantry, two lifts, a new restaurant and a new roof-mounted floodlighting system. The money was to come from the club's development association and thus not effect team re-building via the payment of transfer fees. However, the plan was never brought into operation due to financial difficulties and only the main stand roof was replaced. Despite the Chairman's statement, the problems of raising revenue stemmed directly from meeting the £1.2M cost of engaging the playing services of Trevor Francis together with a three year salary of £100,000 plus bonuses. The re-modelled stadium would have looked symmetrical and attractive as shown in the artists' impression at the conclusion of this chapter, but it was not to be. To return to our interview:

Observer: "What other improvements are in hand?"

Respondent: "It was decided to demolish the Platt Lane stand and build completely new accommodation the week beginning 13th July 1992 with a completion date fixed for February 1993. This totally new accommodation is all seated and include 48 executive boxes. It is designed to provide facilities for the disabled and will have a family section larger than those previously provided. In design it will be cantilever."

This stand, now known as the Platt Lane Stand or Umbro Stand, engendered at that time considerable pride and excitement at all levels of the club. For example, at the club's Annual General Meeting in 1993 the then Chairman, the late Peter Swales said:

"On completion it will be one of the finest in the country. The provision of 48 executive boxes, each with their own viewing balcony, will add further to the excellent facilities of corporate hospitality at Maine Road and guarantee an additional source of income for many years to come."

No expense was spared in the construction of the stand which utilised the skills of over 2,000 workers and has heated public concourses provided by a warm air circulatory system. Spectators have a choice of six catering outlets on two levels providing quality food and drink. In addition to an adjacent Manchester Evening News family stand, the stand incorporates a disabled persons' balcony providing purpose built accommodation for those in wheelchairs with a lift installed to provide access and egress.

The new stand saw its first paying customers on Sunday 7th March 1993 at City's FA Cup Quarter Final against Tottenham Hotspur. It turned out to be an auspicious date in more ways than one! Why? Headlines from Monday's papers on 8th March described in colourful clichés, fans spilling on to the pitch from the new stand initially in a 'rite of jubilation' after the first City goal and then in a 'rite of degradation' after City's second goal, scored at a point in the game when they were clearly the losers being 4-1 down. The fans from the stand were joined by approximately one hundred from the Kippax. Thirteen mounted policemen entered the pitch from the gap between the Kippax and the stand and eventually restored order. The reader of this book will by now be aware of the danger of explaining the reasons for this crowd turbulence in simplistic unitary terms. Tabloids have no such scruples! For example, the Daily Mirror 'cornered the truth' with the ex-cathedra pronouncement on 8th March:

"Idiotic Manchester City fans who blatantly tried to save their team from an FA Cup exit by getting the game abandoned also tried, without success, to spark violent confrontation with the 7,500 Spurs fans."

We have seen however, in Chapter One, that a number of psychological and social processes play their part in crowd disturbances; in particular, we have underlined the importance of past memories and recollections which generate a reactive response in some fans. In this instance, the reader should be aware of crowd violence at City's home league game against Spurs on 28th November 1992, initiated by the visiting fans, and fighting in the City centre after Manchester United played Spurs on 9th January, 1992. The psychological and situational predisposition for disorder may perhaps be best understood in terms of these past events. In addition a commentator remarks:

"Forged membership cards are common currency at Maine Road. Anybody could get a ticket for the game. A lot of

unfamiliar faces. The last time many of these attended a game they were wearing Pringles, Fila and Kappa tracksuits and Farrahs. In other words, the game attracted the element of society most likely to cause trouble and because of the point above, they found no difficulty in entering the ground."

Thus, both the 'perennials' and 'annuals' of human social life colour the organisational arrangements designed to ensure the safety and comfort of spectators in ways that are not easy to predict. A new stand is a major capital outlay and disruption is a disappointment, but in practical terms it can also be a headache for ground staff particularly when the police response is that of a mounted cavalry charge! As we have seen, the disruption in question brought police horses onto the pitch and caused considerable damage to the playing surface, with the pitch compacting into a solid mass. Even in normal circumstances, the problem of drainage at Maine Road is a recurrent one as the pitch is actually ten feet below pavement level and is built, as we have seen, on clay foundations. A problem in the opposite direction is that the under-soil heating which was installed in 1977 keeps the ground playable in winter but tends to dry out the pitch too much in prolonged cold, dry spells. Any damage to the playing surface adds to expense and presented considerable challenges to the ground staff.*

In addition to such expenditure, considerable expense is also involved in meeting local authority safety requirements. The day-to-day financial attrition of such arrangements should not be underestimated. In this regard, the official continues:

Respondent: **"The whole structure of the North Stand and its seating layout had to be revamped. Gangways were not correct and general safety had to be upgraded: we spent £100,000 on the stand. Exit gates were put in the perimeter wall and fences which were**

* *Stan Gibson, head groundsman, retired in 1997 and was interviewed for City's Official Magazine in which he gives an interesting account of the challenges he had to face.*

constructed, are now having to be dismantled arising from new specifications since Hillsborough."

Observer: "Any other improvements you would mention to ease the situation for the spectator?"

Respondent: "Our floodlighting has had to be improved. A new CCTV system was put in with police approval. A new police control room has been constructed and numerous other jobs have been undertaken."

Observer: "What other jobs?"

Respondent: "Well, tremendous improvements in toilet facilities which are not directly related to crowd safety; really to comply with what is required in this day and age. Snack bars in the main stand have been modified. As of now (1992) we are spending £120,000 on two sets of toilets and £50,000 on first aid facilities."

In addition to these improvements, the club had decided to spend £40,000 on a standby generator in case of a cut in power supply so that an emergency back-up system could be called upon to illuminate the ground and its adjacent environment. In addition, to comply with the Taylor Report, the club installed a new Public Address System to cover both inside and outside the ground at a cost of £120,000. These changes are not dramatic or newsworthy. They do however constitute a significant financial drain and are ongoing, for example, in response to further questioning about ground improvements, the official concludes as follows:

Respondent: "A mammoth amount of work on ground improvements has gone on and is going on; for example the local fire authority came into the offices and we are having to spend £30,000 stripping out all wall coverings and refurbishing doors to make them fire resistant. £20,000 has been spent on a fire alarm system for the main stand. We will also have to install one in the North Stand in the not too distant future …… In 1975, 20% of crush barriers had to be tested each year and that has been increased to

25%. The only stand we have with crush barriers is the Kippax but also in the new code, the handrails round the stadium have to be tested ….. ours will not meet the standards so we are having to replace them at a cost of thousands of pounds … we have so far spent £50,000 on replacement handrails. Since the 70's we are talking of an expenditure of roughly £4m. Add that the £6m for Platt Lane and the Kippax will cost from £8m to £11m, depending on how we develop it and to what level."

Changes also came about with regard to policing at Maine Road in the 80's and 90's. With the advent of the football licensing authority, the trend was for the police to move out of football grounds in order to take up regular duties. The Home Office placed the onus on the clubs to appoint a safety officer and to improve their stewarding and security under the direction of this officer. In response to these changes, Manchester City appointed its first safety officer in the early 90's and he immediately put the whole stewarding and policing of the stadium under review. His opinions have been previously quoted in Chapter 1, and as a former superintendent of Greater Manchester Police, his task was to liaise with the local authority and GMP to ensure the safety of spectators and increase the clubs involvement in stewarding. Plans varying from ensuring the comfort of spectators to contingencies for major disasters were developed, not only at Manchester City but at grounds throughout the country. During an interview with the author shortly after his appointment, in response to a question about his role and the expense of putting into practice safety related issues, he provided the following opinion:

"Over the last 2-3 years the Audit Commission reported that the police should charge full rates; this is currently £22/hour. So for one match day, which lasts approximately five hours, each police officer receives £110. For Manchester City this full cost recovery began straight away, whereas other clubs could phase in the cost of policing. This turns out to be very expensive for City.

The Greater Manchester Police statement of context, which was written by police lawyers, states that the police are the

ones who decide how many officers should be on duty at each match and that the police are the ones that give advice to the stewards. They ensure that all the stewards are capable and good at their job. The general rule now is low profile policing and high profile stewarding. My view is that most of the stewards are in it just for the money rather than to watch the match.

The current maximum crowd capacity is 26,000 and the class of the match, 'A', 'B' or 'C' will indicate the number of police needed.

> Low-risk match (e.g. City v Wimbeldon) = 'A'
> High-risk match (e.g. City v Manchester Utd, Leeds or Newcastle) = 'C'

At the start of the season, a match would need 177 constables. Last week at the match against Swindon we had 36 constables and next week for the match against Wimbeldon, we will have 25. This is because the police are beginning to have confidence in us in handling the game on our own. At the start of the season for a 'B' classed match we had 90 constables and now we have 55. We also have ten cameras now with two of them outside, so that a better view is had of the crowd. It is also easier to spot offenders if they are sitting down. The problems we have are that there are too many adults in the family stand – due to cheap family tickets. Some of them are difficult to deal with and are abrasive and offensive to other people in that stand.

Looking back, because of the trouble in the 70's, the police had to play a large part in crowd control, but nowadays with a much better behaved crowd the police are sometimes too heavy-handed, lack tact and over-react to situations. Because of this 'over the top' attitude, they can cause trouble themselves; of course this is not the case for all of them. It is hard to deal with policemen with this attitude; with a steward you can just sack him but with police you can only put in a complaint, which is very time consuming.

Again, it is a personal view but in terms of ensuring the safety of the crowd, there should be a good balance between stewards and police. Of course there will always be police at football matches but at the moment, the police have far too much control over when matches are played. This is because you need to give the police eight days' notice before they will say 'yes' to a match being played. It should, in my view, be the club who determine the time and day of the match."

Such a response has to be contextualised within the reality of a Greater Manchester Police Authority policy which covers ten urban districts of which Manchester is but one. To illustrate, a senior policeman from a neighbouring authority, Bolton, which has a tradition of First Division/Premiership football comments during an interview in the early 90's:

"Tasks previously undertaken by police are now undertaken by stewards. The division of responsibilities is essentially pragmatic; if it is a question of public order then the police will deal with it, if the issue is essentially centred on the ground, then the club will deal with it provided it is within their compass. A safety officer, previously a policeman, has been appointed and he works hard to bring the stewards up to scratch. I think this is a very positive step. Police over time have probably become over-involved with football. A lot of our work was basically enforcement of ground regulations, which would be carried out by stewards. Against this, you should be aware that there has been a total change of policing football since you conducted your research in the late 1970's – based on two major enquiries; the Popperwell Enquiry dealing with the Bradford City fire and more recently heard Justice Taylor's Enquiry into the Hillsborough Disaster. The Green Guide on the construction of stadia and safety precautions to be taken, has been issued, so there is a national series of recommendations and guidelines on how we will move forward together.

The major influence on our ability to combine the work of police and stewards at this ground, as at others like Old Trafford and Maine Road, is the use of closed-circuit television (CCTV). Within Greater Manchester in the 1980's, we developed a programme to train police officers and others who would be concerned with stadium development and spectator safety in the use of CCTV. Now Burnden Park, like Maine Road and Old Trafford has been provided with a comprehensive and flexible system which allows the ground commander from his position in the Control Box to monitor every area of the ground. The control room was placed in relation to our request to the club and to our specification so that, in terms of crowd safety and crowd control, we have everything that we could want and all the support that one could wish for from the club in this aspect of our work.

That facility is invaluable – enormous strides have been made and we can say that we have actually policed trouble out of football grounds since the 1970's and which has enabled us to replace police officers with stewards and the intention is for that process to continue until the grounds in Greater Manchester are self-sufficient – self sustaining in terms of their own internal policing. People are sometimes persuaded that the problem of hooliganism has disappeared, but that is not the case. We have Football Intelligence Officers working to every club and we now have a national structure with a National Football Intelligence Unit based in London. Because we have become more sophisticated in the way we transmit information around the country, we are able to identify the problems at source and to police them out by and large. We still do have trouble with football supporters in certain areas and there is clear evidence of a hard core, organised hooligan minority but this can be targeted and dealt with more easily than before instead of dealing with it on a week by week basis".

Official: "Do you see any problem in this approach and the freedom of the individual in a democratic society, i.e. the 'big brother is watching you' syndrome?"

Respondent: "This is a question we have addressed on a number of occasions. We are fortunate again in Bolton because we had the first CCTV system in operation in the North of England set up in the Town Centre. This system was installed in the early 1990's and

we have had total support from the community. We take the
view that it (CCTV) is in every area of public life – shopping
centres, banks, building societies and so on – and it sees
nothing more than a patrolling police officer would see if he
was standing at a given point; it means that the police can
maximally deploy their limited resources effectively; you can
anticipate a requirement by seeing it in advance and the
public are delighted with it. They regard it as an extra
measure of protection. Probably a total reversal of the views
we might have expected in the late 1970's or early 1980's."

Following on from this interview, an interesting insight into the
emerging role of the steward is provided by *Libero!* the football
supporters' network through their magazine, '90 minutes'. Framing
the rhetorical question, 'who would be a steward?', their reporter
spent a match day with stewards at Maine Road, in the mid-90's,
with the expectation that the answer would be:

"... policeman, social worker, bouncer and first-aider all
rolled into one and you're not even expected to watch the
game and then there's that fetching orange jacket to wear!"

We may present the results of this experience by presenting a
largely unedited account of the article as follows:

"Post Hillsborough and the Taylor Report, the police are now
less conspicuous, playing second fiddle to the men and
women in orange coats. Since 1995, the Football League has
run official programmes for all stewards to try to equip them
with the necessary skills and techniques to control large
crowds. With football becoming big business and undergoing
a process of 'gentrification', supporters' behaviour is often
near the top of the agenda, with standing up and swearing
(an obligatory part of the old match day experience) often
regarded as illegal contraventions of modern-day ground
regulations. Interestingly, clubs can take out or add clauses
to these regulations as they wish ..... Lesson number one –
stewarding is not a big earner. Rates for a five hour shift
vary from £15-£30 ... crowd and exit stewards get £15, gate
and perimeter £20 and senior and supervisor stewards -

vary from £15-£30 ... crowd and exit stewards get £15, gate and perimeter £20 and senior and supervisor stewards - £30. Most of the Maine Road stewards are either City supporters or just love the challenge of the job.

The 'match day order' forms the basis of the briefing all stewards are given before each game at City and ends with the words... "Our aim is to be firm yet fair and friendly. Positive, yet pleasant and polite. Consensus not confrontation." So do City's stewards live up to this aim and to what extent can fervent devotion to your team be construed as bad behaviour? Are there points of tension between the stewards and the police? "Ideally we're aiming for no police at all in the ground", says one steward. "And as we've taken everything off the heavy handed boys in blue, they've been denied the chance to needlessly eject fans". A graphic example of this occurred in the match against Southend, when City's opening goal revealed a few Sky Blues were in amongst the 'Shrimpers'. Club regulations stipulate that, "transferring from one area of the ground to another without the permission of a steward, police officer, or other authorised agent of the club is strictly forbidden". The stewards quietly and quickly escorted them to a City seating block, but the police sergeant on duty wanted them ejected and stood toe to toe with a senior steward arguing the point. Pragmatism won the day and the fans stayed.

The result of this difference of opinion between police and stewards indicates that it is indeed the stewards who are the main source of authority in the ground, currently. Police are only really used for public order incidents and arrests.

When it comes to supporters standing up and swearing, City stewards express the view that to get thousands of animated supporters to sit down could create a flashpoint or confrontation. During the FA Cup game against Watford, the police wanted the stewards to get 2,000 visiting fans to sit down but the senior steward told the police, "These boys have travelled a long way and are used to terraces in the Second Division, so if you want them to sit down, you do it." As one steward explains, "As long as they stay in their

blocks and don't block the gangways, then standing is usually OK."

Swearing, or the "use of foul and abusive language" under the Football (Offences) Act 1991 is strictly forbidden and, in this family-friendly age, is regarded as an affront to women and children. But are they all so easily offended? A Middlesbrough fan with his young son told us, "You just can't help swearing", whilst a mother and daughter supporting City admitted, "We love a good rant and a swear at every game". A supporter who sits in the Junior Blues area says, "I take my two lads and I just can't help swearing. It's part and parcel of football culture."

Manchester City's deputy head steward feels that the odd character amongst the fans, like Sheffield Wednesday's bare-chested 'Tango Man', helps make both the game and his job worthwhile and that any attempt to arbitrarily clamp down on them will only detract from the atmosphere at grounds. During the Cup game against Watford for example, the control room picked up something on CCTV and radioed through to have it stopped. Two very large men were apparently continually bearing their chests, one a Watford fan, the other a City fan. This steward informed control that nothing untoward was happening. "It was just two rival fatties comparing and rubbing their beer bellies", he laughs. The Battle of the Bellies was allowed to continue. Whether all club stewards are as sussed as City's appear to be remains to be seen, but if they were then vociferous fans could enjoy the game a lot more."

It seems clear that policing and stewarding responses to certain types of fan behaviour vary from club to club. On the one hand, there is the pragmatic approach of 'consensus not confrontation' while others are essentially formal and regulative, coming down firmly on any behaviour that could be construed as contravening ground regulations whether it be swearing, standing up, gesturing or a person in the wrong seat. The end result of the latter approach is, according to its critics, the stripping of football of much of its passion and diluting the emotional charge inside grounds; that is removing the 'atmosphere'. A concern with the safety of spectators was understandable during the 80's and early 90's because since the early research was undertaken, as described in the previous chapter, a number of disasters have taken place in sports stadiums in general but particularly in soccer grounds. Most notably in 1985 at Birmingham City's ground, at Bradford in the same year and again in 1985 at Heysel Stadium in Belgium. The problems at those grounds have however, been dwarfed into insignificance by the disaster at Hillsborough on 15th April 1989, when over one hundred people were killed. Clearly soccer clubs had to respond in a meaningful way to those problems and Manchester City was no exception. So what, in *Libero!* Terms, does it mean to have 'sussed stewards' and how does this relate to policing City in the Millennium?

Let us take the last question first and skip forward some ten years to 2002 to a group discussion convened at the request of the author to discuss policing at Maine Road. While it would be relatively straightforward to summarise the content of the discussion and present a synopsis of that summary here it would not have the immediacy or authenticity of a verbatim account of what transpired. Consequently the latter is the preferred mode of transmission; suffice to say, by way of introduction, that the officers involved were unknown to the author prior to the meeting, that the meeting took place in the command centre used for policing the ground and that all officers were currently 'operational' with regard to policing City's ground at a variety of levels. The three officers involved, termed R1, R2 and R3 occupied the ranks of Constable, Sergeant and Inspector. Having familiarised the officers with the earlier research as described in Chapter One, the author (O) opens the discussion with the following question:

O: **"What changes have taken place in policing football at Maine Road since the 70's?"**

R1: **"We do not draw the manpower from as far away as we used to. It is mainly drawn from local divisions, unless it is a very heavily policed game. When you attended pre-match police briefings in the 70's, there were two assigned to traffic control points with keys to suspend traffic lights to assume manual control as they once were. The only traffic operation now (2002) is to assist** coaches exit the area without too much difficulty. Crowd control is very much intelligence led now. Every force has officers who work closely with their football clubs and we base our policing on their estimates and local knowledge about their fans when they visit Maine Road. Typically, we meet with the club and still categorise the games 'A', 'B' or 'C' – 'A' being the least problematic and 'C' requiring the heavier policing, the highest risk. We agree the level of manpower for the 'A's and 'B's while the 'C' category games are open ended. The manpower is then arranged through the four sub-divisions of the South Manchester division. Our function here at Moss Side is a planning role arranging vehicles, radios and so on.

On the day of the game, officers report to St Edward's School which is a primary school just adjacent to the ground and the police commander, who will be a superintendent or chief superintendent will brief the men."

R2: "To take up this point... the briefing is an extension of a written operational order and is done through a laptop computer and psychlops projector, quite different from what you previously experienced. It is very sophisticated and includes photographs, charts and so on. There are still specific deployments for officers however the briefing is on a standard format. Our objectives are set out for that game and the methods we are going to employ to achieve them; three phases are employed to contextualise this, before, during and after the game."

R3: "You do a safety section as well, don't you?"

R2: "Yes. We cover administration, what the officers are going to wear, where spare kit is going to be stored, where vehicles are going to be parked and so on. Communication covers radio channels and then a full safety briefing, outlining contingency plans, emergency message transmission and so on. Probably more detailed, exhaustive and sophisticated than in the 70's.

This takes from fifteen to twenty minutes and is scheduled for at least two hours before the kick-off; takes place for all officers regardless of whether they police the ground regularly or not."

R3: "It is very slick as well. The time involved, relatively short, does not indicate the quality; it is prepared well in advance. The commanding officer on match day will be reading notes as graphics are portrayed and it really is a slick operation."

R2: "We also have built in 'audit' whereby officers from our training unit will conduct a 'dip sample' of officers – that is, ask officers at random specific questions about the briefing. We are aware that they are local officers and will work a lot of games and we don't want complacency to set in. These outside officers will also form a view about the overall arrangements for the game and how effective and efficient they are and report accordingly."

R1: "They adopted this procedure a few years ago but more informally, for example, a sergeant, now an inspector, used to consult with a handful of bobbies. In my case, I worked a perimeter gate on the old (terraced) Kippax and he would appear and ask me questions such as, "What is the capacity of this area behind you?", "What would you do if so and so happened?" You were supposed to know."

O: "Let us turn now to more general issues, the balance between public order issues and what may be termed enforcement of ground regulations. This, of course, brings in the role of stewarding."

R2: "It's very clear that the activity on a match day is a profit making one on private premises. Thus, the main, no the sole responsibility for spectator safety lies with the club. The police support that function. In the case of City, their stewards are particularly well trained. They were one of the first clubs to receive the Footballing Stewardship Safety qualification and are now self accredited. Most of the club's stewards are qualified and have NVQ's in stewarding. Thus, the police have less presence and responsibility than they used to and their disposition is specific to problematic areas."

R1:   "I have worked the ground for many years: over 30 in fact. When I first worked there, there were police officers in every stand but now it is much more limited, as it is at Old Trafford where I have also worked."

R3:   "The club's stewardship operation is as elaborate now as the policing operation and is conducted under the supervision of a safety officer who identifies key roles, appropriate expectations and briefs individuals about their duties, for example as guides, specifically to respond to incidents and so on, as well as overseeing the variety of strategies for crowd control and safety that are available."

R1:   "There is no doubt that stewarding at Maine Road is far more professional now, light years away from how it began. I have seen stewards, when I was policing on match day in the past, go and collect their bib, get their free programme, obtain tokens for free refreshments and walk round to the Kippax. Once there, they take the bib off, put it in their pocket and stand with their mates and watch the game as a subsidised, non-paying spectator courtesy of the club! In those days a lot of people who volunteered to be stewards simply wanted a free ticket for the match and it was a bonus if free refreshments were thrown in. Crowd control was not their motivation."

R3:   "Your (O's) initial comments referred to a possible scenario where the stewards would take over completely from the police in ensuring spectator safety. With regard to a major sports complex like Maine Road, this is more visionary than reality; it is a utopian state! Having policed a variety of different fixtures at Maine Road, I can sense those clubs which do not have a police presence at their home fixtures. The standard of their fans' behaviour in general when they visit Maine Road is significantly different and poorer from those who have experienced a joint police/stewarding operation at their own grounds."

R2: "Remember there are clubs who have gone down this road and have big problems, for example Birmingham, Coventry and others not policed."

R3: "The police/stewardship balance effects the tolerance level of crowd behaviour. In theory, it is the club who should set the level of what is acceptable behaviour on their ground for a fixture – we may call this the tolerance level. It shouldn't be for the minority, disruptive element to set the tolerance level. This is more easily achievable in a joint stewarding/police operation. A police presence certainly gives the stewards more confidence and assurance in dealing with the crowd because they know they have police support who have batons and power of arrest. Stewards do not carry batons."

R2: "This is exemplified in the match control room. Up to Hillsborough. It was known as the Police Control Room and now, it is the Match Control Room. The police have an area for their communications and control systems and the club have their area for CCTV and the ambulance section have a small area as well to serve their specific needs. It is thus an integrated match control facility and not one where the police have primacy."

R1: "There was, some ten years ago, an honest belief within some clubs and even held by senior police officers, that the police should withdraw from football grounds and let the clubs be autonomous from every point of view. I think now however, there is a realisation that a mixed portfolio of 'private' and 'police' arrangements is the optimum 'modus operandi' for crowd control."

R3: "Also remember that local policing, especially at grade 'C' matches, is a considerable expense for the club. The latter thus face a commercial dilemma because to reduce policing, may result in a cost saving, however, they may be faced with a major public order situation which is beyond their competence in crowd control and marshalling and which in itself either directly or indirectly lead to lost revenue. We have seen this also with regard to the on-site sale of alcohol. The initial concept of 'no alcohol for sale' at football grounds was not viewed favourably from a commercial point of view and was subsequently modified. I think you have to reach a happy medium between commercial and safety expectations. There are pre-defined times when police will take a firm stance and indeed will have no option but to take such a stance!"

R2: "Yes, it's a very clearly defined hand over. If the ground safety officer or his nominated deputy cannot deal with a particular incident with the resources available to him, then he will formally hand over control to the police. This is clearly documented."

O: "Perhaps this is a good point to review last season's games (2000/01), say January to the end of the season with respect to specific situations when such transference may have been necessary that is, when what was termed 'riot and tumult' occurred, or did it? You will recall this was City's relegation period, which resulted in their eventual loss of Premier League status. Can you highlight any problems, which may have occurred at these fixtures. To focus discussion we can take the following local press release (Friday 2nd March, 2001)".

At this point in the discussion, matters are halted while the observer circulates a copy of the release to the three officers and gives them time to read it. It is given in full in Chart 4 with only names being omitted.

Police fear a riot at drop-zone City

POLICE fearing a full scale riot at Manchester City on Saturday have been thwarted in a legal bid to impose a booze exclusion zone around Maine Road.

Magistrates blocked a request by officers to close 18 pubs and off-licences earlier in the week, saying they had to wait until nearer match day to argue their case in court.

But officers have now decided not to go ahead with the application, opting instead to increase police activity on the day to ensure no trouble breaks out.

• POLICE are cracking down on a rise in car crime around Manchester City's Maine Road ground on match days.

An inspector who is coordinating the operation said: "We have put more police on the streets but the pubic also has a major role to play in cutting crime.

We are urging people who park their cars near the ground not to leave any valuables on display in their vehicle which might tempt opportunist thieves.

Items which are regularly snatched include mobile phones, coats and bags which could easily have been hidden from view in the car boot."

A City director said the problem of car crime on match day is faced by most major clubs.

GMP believe fans' frustration at the threat of dropping out of the Premiership could trigger clashes with rival supporters and police. The game against Southampton has now been reclassified as having a higher chance of trouble.

The claims made in court were angrily dismissed by City's chief operating officer who defended the record of the club's supporters.

The row flared after police appealed to magistrates to close pubs and off-licences near the Maine Road ground for nearly 12 hours between 7am and 7pm on Saturday.

An inspector said extreme measures were needed to avert a riot – and fellow officers had been forced to deal with riot situations at City's last two home games.

The inspector applied for a ban under SECTION 188 of the Licensing Act 1964 if a "riot or tumult is happening or is expected to happen".

He told the court: "There have been riots. We will show that a riot and a tumult has occurred at the last two matches".

But the bench refused on the grounds that the legislation could only be used when the threat of disorder was more immediate.

An inspector who supervises all football matches at Maine Road said his officers had faced increasing hostility, been kicked and attacked with bottles and wooden stakes in recent weeks and facing 1,500 fans "baying for blood" at the Coventry match last month.

But a City executive said police told the club they were applying for the ban because pubs had been flouting drink regulations on match days. Our fans, he said, had an 'exemplary' record for behaviour in and around Maine Road.

The licensee of the Sherwood Inn in Claremont Road said she was glad police failed in the bid but was happy to discuss the situation at any time they wished.

"We're always happy to cooperate with the police" she said. "I've never had any problems here".

The Landlord of the Parkside Hotel said: "I've been running this pub since just before the season started and we have had no trouble whatsoever. We were stunned about this. Closing would cost me about £5,000 in takings – and match days help tide me over".

The discussion now continues:

R2: "The games you specify were characterised by generally poor crowd behaviour and this was definitely down to the results."

R1: "True, but there were many incidents associated with some of those games, which point up a more complex picture. The January 13th game (2001) against Leeds is a good example: if I remember rightly, Manchester United were also playing away at Bradford. I don't think we had any major disorder problems at the ground but one or maybe two coach loads of Leeds supporters stopped off at Rochdale on the way to the match and went into a pub. The Manchester United hooligan group got on a train bound for Bradford, which actually goes through Rochdale. They were obviously aware of the Leeds fans in Rochdale, got off the train there, sought them out and there was considerable disorder. The problem was, thus, not 'City related' though ostensibly it involved that match; it was caused by United supporters but also by Leeds fans and their coach companies disregarding legislation as enshrined in traffic commissioners' guidelines in respect of conveying football fans. In brief, they shouldn't stop anywhere within a ten mile radius of their destination and certainly shouldn't stop at licensed premises anywhere on their journey. Now when we spoke to the coach companies, they said Rochdale is over 10 miles from Manchester and we didn't drop them off at the pub anyway. The fans' request was to stop for some lunch at Rochdale and to shop. That was the main problem for that match. Also remember that a year prior to that game, City played Leeds in a FA Cup game and there was serious disorder around the ground – and fans remember!"

R3: "What was happening around that time – in date order, home games against Leeds (lost 4-0), Coventry (won 1-0), Liverpool (draw 1-1), Spurs (lost 1-0), Southampton (lost 1-0), Aston Villa (won 3-0) and Arsenal (lost 4-0). The season was going badly for City and there was a gradual panic impact on spectators who saw their club facing the drop, once again to a lower division. It is necessary again, to stress the primacy of context; over a five-year period they had seen a traumatic decline in playing standards with successive relegations then a sustained and meteoric rise to the Premier with expectations that they would finish among the top clubs and bring European soccer to the fans. At the time you mention, they find themselves past Christmas and looking at a dogfight to stave off relegation, once again. As I have pointed out, from 31st Jan to 11th April, there was a succession of bad home results, hope was fading fast, there was desperation among the fans and mounting frustration among the mass of spectators. From an objective point of view, as a member of a management team policing these events and discussing issues with the club, there was a growing concern that disorderly behaviour was becoming more evident. In addition, the presence of alcohol was becoming more prominent and public houses were becoming focal points for the expression of this discontent. In the light of this situation, we recognised the need to be proactive and put in interventions before the trigger was pulled for a major incident; 'positive policing' if you like. In particular, we were looking at the Southampton game scheduled for 3rd March and were very fearful that if it was a reversal for City, it would signify relegation, thereby acting as a trigger. In fact we upgraded that game (from 'A' to 'B") and though it was a reversal, all the other results did City a favour, so it did not have such a disastrous impact on City's overall league position."

R1:   "What you need to bear in mind is that during this period, the City and United hooligan groups – and believe me, though small in number, there are such groups – were more active than they are at the present time. There had been a number of incidents in the City centre where one group had been waiting for the other; the relevance of this is that one of them was actually after that Southampton game. Really nothing to do directly with that game or the policing operation for it. The circumstances were that United were away to Leeds but had an early kick-off, while City had a normal 3.00pm kick-off at home, so when City's game finished, the United hooligan group had already returned to Manchester and located themselves in the Grafton public house near the Manchester Royal Infirmary. The City group were meeting in the Phoenix pub on the junction of Booth Street and Oxford Road about half a mile away and there was a confrontation – the United group descending on the Phoenix and attacking City fans with tables and chairs. A police operation was mounted and maintained order, but that was an incident after the games had finished and wasn't directly associated with the match. It was however typical of that period with United and City fans taking every opportunity to confront each other. Now City v Coventry had two episodes which gave rise to considerable concern but which I cannot discuss now as judicial proceedings are still pending. But I will be happy to do this after they are concluded in April (2002). The Liverpool game was characterised by rivalry; it was an evening game with no massive problems but I do recall an incident on the coach park. This is an illustration of how easily things can flare up. The visitors' coach had a large skylight in it; some youths were hanging out of the skylight and were baiting passing City supporters, singing songs about relegation and so on."

R2: "Just to interject, you have to frame that in the context that City played Liverpool in the last game of the season when the club was relegated. Fans remember incidents that took place then and that they were relegated against that club."

R1: "As I was saying, there was this provocation and the tension mounted with a few missiles being thrown at the coach. The police then had to become involved and diffuse what was becoming an ugly situation by dispersing the City fans on the Kippax car park and actually go onto the coach and sort out the provocateurs who had created the problem. This was not a job for stewards.

Now against Chelsea, the final game of the season, it must be remembered that City fans always have had a tradition of invading the pitch at the end of the season. This stopped when the perimeter fence was erected but began again when it was taken down. In this last game, Chelsea had beaten City and the City fans, as was their tradition, invaded the pitch and did their thing. However, quite a few Chelsea supporters remained in the ground, contrary to advice and the City fans became bored; Chelsea fans lingered and showed a morbid fascination with what was going on, on the pitch. City fans began picking divots up to keep as souvenirs but seeing Chelsea fans as targets, began throwing them in that direction. This then escalated to coin throwing, advertising boardings got kicked down and broken up, a couple of plastic seats were thrown at police horses which were drawn into the ground at this time and finally one group of City supporters outflanked the line of police and stewards, protecting the Chelsea supporters in the North Stand and entered that stand on the other side of the goal posts. They approached the Chelsea fans who decided to defend themselves and fights ensued."

R1: "This disturbance followed a well defined curve which we have often observed. You can sense something is building up from increased noise levels from the crowd, heightened arousal; the throwing of missiles follows and there comes a point when it comes to its peak and can't really get any greater because police resources outweigh the opposition and extinguish it."

R2: "It is fair to say that on this occasion, there was hand to hand fighting. On the arrival of the first police officer, it stopped. The stewards were unable to control or contain it and were attacked. Again, it showed clearly the limits of stewarding. The stewards do not ultimately have the power of arrest and people are aware of that; even if they did arrest, they would be in the same position as the police, your numbers start diminishing and are depleted once you begin arresting. Consequently, you can never correlate the seriousness of disorder with the number of arrests; once you begin extracting individuals your resources are depleted. Remember for every prisoner, you lose two officers. If you lock up ten people you have twenty officers out of commission, also what do you then do with them? As soon as they are arrested, there is a duty of care; you cannot just throw them in a cage and go back for another ten. We can only police an event within the realms of the law: these are the dilemmas of control. It becomes an art form and very complex."

O: "Let us now leave the question of the 'myth' and 'reality' of mobs and the issue of riot and tumult, and look ahead positively. Is there any forward planning with regard to police arrangements for City's intended move to their new stadium for the 2003/04 season?"

R2: "Various features have been designed into the stadium. There will be additional CCTV cameras, all of which are not required for the Commonwealth Games as such. There are communication systems and facilities within the stadium which are designed with its football use in mind. There are cell areas or detention rooms actually in the stadium, which hopefully will not be needed for the Games; of course there will be a ground control box with state of the art facilities and briefing facilities."

O: "Will there be a standing area for supporters?"

R2: "No."

R1: "I have been a football supporter from being a child and as a supporter, rather than police officer, I would much prefer to stand at a football match. The main reason for that, is it gives me more control – particularly when I go to a strange ground. To illustrate by way of the reverse, I bought a ticket to watch City play Southampton and spent a lot of money and time getting there. On arrival, I found I was sat at the front with the pitch at head level. It was a terrible view – a waste of money. Now on the terrace, I would have had more flexibility. Also if I didn't like the behaviour of those around me I could just move ten or fifteen yards away from them. But if I am sat next to them, this option does not exist. Also, there is the opportunity of attending a match on a casual basis with friends whereas today it is not possible. However, from a police officer's point of view, it is easier to spot those misbehaving when they are seated compared with standing. Sure it may be harder to get them out, but I think it has resulted in improved behaviour and safety overall."

R2: "Standing leads to uneven densities, which from the police point of view is difficult to manage and access. There are, of course, problems of those standing in seated areas, particularly where there is a mixture – some standing, some seated – it leads to disorder and this problem needs to be addressed."

R1: "I think the main problem with the old terracing was that the clubs had unrealistic capacities. Now straight after the Hillsborough Disaster, the Kippax Stand was slashed from a capacity of 25,000 to 19,000. The difference was immediately noticeable – you felt a lot more comfortable."

R3: "I listen to what you say and I agree with some of it, but I do not see that there is any future in standing at football grounds. The old image of clothed caps, orderly masses, self policing in shanty stadia, no longer applies. I personally have a young family who are football supporters and expressing a personal view, want to be able to take them to the ground where, yes, they can sing and shout but where they can sit and be familiar with, and safe, in those surroundings and to enjoy the experience. Not to be stood behind barriers, to lose them in crowd surges and so on. I wouldn't go to a football ground to stand."

R2: "I would go to a football ground to stand but not with

children. I would prefer to sit, because I feel if you give people a decent seat in a clean, tidy area with good toilet and refreshment facilities, then you will guarantee a level of behaviour which is acceptable. We have found it in the North Stand at City. We were having problems there. It was getting to be a 'no-go' area called 'the cave'. With some very simple environmental changes, painting it, putting lights in and so on, it has dramatically improved behaviour in that area."

R1: "I don't think they will ever go back to terracing and after Hillsborough, I can understand why not. However, I do believe that if grounds had small terraced paddocks with sensible capacities, it would be okay. Just because people are stood up does not mean that they will behave badly, for example, urinate where they stand. To support my point, when I visited Southampton last season (2000/01) as a spectator to the all-seater stadium, the City fans were on the lower and upper tier. I was on the bottom tier and got drenched with urine coming though the ceiling because those City fans sitting above could not be bothered to get up and go to the toilet. That was in seated accommodation, so I don't think that seating is the main factor governing behaviour."

R3: "Could be related to club culture. There are some clubs, for example Ipswich, where you don't have a degree of concern. Norwich is another and so on. When away from home, their behaviour wouldn't generally be of the kind described by my colleague. With City, there is a small unruly element and you do have a lower standard of behaviour among these than might reasonably be expected. There is also a small sinister element who we know, during the summer of 2001, stopped off at Oldham where there were politically motivated disturbances of some magnitude."

This last point illustrates the further levels of crowd functioning with which we began this chapter but at this juncture, rather than expand this analysis, we will retain our focus by considering the first question which preceded this discussion; namely current arrangements for stewarding at Maine Road. The safety officer we have previously quoted left his post in 1999 and a new man was appointed. Who is this new man, what procedures has he put in place and how might this be viewed as an 'ideal model' which other clubs might employ? In view of the consensus view, from a number of varying perspectives, that the policing and stewarding arrangements at City are currently in harmony and exemplify 'best practice', it is appropriate to pursue the theme of this chapter by initially presenting interview data secured during early 2002, with the new safety officer and to follow this, as was the case with the Chairman of Manchester United, reported in 'Manchester United at the Millennium' with more systematic investigation of his pattern of occupationally related interests to illustrate an ideal role model. First for the qualitative information; let the safety officer (R) introduce himself and we can key his remarks into a plan of the stadium as shown at the conclusion of this chapter. The interview was conducted at Maine Road and as with the previous respondents, the interviewee and his background were previously unknown to the author:

Respondent: "I was a police officer for thirty years and finished my career some three years ago, at Wigan. I have been involved in policing football at every ground in Greater Manchester. I was a member of a special contingent of police officers who went across and policed the Cup Semi-Final between Wolves and Spurs at Hillsborough in 1981. It would be fair to say that while I was a sergeant and inspector, a lot of my football policing experience was gathered at Old Trafford. I spent ten years in the old Stretford Division and policed the ground at the Stretford End – between 1976 and 1986. Later on in my police career, I returned as part of a team which was then trying out what was, for the time, the innovative use of CCTV for crowd control. It was a portable system sponsored by the Football Trust and it would be taken down after every game and transported to other clubs, for example Oldham, City and so on. I must confess that I am a City supporter and consequently, by opting to work at Old Trafford, I could attend City's home games as a paying spectator! My overseas experience involved accompanying United supporters to St Etienne in France – a notorious game in terms of crowd disturbance, which resulted in United being thrown out of the tournament. Subsequently, I was a key witness for them because, to be fair, it was the French fans who instigated the problem not the United fans and as a result, United were allowed back into the competition."

Observer: "So, some twenty five years' experience of operational issues concerning crowd control at football matches?"

Respondent: "Well, more than that because when I joined the police in 1969, I used to police this ground, Maine Road, on a regular basis. In those days, it was not of course Greater Manchester Police but Manchester and Salford Police and United's ground was outside of Manchester and hence policed by Lancashire Constabulary. At the opposite end of the time frame, I finished up policing both football and rugby crowds at Wigan."

Observer: "Any other connection specifically with City?"

Respondent: "Yes, I have worked here behind the scenes looking after the ball boys and the press room as well as the Junior Blues as a supporter for nigh on twenty years. When the club approached me to fill the vacancy of safety officer, which had occurred in 1999, I accepted. It was, thus, an opportunity to retire from the police with a full pension and have a second career with a club that I had supported since being a youngster. So I retired from the police on 1st August 1999 and took up this job on the same day. A baptism of fire, in a way, because two days later we played Liverpool here and I was in charge! Having said this, I received some tremendous help from within the club and from the senior stewards and on the whole, the transition was non-problematic."

Observer: "How have you progressed matters since then?"

Respondent: "Well, the first job was to put flesh on the skeleton contingency plan and to formalise it in written form and thus, allay the concerns of the Manchester Safety Group. Though training of stewards had been undertaken, what I felt was needed was a more systematic approach backed by checkable evidence of what had been achieved. In other words, instead of an entry on a computer that a particular steward had completed modules 1, 2, and 4 say of an in-house training system, why not take advantage of existing independently audited provision with detailed records?"

Observer: "What provision?"

Respondent: "There was an 'off the shelf' football stewarding qualification recognised by the Football League, the Football Association, the Premiership, the Football Trust and the Football Licensing Authority. As this was in place, why not take advantage of it? I saw it as an insurance for the club even though there was no precedent; historically the other three big clubs in the area had resisted signing up to it. My aim was to achieve a nationally recognised accreditation and consequently, I set up a system in order to achieve this."

Observer: "Which was?"

Respondent: "Initially the establishment of a training team, consisting of a senior fire officer who is my deputy safety officer and a safety officer in his own right, until recently at Leigh Rugby Club, another trainer from the fire brigade and another trainer from Greater Manchester Police. Together, they form my training team and have all got accreditation in terms of NVQ's and are recognised assessors for D32, 33, 34 and so on. As a result of this initiative and adopting a cascade model of curriculum delivery, flowing down a hierarchical staffing structure, we have obtained the stewarding qualification in a very short time; were the eighth club in the country and the first club in Greater Manchester to achieve it. The audit trails associated with the award have now diminished so that when we forward the club's name for certification, we receive it without a request for an audit, indicating and reflecting their vote of confidence in our procedures and training content."

Observer: "A content which involves?"

Respondent: "Well, seven modules, though in reality it is six because module 'O' is a familiarity module, taught by the training team who are responsible for keeping paper records and creating a personal file for every steward. Thus, if we wanted to demonstrate to any legitimate interested party that a named steward had successfully completed the training, that these were his exam results, they are available. In terms of content, the modules cover contingency plan, fire awareness, first aid, customer care, familiarisation of the stadium – all these sorts of issues which are part of the approved syllabus in the National Training Package, which has been dovetailed into what we require as Manchester City Football Club. The approach is sufficiently flexible to allow it to be tailored to our specific needs while providing a uniformity of provision, which allows for transferability between clubs. Thus, if a steward transferred to say Stockport County, he would not have to repeat all the modules but perhaps only one or two, which would bring him up to speed with regard to the particular circumstances of that club. Similarly we employ students as stewards and when they return home, they have a qualification which is common currency for their employment on a part-time basis in Derby, Southampton or wherever they may live."

Observer: "This training, I assume, takes place while they are actively stewarding, not prior to it. It thus leaves open the question, how do you become a steward, say at Manchester City?"

Respondent: "First you fill in a 4-page application form and apply to the club to be a steward. It is something we have devised ourselves and doubles as a personal record: similar to the one used by the police. We don't interview on a personal basis but invite applicants to a series of open meetings at which I give a presentation about the role of the steward, expectations and so on and this is supported by inputs from senior staff who are there to support me. A variable format is employed to involve as many people as possible and enhance the teambuilding ethos of my safety organisational structure. The novice stewards then stay with an experienced steward for two or three games and then sign up for training either during the week or weekends. Modular delivery is accompanied by coffee and biscuits and I would like to think that we create a quiet supportive atmosphere, in which learning potential can be maximised with consequent benefits – often intangible – which accrue to the club. Remember, myself and my team are responsible for the safety of some 34,000 people, not the 11+ squad who actually deliver the product, that is the game, under the guidance of the manager and his staff."

Observer: "In terms of recruitment, if an applicant has a criminal record does it militate against their becoming a steward or, and this is a serious question, can it actually be an advantage if the individual has actually been convicted under the Football (Offences and Disorder) Act 1999; in short, poacher termed gamekeeper?"

Respondent: "A criminal conviction is not a bar as it is defined by the Rehabilitation of Offenders Act, but I would have some concerns about employing soccer hooligans as stewards. If I read you rightly, you are referring to what may be termed colloquially, 'been there, done it'. No, I wouldn't see it as an advantage, nor for that matter would it for itself be a disadvantage but I really don't think that in my circumstances here, such recruitment would add value to present practices. Mainly because you must realise that stewards are drawn largely from a supporter base which is very loyal, fanatical and reasonably well behaved within the parameters of football match attendance. We do not have a large, hardcore hooligan group at City; at least that is my opinion.

What we do have is a number of supporters who enjoy alcohol and sometimes this can effect their behaviour at away games; remember we travel away in large numbers hence our usual 'C' classification of the recipient club. We took 5,000 to Preston, 6,000 to Sheffield Wednesday and can sell most of our away tickets. Maybe in the Premiership, you know we are now in the First Division, maybe we would be classified as a 'B'. There are also one-off situations, for example, we do not request tickets for our supporters and will not be allocating tickets to Millwall which is our next home fixture, because of the past behaviour of their fans. Our tickets are not on open sale and consequently touts will have trouble getting hold of them and selling them openly on the day, which is, of course, a recipe for disaster at a football match."

Observer: "So much for recruitment and training and the nature of the fan basis: to re-focus, could you describe the structure of stewarding at City for the uninitiated? Perhaps relate it to the physical layout of the stadium?"

Respondent: "Yes, I inherited a structure which was viable at that time. My initial action was really an audit of my human resources both in club and from outside agencies: this was not as simple as it sounds because the posts are part-time and people may only be here for a couple of hours at a given time, making judgement difficult. There has been no great change in personnel as a result of that exercise, but we now have a clearly delineated organisational chart with myself as safety officer, a deputy head safety officer or head steward, a head steward of the corporate areas who will give leadership there – remember boxes can be occupied by away supporters in home areas – then a head operational steward. The latter is also the deputy safety officer; under him are five senior supervisors, one for each stand apart from the Kippax, which has two senior supervisors, one on each of the middle and lower tiers. The top tier is corporate hospitality. Under each of these senior supervisors, there are supervisors and underneath them, the operational stewards. This gives in the region of about 200-220 stewards: we may call these City stewards.

Now in addition to these, I contract with an Agency to supply a further 100 students who perform specific tasks. Let me describe their role. They are supplied by a company called Showsec International, who steward the Manchester Evening News Arena and will also be involved in stewarding the Commonwealth Games. For me, they effectively steward the segregation line between visiting and home fans in the North Stand. I also have initiated a search of home supporters on the North Stand, as I had concerns about bottles being brought in, not to be used as weapons, but for drinking. Of course, alcohol is not allowed to be brought into the ground. That is the stand that is going to cause me problems if any occur because it is where the visiting fans are located. The agency stewards conduct the searches. City stewards greet the visiting fans and steward that part of the ground after their arrival and the relationship built up outside the ground can be maintained and indeed built on inside the ground. I want good relationships with visiting supporters who come here year in, year out and thus, strive to do it via my stewards. I also have three response teams whose roles are specific; they are there for checking tickets and preventing abuse and will also go into potential trouble hot-spots, areas of the crowd from which we have had complaints, for example, racist language, arguments etc."

Observer: "Are these response team stewards specifically equipped to deal with crowd problems in terms of their personality dispositions and/or physical attributes?"

Respondent: "Yes, both. Certainly they look 'mean' and I make no apologies for that. Sometimes you need that kind of presence but also they are intellectually bright not conforming to the 'old bouncer' stereotype. They are imposing enough and have the right attitude to persuade people to alter their behaviour but in a courteous, not heavy handed way. I insist on this. This is a family club and our supporters are part of that family. My match day order says, and will always say, 'Please treat people as you would expect your own family to be treated while you are here'. The drawback with agency stewards is that you don't get the consistency you would like over a given period.

I also have a reserve of half a dozen or so stewards who will fill in the gaps. For example, an exit gate steward may not have turned up and then I can allocate one to that job after appropriate briefing by the senior supervisor. Finally, I have a minimum of three people in each corner of the pitch whose job is highly specific; they deal with any pitch encroachment. They do not have a steward's jacket but have a club jacket with MCFC security emblazoned on it. Their remit is to remove any unauthorised person from the pitch as quickly and quietly as possible."

We may break into the interview here to provide an organisation chart which shows the distribution of roles related to safety and control aspects on match day.

CHART 5: MCFC MATCH DAY ORGANISATION CHART

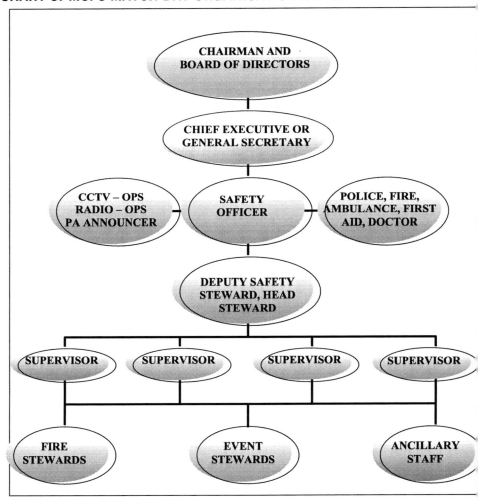

The reader will see from the glossary of terms in the text that we break up the concept of role into role demands, role conception and role behaviour. Role demands and behaviours of stewarding may be set out in the following two charts:

CHART 6: ROLE DEMANDS OF THE SOCCER STEWARD: MANCHESTER CITY MODEL

❖ To control or direct spectators who are entering or leaving the ground, to help achieve an even flow of people to the viewing areas

❖ To carry out pre-match safety checks as directed

❖ To recognise crowd densities, signs of crowd distress and crowd dynamics so as to help ensure safe dispersal of spectators

❖ To be able to respond to any emergencies, e.g. raising alarms or tackling the early stages of fire

❖ To staff entrances, exits to and from the viewing accommodation and other strategic points, especially ext doors and exit gates from the ground which are not continually open whilst the ground is in use

❖ To enforce the Ground Regulations as necessary and where appropriate offences under specific football related legislation

❖ To assist or liaise with police as appropriate or as requested with crowd control

❖ To undertake specific duties in an emergency

❖ Prevent overcrowding by ensuring the crowd limits in various parts of the ground are complied with

❖ Prevent spectators, as far as possible, from climbing fences and other structures and from standing on seats

CHART 7: ROLE BEHAVIOURS OF THE SOCCER STEWARD: MANCHESTER CITY MODEL

❖ Ensure all approaches and emergency exits are kept clear and that vehicles are correctly parked

❖ Assist in the diversion of spectators to other parts of the ground including the closing of turnstiles when the capacity of any area is about to be reached

❖ Be able to find and to operate effectively, fire fighting equipment in the designated area

❖ Find the location of the first aid rooms and any first aid equipment kept elsewhere

❖ Be fully conversant with any messages or signals used to alert the staff that an emergency has arisen

❖ Be capable of recognising potential fire hazards and suspect packages, reporting such findings immediately to their Supervisor, Head Steward or the Ground Safety Officer

❖ Comply promptly with any instruction given in an emergency by a police officer, your Supervisor, Head Steward or the Ground Safety Officer

❖ Remain at allocated posts as instructed unless otherwise authorised by a Supervisor, Head Steward or the Ground Safety Officer

❖ Report to a Supervisor or Head Steward any damage or defect which is likely to pose a threat to spectator safety, e.g. a damaged barrier or unsafe signage

❖ Assist in the identification of spectators who are banned from the ground or who do not possess tickets at all ticket matches or who are in possession of forged tickets

The interview may now be continued in the following fashion:

Observer: "Perhaps having described the structure and role of stewards, we can now move to the interface between police and stewards. To what extent are these roles complimentary or antagonistic?"

Respondent: "My personal view is that at City, there will never be on a continual basis, a police free game. You could probably get away with it once, perhaps twice, but after that I think it would become an 'us and them' situation, the 'them' being the stewards. If there has got to be a 'them' then I would rather that be the police so we can maintain the warm socio-emotional relationship between club stewards and supporters. Also it would make the recruitment of stewarding, which is difficult at the best of times, even more difficult. It takes an unusual sort of person to be a steward; the motivations are various. Some do it because they support the club, some because they like the companionship, some because it is paid, some like the power bestowed by donning a uniform, some to fund their education (students) and so on. I do not really want the power syndrome mentality and take steps to discourage it, if I see it. Thus policing and stewarding are complimentary but different. The police attitude here is that the stewards should be the first point of reference but that if it becomes too difficult then they can be called upon as a back-up to assist. This I regard as healthy and is an ideal type relationship; ideal because, not at the command level, some police at the operational level, are reluctant to become involved and do not see such involvement as part of their role. I fail to understand this, because if an identical incident to one that occurred at a football ground happened on the street, then they would be the first to take action. In a football ground, some officers do not see such intervention as part of their responsibility. This sometimes reflects inappropriate leadership.

Let me illustrate this point from my own experience of policing football grounds. At Old Trafford when policing a United game, you could tell when you had a good sergeant on because the police officers would be strung out across the forecourt; a disinterested sergeant or inspector would be reflected in a different disposition of men – gathered in bunches. Thus, when I was chief inspector working at Old Trafford, and this is quite recent in 1997, I could tell whether I was going to have an easy day or hard day because of the way the person in charge had deployed their staff. Here at City now, we are reaping the fruits of our labour in terms of building a strong healthy relationship between police and stewards; in summary we would be the first point of contact for dealing with the crowd and the police would be our back-up or support.

On match day I see my role as being in control and therefore logically I remain in the match control box. This reflects the fact that first and foremost, the safety of the people at the match lies with the club and therefore it lies with me, as their safety officer. I am the one who sees the referee before the game to brief him not the police, though sometimes supported by them. I tell him where the away supporters are and can refer to the document which has already been sent to him to brief him on what the evacuation policy is, what the code word is for an ongoing emergency, where the blue lights are and a steward is specifically appointed to act as ground chaperone for his visit. He is suited up rather than wearing a uniform, meets the referee on arrival and also his assistants. He positions himself outside the referee's changing room and will be in the tunnel when the referee comes off at half-time and will make a judgement whether to go onto the pitch 10 yds, 20 yds or more depending on the referee's performance, with a senior steward. He will also be there at the end of a game and throughout, will have a direct live emergency communication channel should he or the referee wish to communicate with me. It also means I can communicate through him to the referee. After the game, he stays as long as the referee stays and makes sure he leaves the ground safely. Let me stress, nobody has told me to do this. It is my innovation here at Manchester City and is a crucial part of our overall match arrangements."

Observer: "Let us move now to actual incidents of crowd behaviour at specific games so that we might further our understanding of collective behaviour and practical matters of control, particularly as these are interpreted by the media. The games I would like you to comment on are those from January 2001 to the end of the season at home, here at Maine Road, which were characterised, by the media, as involving 'riots and tumult' with action being taken by the police to suspend local licences on a particular match day. I have already spoken to the police and obtained their perspective."

Respondent: "Well, the first point is that results do undoubtedly have an affect on behaviour and the attitudes of spectators. Let me give you what might appear to be a trivial matter but which has actually happened; if a supporter trips up on exiting the ground, you are unlikely to hear about it if we have won but if we have lost, you might get a letter of complaint or even a compensation claim. My post bag is lighter this year (City were having a successful season being top of the division at the time of the interview) than it was last year; I do not deceive myself that the comments we have received about the excellence of our stewarding are solely down to me and the changes I have introduced. It is partly because of the results this season and the way the team is playing even when they have a reversal; that is, they are still playing good football. We sometimes forget that, that is what spectators come to see good performance which entertains. To return to your point, I feel that the description of 'riots and tumult' is an over-reaction: while undoubtedly there were some difficulties arising from the threat of relegation, there was also the lighter side. Let me illustrate by way of anecdote if you like, while making no claims to systematic observation. We were playing Arsenal and were losing 4-0 within twenty minutes, the eventual score. We had one lad who ran onto the pitch and sat down – he was removed; then we had two streakers, one male and one female. The City supporters were chanting, not City Aggro, the old Kippax battle cry, but "boring, boring Arsenal; we can play you every week". This sense of collective humour was absolutely unbelievable in the light of the prevailing match circumstances and it made the hairs on my head stand up. The Arsenal fans responded in various non-combatant ways, and the City fan who had sat down in the middle of the pitch in silent protest – causing no problems whatsoever on being removed – actually got a standing ovation from the Arsenal fans. That is the crowd attitude we would love here every week. So, while there was heightened crowd disaffection over the period you mention, I cannot honestly blame the City supporters and would not, on balance, accuse them of rioting; certainly not in terms of what I have seen in my thirty years policing experience prior to my present job.

You mentioned the last game of the season against Chelsea, which we lost and were relegated. Now there was a pitch incursion as usual – the previous two seasons to celebrate, that season to conform to tradition because it's what they do anyway. From the tenor of your remarks you seem to think that the mounted police coming into the stadia was a reaction to riot and tumult; it wasn't. In fact it was pre-planned; that is, if necessary they would be there to protect the Chelsea supporters and consequently the provision was proactive and not reactive. The horses were in place ready to come in.

There were approximately 33,000 people in the ground on that day and the majority went home peacefully and of the 1,000 or so on the pitch, they were initially 'sons and daughters'. Then we got a criminal element who started to throw lumps of turf at the police horses and then into the Chelsea supporters who had, for their own reasons, stayed behind; in fact, very few divots reached them. To Chelsea's credit, most of their supporters had left the ground as requested but a minority decided to stay and there was an attempt by some City supporters to attack them. It didn't actually work and that was the end of it. The difficulty was that it was shown on National TV and I have seen far, far worse cases of disorder at football grounds which have themselves not been classed as riots; in my experience I would regard what happened as 'annoying', something that was unfortunate but by no means a major crowd conflagration, confined and limited as it was, to a small section of the North Stand. We identified some of those involved and they have been successfully prosecuted.

My personal view of the proposed ban on serving alcohol at local pubs on a particular match day, was that it was not thought through sufficiently. In fact the court demonstrated that, but for different reasons. I think the legislation invoked was inappropriate. Even if you stop people drinking before or after the games in pubs near the ground then they will drink regardless, away from the ground and probably nearer to the City Centre on another police division. It puts the problem on the agenda of another police commander who would not really welcome this particularly if it is in a City Centre location, which constitutes the crossroads of routes for travelling fans with various club loyalties and identities. It puts the potential for disorder higher up the scale and thus does not solve what is perceived to be a problem; indeed it may create one where none existed. This is my personal view.

Now, again referring to the time period you mention, we did have a problem here with regard to the visit of Coventry City but that was caused wholly by Coventry City supporters. It was nothing to do with this club. There were 4,000 visiting Coventry fans who were 'up for the Cup' and the vast majority of them were well behaved. We had actually played them three weeks before at Highfield Road and the safety officer there reported that both sets of fans were well behaved and in fact were singing Christmas carols together; no signs of animosity or major disorder. We have played them since the game in question, at home in the FA Cup and again, without incident. However, there is an element who were specific to that fixture; they hired a coach from Leicester, a rogue coach, who were videoed by the police and gained access to the ground. Now, when City scored a goal, much against the run of play, we have been outplayed all the game, it had to happen of course at the end where all the Coventry supporters were, and in the last minute of the game, some of them reacted and breached the segregation line actually in front of the match control room where I was stood and started to attack seated supporters in the main stand. That resulted in some of the home supporters in the main stand going to the defence of those being attacked; police moved in quickly and mounted a couple of charges at the Coventry supporters and a number of arrests were made and those responsible are due to appear at Manchester Crown Court."

Observer: "Quite different then from the media account which put the cause of the disturbance down to the threat of relegation?"

Respondent: "Yes."

Observer: "Let us now look forward to the change of ground, the season after next (2003/2004). Will all your good work be undone?"

Respondent: "No. I see the move in physical location being paralleled by a move in my organisational structure for safety and control. We will still need agency stewards and I may have to recruit more to help with the more difficult areas of the new stadium. When I say difficult, I do not mean in terms of crowd trouble but where sight lines are problematic. There will be a control box and though the stadium is there to stage an athletic event, it was designed with football in mind; the planning process took place well before I was appointed so I have had little input to design considerations. However, having seen the plans and the design of the control room, I am happy for them to stay as they are; perhaps the control room could have been built a little more forward into the stadium to give improved all round vision but aesthetically, from the architectural point of view, it would have detracted from the overall conception. That said, the stadium was built for the Commonwealth Games and it is a minor point. On the plus side, I currently have 16 CCTV cameras but in the new stadium, I will have something like 67 cameras. There will be a turnstile monitoring system similar to what I have here but there is also an exit gate monitoring system which I haven't got. There are also cell areas but we may not need these. Consequently, the transition should be relatively smooth; in fact I have been asked to provide some of my stewards for the Commonwealth Games because they are qualified. My view is that yes, we will provide some stewards and make my training team available but I have not involved the club in that because stewarding an athletic event is, in my view, somewhat different from stewarding major league soccer."

Observer: "Do you see the new stadium as providing an opportunity for standing spectators when it is handed over to football?"

Respondent: "This is a personal view. I do not think that standing will come back. In fact I think it would be a backward step. Even in what might be considered as a model standing area – the old scoreboard end at Old Trafford, there were still problems of identifying missile throwers; there were coins thrown and you will recall the famous picture of the 70s of a spectator with a dart stuck in his forehead. One of the difficulties I had in policing the standing spectator, and I can only draw on my direct experience, was to cope with the crowd densities and configuration. For example, in the Stretford End, they would form a sterile circle* and one of the things I had to do was realign the fans and give them a verbal warning to make room for others. I would come back, no change, so we would eject six and warn them again; come back, no change, so eject another six. The third time I would come back and the configuration would be altered. You had to go through that process. I suspect that such crowd configuration, accompanied by surges, would appear again over time and balancing the situation up would not favour its re-introduction. I have looked at the combination of standing and seating arrangements in Germany but a German approach would probably not result in safe standing here because there are cultural differences and expectations. If a decision was made, it would have to be a government one and a brave one at that, in the light of Hillsborough. So I don't favour terraces or fencing. Seating is much easier from my point of view as a safety officer."

Clearly, this informed opinion has to be taken seriously. However, the problem of ensuring fans remain seated is a difficult one to manage, particularly where sight lines are easily obscured. Thankfully, this situation should ease when City move to their new stadium as viewing positions and sight lines are set at a high level as the reader will be made aware in Chapter Four.

*Interesting corroboration of the crowd configuration described in the book, 'Manchester United at the Millennium', by the author.

In view of the general acclaim afforded, the Safety Officer's role at Manchester City and the system of stewarding and policing at the ground which is often cited, even from what are often conflicting ideological viewpoints, as 'best practice', more systematic investigation is warranted. As a start, we may follow the procedure adopted for elucidating the ideal characteristics of the football chairman's role (See 'Manchester United at the Millennium', 2001, Chapter 4), using the Chief Safety Officer's responses to an Interest Inventory to provide a pen portrait of his work-related characteristics and leadership style. By this means, we hope to provide a benchmark for others who might seek to successfully follow in his footsteps. We rely on results which are 'objective', in that they arise from the administration of the Strong Interest Inventory backed up by an interpretive manual written by the author. Answers to the Inventory are provided by simply indicating one of three responses on a pre-coded sheet, in response to questions contained in a test booklet grouped into eight sections; the sections being occupations, school subjects, activities, leisure time, types of people, preference between kinds of activities, self ratings of characteristics and preferences in the world of work. We may draw on the report prepared for the Chief Safety Officer, with his permission, to provide an ideal profile of a Chief Safety Officer's role at a major league football company. We say 'ideal' because of the weight of experience and rank that the individual brings to this job and it's rating as excellent, both internally by the senior officers of the club and externally, by police, safety committee and a radical spectator movement.

In order that the reader may be fully conversant with this approach and its attendant results, it is necessary to point out that the underlying theory on which the Interest Inventory is based, is that each person can be described in terms of a relative similarity to one or more of six idealised occupational interest/personality types. It is further assumed that each 'type' of personality seeks out a different kind of occupational environment consonant with his type, so as to reduce psychological discomfort. In brief, and in non-scientific language, if a person is 'round', he/she attempts to find a round hole; if he/she is 'square', attempts to find a square hole and so on. Thus, according to this theory, 'personality type' contributes as much as 'job requirements' to establishing the particular 'tone' of an occupation or specialisation within an occupation, for example, within the general category of security personnel, a chief safety officer of a football stadium.

Six 'ideal' personalities with their vocational orientations, known as General Occupational Themes (GOTs) are described in the form of a hexagon presented in the following figure.

CHART 8: AN INTERPRETIVE SCHEME FOR PERSONALITY ASSESSMENT

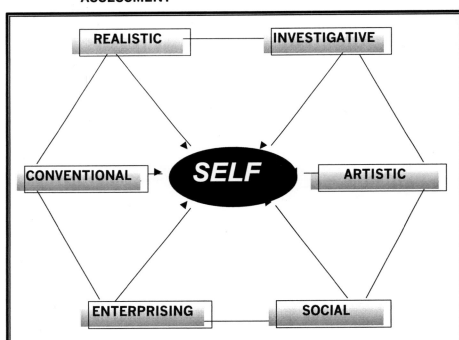

The 'types' most similar to each other in the figure are adjacent; those most dissimilar, opposite. Brief descriptions of all six themes may be given as follows:

REALISTIC	:	building, repairing, working outdoors
INVESTIGATIVE	:	researching, analysing, inquiring
ARTISTIC	:	creating or enjoying art, drama, music, writing
SOCIAL	:	helping, instructing, care giving
ENTERPRISING	:	selling, managing, persuading
CONVENTIONAL	:	accounting, organising, processing data

Few people are 'pure types' and consequently exhibit in varying degrees combinations of these occupational themes. This hexagon is used to order and describe the personality orientations and occupational interests as interpreted from the 317 questions on the Strong Interest Inventory. It needs to be stressed that 'interests', not 'abilities' is the focus and that this approach is objective rather than involving 'subjective' ratings of performance.

TABLE 1: CHIEF SAFETY OFFICER: MANCHESTER CITY PLC
TOP THREE OCCUPATIONAL THEMES (GOTs)

THEMES	RESULTS	COMMON OCCUPATIONAL INTERESTS	COMMON LEISURE INTERESTS	DESCRIPTORS
Enterprising	Average Interest	Business Politics Sales Marketing	Golf Tennis Squash Clubs Community organisations	Assertive Adventurous Energetic Talkative Self-confident
Realistic	Average Interest	Agriculture Forestry Technology Skilled trades Law enforcement	Fishing Camping Hiking Building Repairing	Practical Reliable Rugged Persistent
Conventional	Average Interest	Data analysis Record keeping Computer operation Clerical tasks	DIY Collecting Civic organisations	Calm Efficient Thorough Conscientious

To develop the information contained in the previous table further, let us focus on the Safety Officer's top two themes, that is, Enterprising Realistic (ER). The two-letter theme code is ER and because they are fairly close to each other on the hexagon, they share some similar interests. People with this code enjoy directing the production of goods or systems in efficient, hands-on ways in an action orientated work environment that produces tangible results in response to a clear chain of command. The role of Safety Officer, as interpreted at Manchester City, is a good clear example of this. The underlying motivator is the Enterprising theme which involves persuading people to do things and selling, in this case, safety systems. As high interest, comparatively speaking, was also shown in the Realistic theme, so using physical skill is a strong motivator as well. The type of work that brings most career satisfaction for the ER type, most likely involves directing the production or persuading others to go along with a tangible end product; in this case, systems designed to ensure the safety of some 30,000 spectators in a confined physical space: the stadium.

Basic Interest Scale Results (BIS)

The Basic Interest Scales (BIS) narrow the broad pattern of interests described by the GOTs by showing the respondent's preference for 25 specific areas of activity. While the GOTs describe what a person prefers to do, in general terms, the BISs provide more specific detail. The following table reveals the Interest Scales from those of *most* to *least* interest to the Chief Safety Officer. Each scale is coded with the first letter of the General Occupational Theme to which it is related. It must be remembered that while the GOTs describe what a person enjoys in general, the BISs describe what that person likes to **do.** Adding results on the BISs to the personal hexagon can provide further insights into interest patterns. Questions are raised as to whether a person's interests in specific activities cluster around the General Occupational Themes in which the person has shown most interest. Alternatively, the question may be posed – are the Individuals' specific interests different from his or her general interests?

If the results from the GOTs and BISs do not cluster, it may indicate a pattern of diverse interests. Remember again, we are concerned with patterns and that terms like 'average' and 'above average' have to be understood in terms of overall configuration and not in orders of ascendancy, as is the case with performance criteria. Thus a series of average scores taken together, does not mean an indifferent profile rather it may be construed as indicating a broadly based occupationally stable personality profile with the individual feeling comfortable when working in a wide range of environments.

TABLE 2: CHIEF SAFETY OFFICER OF MANCHESTER CITY PLC: BASIC INTEREST SCALE RESULTS

Results Show Very High Interest In:

Theme Code	Basic Interest Scale	Typical Interests and Activities
R	Agriculture	Working outdoors
E	Sales	Selling to potential customers

Results Show Above Average Interest In:

Theme Code	Basic Interest Scale	Typical Interests and Activities
E	Organisational management	Managing/Supervising
E	Public speaking	Persuading, influencing
R	Military activities	Working in structural settings

Results Show Very Little Interest In:

Theme Code	Basic Interest Scale	Typical Interests and Activities
I	Mathematics	Working with numbers/statistics
I	Medical Science	Working in Medicine or Biology
C	Computer activities	Working with computers
S	Teaching	Instructing young people

This second stage in charting the ideal role model of the football Chief Safety Officer clarifies whether specific interests are different from the general interests we have already identified. It will be seen from the table, that the top five specific interests all cluster around the Realistic and Enterprising Themes and that the 'ideal type characteristics' of the major league Safety Officer's role, involve an enjoyment in working outdoors, selling to potential customers and persuading/influencing other people. These activities are best deployed in a setting involving a clear hierarchical structure involving the Chief Safety Officer in managing and supervising the systems set in place for crowd safety. At the opposite end of the pole, is a strong dislike of mathematics, working in medicine or with computers and with teaching young people.

Personal Style

The four Personal Style Scales furnished by the Strong Interest Inventory provide additional insight into how comfortable our Chief Safety Officer is in activities and situations in which he finds himself at work, home and leisure. In essence, these results show or suggest how he likes to go about doing a particular job or task. The results may be set out graphically in the following chart.

Clearly, the expression of a personal style in the work setting is constrained by environmental circumstances. Thus, while the person in question may have a leaning towards a learning environment which is practical rather than academic, expectations of others, for example, parents and adolescent offspring may determine the opposite; in the extreme case, a boarding school situation based solely on 'cramming' to obtain the best possible external examination results. Similarly, 'high risk taking' as a preferred style might be out of place in a bank environment, as recent events in Singapore and Ireland have shown! It would certainly not be appropriate to derive procedures and systems where the safety of others is involved, as with the job of Chief Safety Officer at a major league football ground. While risks may have to be taken from time to time, they have to be calculated ones based on the best possible intelligence.

CHART 9: PERSONAL STYLE SCALES
CHIEF SAFETY OFFICER, MANCHESTER CITY PLC

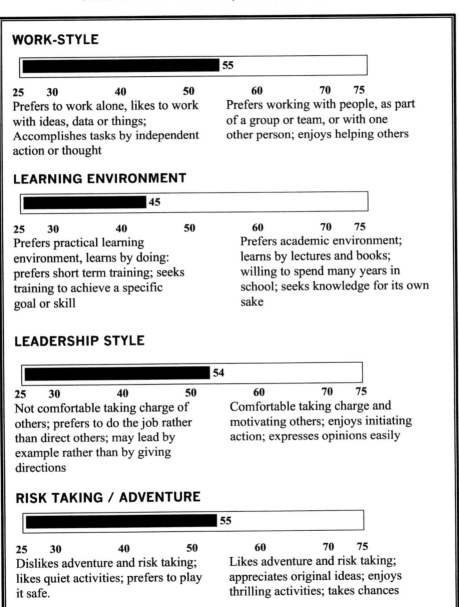

WORK-STYLE

| | | | | 55 | | | |

| 25 | 30 | 40 | 50 | 60 | 70 | 75 |

Prefers to work alone, likes to work with ideas, data or things; Accomplishes tasks by independent action or thought

Prefers working with people, as part of a group or team, or with one other person; enjoys helping others

LEARNING ENVIRONMENT

| | | 45 | | | | |

| 25 | 30 | 40 | 50 | 60 | 70 | 75 |

Prefers practical learning environment, learns by doing: prefers short term training; seeks training to achieve a specific goal or skill

Prefers academic environment; learns by lectures and books; willing to spend many years in school; seeks knowledge for its own sake

LEADERSHIP STYLE

| | | | 54 | | | |

| 25 | 30 | 40 | 50 | 60 | 70 | 75 |

Not comfortable taking charge of others; prefers to do the job rather than direct others; may lead by example rather than by giving directions

Comfortable taking charge and motivating others; enjoys initiating action; expresses opinions easily

RISK TAKING / ADVENTURE

| | | | 55 | | | |

| 25 | 30 | 40 | 50 | 60 | 70 | 75 |

Dislikes adventure and risk taking; likes quiet activities; prefers to play it safe.

Likes adventure and risk taking; appreciates original ideas; enjoys thrilling activities; takes chances

It will be seen from the foregoing figure that, in terms of typical work style, the Chief Safety Officer enjoys working with others on teams, committees or group projects. He enjoys the 'give and take' of group discussions and believes the best ideas or solutions occur when those working on a task can meet to discuss their ideas. With regard to an optimum personal working environment, his score suggests that he enjoys learning by attending lectures or by reading as well as by hands-on experience. He is thus comfortable in a variety of learning environments. His leadership style indicates a comfort zone involving aspects of an outspoken and directive leadership style but is not totally committed to this. He tends to use a variety of styles depending on the situation or on the people he is working with. Finally, his risk taking/adventure scale score suggests he enjoys some risks or adventures now and then. Before jumping into something new however, he typically takes time to think about it and to prepare adequately. Overall, he is prepared to take, what may be termed, 'prudent' risks, but overall, his score is in the medium range.

Clearly, the above account is only a partial picture of the parameters of the Chief Safety Officer's role and what he brings to it in terms of individual attributes for in no small measure, his actions are circumscribed by the setting in which he has to operate. As we have seen, earlier in this chapter, policing and stewarding in large sections of standing terraces such as the old Kippax, is problematic to say the least. The Safety Officer's task is eased when such parts of a ground are re-developed as happened with regard to this particular stand; an aspect of ground improvement we will now turn to.

The re-birth of the Kippax

Having described the Kippax and its social configurations in the 1970's, in the previous chapter and slipping back in time from the discussion and results described above, we may now turn to its re-birth in seated form; such a re-birth was not accomplished without problems and pains. To help describe what is involved in the construction of such a stand we will now present an account of an interview with the partner in the firm of architects, Howard & Seddon of Manchester who were responsible for designing and overseeing its construction by the building firm, Sir Robert McAlpine. The interview took place in early 1996 and may be reproduced in edited form to provide a succinct account of this redevelopment. In conducting the interview, emphasis will be placed on safety aspects and the relationship between management decisions and change in design and building.

Observer: **"How did you become involved in designing the Kippax Stand at Manchester City? Are you the only architect for this project?"**

Respondent: **"We have been involved in designing the Kippax stand since 1992 or 1993 I think. We carried on from being involved in the Umbro stand. We started to build the Kippax stand with Peter Swales still being the Chairman and while we were doing that, the new management team came in and requested us to redesign the stadium in ways which conform to new safety requirements. So we were involved in the stadium and we were the only architects involved for around 5-6 years."**

Observer: **"Could you say something about the change in the management team and the effects of the team on your job? Are the builders, in any way, also affected?"**

Respondent: **"When the new management came in they reviewed the old management plan and the new management had more expectations for a higher profile building and better arrangements with respect to VIP facilities, restaurants and public utilities. We had to increase the height of the building by a floor in order to accommodate this major change which directly caused a major increase in costs. We needed more time on the drawing board so that as changes were made, the design remained the same. However, the builders were not involved at this stage."**

The reference to the 'new management' is fully described in the following chapter and that chapter begins with a succinct description of organisational change in terms of 'transitory associations'. The 'new management' was brought into being by such an association but once formed and in place, had its own ideas and plans to put into operation. These social considerations point up the complexity of making what appears to be a straightforward physical change in stadium layout; that is, the human factor can bring about a fundamental re-appraisal of established plans and procedures. Let us now refer back to the interview by leading with a question relating to the interplay of roles – in this case, that of the builder and architect.

Observer: "**What is the role of the architect in the development of a stadium such as this and how does it relate to the builders' role?**"

Respondent: "**The architect's role is to design a building to the client's requirements or what he perceives to be the client's requirements. To design a building, we must first get planning permission from the local authority and then produce all the technical drawings. We are also responsible for co-ordinating a team of engineers which includes mechanical and electrical engineers and other relevant personnel in drawing up a detailed design for the project. Then we choose a builder and through the builder the cost and price for the project is determined. We must present the cost and price to the client for approval and then employ an administrator on site to make sure everything goes according to the design plan required by our client. The builders are not involved in the designing schedule. It is out task to ensure the builders do not change the design too much and this takes a long time because we had already on what to do in the first place and the changes we were asked to make were considered major ones. Also, the new management wanted to start the building as soon as possible and that puts a lot of pressure on us. Our true requirements are to make sure the client is satisfied and happy with the ongoing project, resolve problems which arise and more importantly review the cost incurred in this**

project so that it's within the budget and time constraints."

This quotation draws attention to the technical aspects involved in this particular role; the design, the necessity for planning permission and the production of technical drawings. Clearly if there is a major change in the design format, then considerable adjustments have to take place. In terms of the last sentence then there is obviously a conflict between 'briefing the client' and the technical execution of the role when major changes are required. We shall see later that problems did arise which required some adjustment, for example, contamination of the ground but more dramatically, the change in management structure was the major change variable. Let us continue with the interview:

Observer: **"How do you communicate with client and builders?"**

Respondent: **"We have a meeting every fortnight on site with the client and builders on the development of the project. We also have discussion with the client about which contractors to employ and other matters like which catering and alternative services to sub-contract. Caterers have a really big role to play in the requirements of the buildings, kitchens, restaurants and other facilities."**

Observer: **"Who are your builders?"**

Respondent: **"The builders contracted are McAlpine Building. They are well experienced with the design of stadia. In addition, they do everything and they are the main contractors. They bring in their own sub-contractors to do the specialised work in the building process and also have consultants as well to look after the site."**

Observer: **"What challenges occurred in the development of the stadium and how were these met?"**

Respondent: **"The challenge was to develop a stadium within the cost of approximately ten million pounds. We had to**

produce a design which meets the change in new safety requirements. A major problem is related to time constraints; we try to meet the deadline for the start of the season and also have to take into account current games. We also have two or three contracts which may phase in at once because we have the demolition of the old stand running concurrently with the building of two or three thousand seats for the new stand and completing the sanitary facilities as well to accommodate spectators in these. Thus at one stage, the new stand was only a shell with seats without any facilities. This was a tough time as mobile units have to be set up at the car park which causes inconvenience to spectators. In other words, the stadium was being used while under construction. This is a standard approach in maximising the utilisation of a stadium within safety requirements. I think this is unique to soccer stadia where we put seats in and keep adding to it; Manchester United did the same thing. Moreover, we have to look deep into the design; there's lots of clauses especially on containment of spectators and we adhere to the safety standards set by the council in following specific guidelines."

Observer: "When did you start to reconstruct the Kippax?"

Respondent: "It was phased in over the whole season and the perhaps the whole year. We started with the demolition and then added in development. This is not the best idea because there are three or four contracts simultaneously and there are different prices charged by contractors. The new management just came in not knowing what exactly was involved in building."

Again, this points up the problem of the insertion of a new management team in terms of the clash between technical expertise and changed expectations. Clearly the problems of re-drafting plans, budgeting and so on, have to be dealt with but at some considerable time and expense. The professional role here is in conflict with the management/client requirements and the conflict has to be resolved in some way. The interview continues in the following vein:

Observer: "Any problems during development/re-building?"

Respondent: "There was some contamination in the ground, but it was not major contamination as it was only ash and other chemicals considered toxic. We had the same thing when building the Umbro stand but it was not classed as contamination in those days just the European law and regulations have changed and come to see it as being contamination. This meant we must have special contractors and special lawyers to dispose of the problem; expense was horrendous and cost a million pounds extra to do it."

Observer: "How is the stand designed for safety? If an emergency happens, how long does it take for people to be evacuated?"

Respondent: "The stand is built to comply with safety guidelines from the council such as the standard size of the width of staircases, number of seats approved in a row and so on; the agreement stipulates that it will take approximately five minutes to complete evacuation from the stand."

Observer: "What is the capacity of the stand?"

Respondent: "The stand was designed to take 11,000 people in three tiers."

Observer: "What are the major improvements on the old stand?"

Respondent: "Before there was no seating. The Kippax stand is now fitted with seats which comply with safety regulations. It's part of the safety guidelines despite some complaints from fans that they prefer to stand during a game. The design of the stand cannot conform to "psychological laws" that suggests people might prefer to stand up. Present legislation requires people to sit down during a game."

Observer: "Are there any special features for disabled people?"

Respondent: "Again, the design has to comply with the guidelines laid down by the council. There are spaces prepared for wheelchairs, about 30-40 of them. Lifts were planned to all levels to ease access. Disabled toilets were also built and other facilities to assist the complete mobility of the disabled."

Observer: "What is special about the Kippax stand?"

Respondent: "The main difference compared to other stands in the stadium is the provision of VIP facilities such as restaurant and conference facilities on the top level. It is much bigger and better than other stands. When compared to other stadiums at national level, the VIP facilities will stand out in that this can be used on non-match days for various functions. Stadiums designed in the 30's and 40's were only for football and the new stadium is a multi-purpose complex with its design suited for community purposes. The management is very keen to make sure that everyone has a role in using the stadium."

Observer: "How much did it cost to build?"

Respondent: "The final cost was around £10.5m and this cost was kept down to the minimum. The stand was designed on a shoestring budget as we were constrained by the limit of spending fixed by the new management. The most important thing was we had a good builder and architect relationship to keep the cost down. In our present economy, we will try to give the best value for money."

Observer: "How is your fee negotiated?"

Respondent: "Actually our fees are fixed. This is stated in the contract with the management and it would have been too time consuming to re-negotiate the fees. We are paid upon completion of the project and also provide a year's warranty to see that everything is in proper order."

Observer: "What kinds of subsidiary installations are used?"

Respondent: "They are not provided in the contract but those installations are optional. However, we do provide facilities which revolve around the mechanical side such as heating, on every level and air-conditioning. One aspect of the stand is that we provide a generator for the production of power to run the lighting, floodlights and heating which is much cheaper. In addition, we also put in redesigned floodlights for the best lighting effect on the field."

This interview points up some of the complexities involved in responding to environmental and organisational constraints. When we look at what appears to be simple ground improvements, the demolition of an existing stand and the erection of a new one, we see that many other factors, physical as well as human are involved. Moreover, the views expressed by the architect, as well as those previously noted for the safety officer, reinforce the notion that the unitary concept of 'role' is an oversimplification. In brief, the architect has certain demands, expectations and so on which circumscribe his role. However, his role conception as we have seen is radically altered by management changes; these brought about a fundamental change in his behaviour, that is, re-designing the stadium according to new directives. Thus the interview provides an apposite illustration of the three specific senses of the word 'role' as described in the appendix namely job requirements and demands, the individual's actual behaviour and job expectations and perceptions. By way of concluding the interview, we may ask about the future development of the ground:

Observer: "Any plans for the future development of the ground? Kippax or more general?"

Respondent: "The Kippax stand is a completely different design from other stadiums because it is the first stage leading to the complete redevelopment of the whole ground. There are plans to take the design and wrap it around the ground to form a massive stadium. The idea is to keep the existing infrastructure at the bottom but take off the roof and complete the wrap around. The extent of construction depends on how the club performs and the revenue which comes in to finance this long term plan. The first idea is to be ready by 2002 for the Commonwealth Games."

A brave new world – Manchester City stadium modified to host an international event as envisaged by its architects in the second Millennium. On the other hand, with a major new stadium under construction in Manchester for the Commonwealth Games, it perhaps makes more commercial sense for City to lease time in this stadium for match days albeit at a psychological cost to the fans. The attractions of this approach are considerable and in fact resulted in a board decision to leave Maine Road in time for the 2003-04 season. They may be listed as follows:

- capacity of approximately 48,000
- available for the start of 2003/2004 season
- 3,000+ car parking spaces
- seats at the side of the pitch
- Metro Link station at the ground
- one mile from City Centre
- surrounded by new Sport City
- funding from lottery money and council
- Maine Road to be taken over by the council

Inevitably, these attractions proved too strong and as we have said, the Board decided to move from a venue which had grown like topsy. A growth well captured by the journalist and author, Mark Hodkinson in his Weekly Times column and his book *Blue Moon*:

"**Football grounds are places of pilgrimage. They are perceived as permanent, largely unchanging against the backdrop of a life that can be uncertain and fickle. Between this game and the next there might be birth and death, new** job or redundancy, marriage or divorce but these lives, rich or fallow will be played out against a fortnightly ritual – same place, same time, same faces.

The condition of the ground is irrelevant. Camaraderie and community is present at non-league grounds where broken terracing and a flimsy fence is the sum total. As it happens Maine Road is impressive though wilfully asymmetrical. Perhaps it is apt that its four stands are so dissimilar for City have been riven by disagreement and ego. When the wind blows and the pigeons huddle beneath them, the mismatched structures become symbolic of the men who have squabbled over this famous club …. Out on the pitch, the stands, by their sheer size conspire to reinforce a sense of smallness on the individual ….. the tallest is the Kippax, traditionally the home of City's most partisan and vociferous supporters. It was flattened in the summer of 1994 and a new all-seat stand built in its place. Where it was once able to house 35,000 supporters, when the ground was first built in 1923 and 18,000 when the old stand was demolished, it's new capacity is 11,000. The top tier would not be the ideal place to hold a convention of vertigo sufferers. The drop to the pitch is incredibly steep but if the game fails to absorb the visitor, the views across Manchester are magnificent…..

Maine Road has been the home of City for more than 70 years but the club may soon be packing away the memorabilia and moving a few miles to the east of the City to a new purpose built stadium though many supporters have a nostalgic affection for Maine Road ….. they know that wherever they play, it is they (the fans) that imbue it with a sense of the sacred!"

The new setting for such a 'sense' is described in Chapter Four, however, prior to that, we need to consider the question of management at Maine Road. By no means a straightforward one!

CR

THE NEW KIPPAX STAND: 1990's

MAIN STAND SHOWING NEW ROOF AND STADIUM CONTROL BOX

NORTH STAND IN THE 1970's

ARTIST'S IMPRESSION OF MAINE ROAD IF REDEVELOPMENT HAD GONE AHEAD IN THE 1980's

MAINE ROAD AS IT IS IN THE MILLENNIUM

CHAPTER THREE ∞

MANAGERIAL SUCCESSION: THE 80's AND BEYOND

Introduction

Just as there are lessons to be learned from soccer crowds about such psychological processes as perception, individual personality, abnormal behaviour, concepts of self, non-verbal communication, social influence, attitudes and prejudice, so also they provide the reader with a glimpse into the processes of managerial succession, organisational formation and development. Academically speaking, there are many accounts of organisational structure and management behaviour, however, Silverman (1970) in the first chapter of his book on the Theory of Organisations, attempts to synthesise the distinguishing characteristics of organisations in the following terms:

"1.　Organisations, unlike other social arrangements arise at an ascertainable point in time. They are easier to perceive as artefacts, consciously established to serve certain purposes, which are generally stated at the time. Their founder(s) further provide them with a set of rules, which generally lay down clear lines of authority and communications with the intention of ensuring that those purposes may most readily be attained.

2.　As artefacts, organisations will be characterised by patterning of relationships which is less taken for granted by the participants who seek to co-ordinate and control.

3.　It follows that a relatively great amount of attention will be paid in organisations to the discussion and execution of planned changes in social relations and the 'rules of the game' upon which they are based."

In terms of management, Torkildsen (1992) comments:

> **"Good management of leisure and recreation is concerned with setting goals and meeting objectives and targets, achieving optimal use of resources, achieving financial objectives, meeting priority needs and offering the most attractive services to meet leisure and recreation demands. In order to manage well resources, services and purpose built facilities, managers need to understand the concept of management and the skills and techniques of management to achieve goals and objectives.**
>
> **The quality of management determines, to a large extent, the type of use and viability of leisure services and facilities ... whether leisure facilities are large or small, whether they are run publicly, commercially or privately".**

(Torkildsen, G. Leisure Management, 1993)

The soccer club is, of course, a leisure organisation and needs to be 'managed' in these terms but its systematic description can also throw into relief what tends to be a neglected area in organisational social psychology, namely what have been termed 'transitory associations', which bring about change as described in Silverman's (3) above, but which have a limited life span and do not exhibit rational management characteristics. Such 'transitory associations' serve as the carriers of ideas and provide the stimulus for management change and renewal by becoming, over time, part of the organisation's formal structure. We describe one such association and the role it played in the structuring and restructuring of Manchester City as a complex organisation later on, but before doing so, it will be observed from the following table that the period, 1980-1990 was characterised by great management changes; no fewer than six managers being appointed during this period. It was also a decade of organisational conflict and dissatisfaction heralded by the sacking of Malcolm Allison and Tony Book, somewhat ironically, during the making of a Granada TV documentary about the day to day working of a major soccer club. After these departures, Norwich City's John Bond was given the job of manager. It is with his tenure that we will begin this chapter. Bond recollects his time at City in Gary James's book.

TABLE 3: MANCHESTER CITY MANAGERS: FROM FOUNDATION TO THE MILLENNIUM*

1.	LAWRENCE FURNISS	1889-1893
2.	JOSHUA PARLBY	1893-1895
3.	SAM OMEROD	1895-1902
4.	TOM MALEY	1902-1906
5.	HARRY NEWBOLD	1906-1912
6.	ERNEST MAGNALL	1912-1924
7.	DAVID ASHWORTH	1924-1926
8.	PETER HODGE	1926-1932
9.	WILF WILD	1932-1946
10.	SAM COWAN	1946-1947
11.	JOCK THOMSON	1947-1950
12.	LES MCDOWALL	1950-1963
13.	GEORGE POYSER	1963-1965
14.	JOE MERCER	1965-1972
15.	MALCOLM ALLISON	1972-1973
16.	JOHNNY HART	1973
17.	RON SAUNDERS	1973-1974
18.	TONY BOOK	1974-1979
19.	MALCOLM ALLISON	1979-1980
20.	JOHN BOND	1980-1983
21.	JOHN BENSON	1983
22.	BILLY MCNEIL MBE	1983-1986
23.	JIMMY FRIZZELL	1986-1987
24.	MEL MACHIN	1987-1989
25.	HOWARD KENDAL	1989-1990
26.	PETER REID	1990-1993
27.	BRIAN HORTON	1993-1995
28.	ALAN BALL	1995-1996
29.	STEVE COPPELL	1996
30.	FRANK CLARK	1996-1998
31.	JOE ROYLE	1998-2001
32.	KEVIN KEEGAN	2001

* We may summarise the message conveyed by the table in the following way:
- Over a hundred-year period from 1889 to 1989, City have had 24 managers. Since the last date, some twelve years ago, they have had eight more representing a third of the 100 year total. We may highlight the pre and post war period as follows:
- Number of managers since the 1940/45 War – 23 over a 56 year period.
- Number of managers before the 1940/45 War – 9 over a 56 year period.

However, it is unclear from this text whether this is interview material given at first hand to James in the mid-1990's or whether it is derived from a secondary source. The style of it's presentation would suggest the former. It reveals the problems which organisations have to face in terms of change and managerial succession. We will quote James's account in full to convey the tension that can arise at senior level during managerial succession. Personality and perception are involved and the induction of the manager can leave lasting impressions which may not always lead to the efficient and effective performance of the club. John Bond recalls:

> "'About six months before I actually took over, I met Peter Swales at the Royal Gardens Hotel in London. City, at that time, were not doing too well under Malcolm and Swales said, 'I would like you to become our manager'. I was at Norwich at the time so we discussed a few things and he promised he'd be back in touch. Well City started to pick up a little towards the end of the season and then I got a call saying, 'We're not going to do anything now. We're going to keep Malcolm and Tony Book on. We can't do anything at the moment, but rest assured that if I do make a move in the future, you will be the first person I speak to'. I understood but I was quite happy at Norwich in any case.
>
> The new season started and Norwich had been surviving quite easily under me, but this year we were struggling. So both sides were having a bad time. Anyway, I came home from one particular match and my wife said, 'You've had a call from Peter Swales. He's going to ring you at nine o'clock tomorrow morning. He wants you to become his manager'. Norwich had no money and weren't really going anywhere, so to be honest, Peter had got me straight away. There was no doubt. It was probably a case of just signing the contract and getting up to Maine Road."
>
> Norwich were determined to keep Bond and offered him a job for life. They also demanded huge compensation from City and pointed out Bond had a seven and a half year contract left to run. The wrangling between the two clubs lasted more or less all season but Swales was determined to

appoint Bond and the deal was done. The new manager felt the City Chairman did not have the full support of the Board. He recalls however, that 'It wasn't that easy to start with as there were one or two directors on the City Board who didn't really want me as manager but Peter Swales had the decision and they were unable to object really. So I became manager, but I remember one particular director saying, "I don't know where the Messiah is who can replace Malcolm Allison!" I sat at the end of the table and he sat immediately on my right and I knew from that day onwards, he was one of my enemies. But he wasn't the only one ...

Another director made a comment about moving from Norwich to Manchester, which implied that I was a bumpkin moving into the big city. To be honest, I treated that with the contempt it deserved. The stupidity of the remark said everything about the man really. At that time it didn't really bother me, as I knew what I could do. I knew I was capable of managing Manchester City and doing well enough for the fans.

A director made a comment after I had been there a while and signed my son on. He said, 'Now, he will have to prove to me that he can play'. I said, 'Prove to you? Who the hell do you think you are? You're a director of this club but it's my job to bring the players in. He hasn't got to prove anything to you, he has to prove it to me'. I then stormed out of the boardroom.'

The purchase of Kevin Bond did not occur until September 1981, but John Bond is adamant that the problems at Board level during his first year or so made him regret leaving Norwich. Not everyone on the Board was against Bond however. In general, the Board appeared to be in support, although one or two felt unable to make a judgement."

After drawing in the 1981 FA Cup Final against Spurs, the City squad returned to their London Hotel and James continues his account quoting Bond verbatim:

"It was really sad. That night at the Royal Gardens was a bitter experience. Unfortunately, I don't think Peter Swales at that particular time, knew how to accept not winning something he thought he ought to have won. I suppose if you had told him in October (1980) when I took over, that City would avoid relegation and get to the Centenary Cup Final, he'd have accepted that. But once we got to the Final, he wanted more. It was a very bitter night for me in many ways. I tried to brush it to one side and get on with having a few drinks, but it was difficult. I remember the attitude of Peter and one or two of the other directors. It wasn't good. They thought we should have won and made sure we knew.

It was sad really. The lads had played their hearts out and were as unlucky as hell. They wanted to win more than any of the directors, but it was so unfortunate for them. I just felt very upset about the whole thing and if I'd had the thinking and the apparent foresight of a Kevin Keegan, I would have walked out on the club there and then. That's what I should have done. If I'd have done that, my future would have been secure in football for evermore. I don't want to boast about what I did in those months to get City to Wembley, because I could also tell you about the things I didn't do and all the bad things I did. I'm just making a statement of fact about what happened that night. I've thought about it so often, what I should have said. At that particular time, I didn't want to be at Manchester City. I'd had enough in those six months I'd been there.

Funny as it may seem, I got on very well with Peter Swales but I didn't like some of the others. There was a lot of snidiness going on and a lot of talk behind my back. They'd talk about the teams I'd pick. I just didn't like the snidiness about the club. It was cold. This is the one part of my life I wish I could go back and do again because I would not do what I did that night, that's for sure. If I'd have realised, I would have actually walked out before the Final. I would never have wanted Peter Swales to think that had any bearing on him because as far as I'm concerned, he never interfered and mostly he allowed me to do what I wanted to do. He was okay, it was the rest of them that I had problems

with. There were some good office staff there, but the other directors ... they never stood up to be counted but were quite happy to be afforded all the privileges that Manchester City gave them in terms of boardrooms, watching matches, going to away games, contact with all the big people in the game and so on. That attitude was not for me".

City lost the Cup final replay and this was to be their first and last visit to Wembley during the 1980's, with John Bond resigning after City's 4-0 FA Cup defeat against Brighton on 29th January 1983 with his assistant John Benson being appointed as the new manager. From the club's point of view, this was financially the easy option but did not save City from relegation to the Second Division and the need to appoint a new man. His successor, Billy McNeill appointed fellow Scot, Jimmy Frizzell as his assistant and their experience of managing on a shoestring came into their own as City's financial situation was, to say the least, difficult with the popular press reporting that interest on loans was topping £1,000 per day. This poor financial position, rapid managerial succession and problems again at Board level during the 1985/86 season, saw McNeill leave his post after the start of the following season; his deputy Jimmy Frizzell took over. However, boardroom problems persisted and crystallised in a fan based protest against the Chairman, Peter Swales as exemplified by a handout distributed over the names of four season ticket holders during April/May 1987. The handout is re-printed in its entirety in the following pages, as it neatly summarises the strains and tensions of organisational functioning at that time.

The season 1986/87 was the first to hold play-offs to decide promotion and City were relegated again after a 2-0 defeat against West Ham. Interestingly, crowd behaviour on this occasion was reported as exemplary and modifies the general proposition of frustration – aggression, which has been described in the previous chapter with regard to the effects of relegation on public order issues. We may quote James to illustrate:

"The Blues were relegated again in May 1987 after a 2-0 defeat at West Ham. At the end of the game, City supporters and West Ham fans, which it must be remembered had an exceptionally poor reputation at this time, climbed over the

fences and onto the pitch. Officials feared that the two sets of supporters were about to fight and were surprised to hear the Hammers chanting, 'You'll be back' and see both groups swapping scarves and souvenirs. It was the kind of moment that should be more widely reported in the media but rarely is and was a sign that the decent majority of supporters were not the caged wild animals the government and media portrayed them to be. City had been relegated but their supporters did not seek revenge. The West Ham fans could have ridiculed but they didn't ..."

After relegation, Jimmy Frizzell was re-titled general manager and Mel Machin of Norwich was appointed the new manager for the 1987/88 season. The following season 1988/89 saw the 'inflatable craze' among the crowd, with giant bananas featuring strongly as exhibits at both home and away matches. Fancy dress as at Hyde Road at the turn of the century, described in Chapter 1 also featured in games such as the one at Stoke on Boxing Day 1988 and the general party atmosphere was reinforced by City's return to the First Division, in 1989, after two seasons in the Second with Mel Machin obtaining an improved contract. The following season saw the defeat of Manchester United at Maine Road by a 5-1 scoreline which is still remembered as City's finest hour and a half by many which dubbed the team 'Machin's Marvels'. However, this form was not sustained and after a succession of defeats, Machin was dismissed; the reason being, 'fan pressure and his lack of spectator rapport'. This came as a shock and led to further protests against Chairman, Swales who had survived the handout campaign. Tony Book was appointed caretaker manager to be eventually followed by Howard Kendall but only after a botched attempt to lure Joe Royle to Maine Road from Oldham Athletic. His successor, Peter Reid was both a player and a manager and brought in Sam Ellis from Bury as his number two.

These rapid managerial changes did not deflect the spectators from the view expressed in the handout, displayed on the following pages, and their protests began to take an organisational form which became known as the 'Forward with Francis' movement, which ultimately brought about major organisational changes, not all of which were planned in the sense described in the introduction to this chapter. It is to this transitory association we now turn.

THE CASE AGAINST PETER SWALES

Peter Swales is constantly reminding City fans of his excellent track record in his 13½ years Chairmanship at Maine Road. Whilst looking through some old City programmes, I came across the City v Southampton programme for Saturday 6th October 1973 which heralded the arrival of the new Chairman of Manchester City – Peter Swales. I think you will agree it makes interesting reading.

Eric Alexander, the outgoing Chairman claims:

> *"We have now reached a stage at the club, by unanimous agreement, where no one man will ever control Manchester City".*

Joe Smith, the President, justifies the choice of Peter Swales as Chairman on the grounds of:

> *"(His) financial wizardy which has enabled City to announce the biggest profit in its history".*

When the laughter has died down – read on, it gets better.

We can examine Peter Swales' record as Chairman under several headings and consider some of his comments in the programme made in his inaugural address to the fans entitled somewhat ironically:-

"IT'S ALL A QUESTION OF FINANCES AND SUCCESS ON THE PITCH"

1. THE TEAM'S PLAYING RECORD
(* footnote at end of Table)

"The object is to make City the number one club in the country."

The team Swales inherited had swept the board in the previous 5 years winning the League, FA Cup, League Cup and European Cup Winners Cup and was widely recognised as one of the best teams in the country*. Swales pledged to improve on that record and promised the fans that if he had not brought success in 4 years, he would stand down. Well it is nearly 14 years and as we prepare to be relegated for the second time, we are still waiting for that promise to be kept. The City team for that day reads: Healey, Book, Donachie, Doyle, Booth, Oakes, Summerbee, Bell, Towers, Lee, Marsh. It is difficult to envisage any of the City team today forcing their way into that side and you could perm any one from that forward line of Summerbee, Bell, Lee and Marsh and justifiably argue that they offered more in entertainment value than all the present City team out together.

2. ATTENDANCES

"It impresses me when our figures go up and they will do so. I'm sure of that. There's no false hope behind that statement".

Peter Swales has consistently claimed credit for improving attendances at Maine Road and even repeated the same boast in the Sunday Mirror of 12th April 1987 following the 4-2 home defeat by Southampton. Let's examine this claim. When Swales took over, City were the third best supported team in the country and the attendances for the first 4 home matches of the 1973 season before Swales became Chairman were 34,178; 30,931; 31,209 and 32,118 averaging out at 32,109. Present attendances have slipped below the 20,000 mark and will fall even further when we are relegated for a second time. Mr Swales is either a good liar or a bad mathematician if he thinks a drop of 12,000+ is an improvement in attendances.

3. FINANCE

"I do not think a football club should run on an overdraft, especially in these days of sky-high interest rates… it's not very clever to run a major business like ours on a vast overdraft".

For once we agree Peter. It's not very clever to be £4 million in debt and to be paying interest charges of £1,000 a day. Mr Swales was the Chairman who sanctioned the Allison lunacy of paying over £3 million for 'world beaters' like Steve Daley, Kevin Reeves and Michael Robinson.

"Think of applying the shrewd transfer style of Burnley to a city club … They have made a success of their methods … Imagine Burnley's kind of operation applied to a city club. This, I feel, can be the answer to making a secure future. What they have done, we can do on a bigger scale".

Well Peter, we all know where Burnley are now but if City are aiming to do it on a bigger scale, then perhaps the Salford Sunday League is our ultimate target.

4. MANAGERS

*"The relationship between Chairman and manager is important.
They have got to have a certain affinity. My role is to make sure
we have the right man".*

Well it's nearly 14 years Peter and we're still waiting for the right
man. We've had Hart, Saunders, Book, Allison, Bond, Benson,
McNeill and now Frizzell. Big names and not so big names but
they've all got one thing in common – failure and bad selection on
the part of the Chairman. The opportunity presented by the
departure of Billy McNeill was thrown away by penny pinching
and appointing Jimmy Frizzell on the cheap – a man clearly
unsuited to running a club of City's stature having neither the
ability nor the personality to run a top club. If Mr Swales was in
any other business than football, then he would have been shown
the door a long time ago with a record like that.

Mr Swales, you claim to love City and have their interests at heart.
If this is the case, I feel you only have one option left open to you.
The fans have left you in no doubt as to what they think of you.
You have destroyed a great club. Do the decent thing – resign and
take your right-hand man Frizzell with you and make room for
somebody else who can start resurrecting the club that we, the fans,
love.

K Doodson
C Johnston
J Hawkins   **Season Ticket Holders**
A Jenkins   **Manchester City FC**

** Pre-War Honours: League Champions 1937: Runners up 1904 & 1921;
FA Cup Winners 1904 & 1934: Runners up 1926 & 1933.
Post-War Honours: League Champions 1968: Runners up 1977: FA Cup
Winners 1956 & 1959: Runners up 1955 & 1981.*

Forward with Francis

The above sub-title may be misunderstood if the reader is not a dedicated soccer fan. It does not refer to a cavalry charge or indeed a set formation in ballroom dancing! Rather it refers to a process of organisational development and renewal, through what we have termed a 'transitory association,' which came to be called the 'Forward with Francis' movement. In brief, it encapsulates in words the need to bring about change at Manchester City. The focus for this change was personified in Francis Lee and arose from a sustained lack of team success, heightened by the re-emergence of rivals Manchester United as **the** major force in the new Premier League. The direction for this grass roots dissatisfaction became crystallised as we have seen in the person of the club Chairman, the late Peter Swales, with some quite venomous criticisms levelled at his handling of club affairs over a sustained period. Let us trace chronologically the emergence and development of what was, somewhat emotionally termed, the 'battle for Manchester City', by drawing on an account from someone who was both a commentator and actively involved in bringing about the change; namely Alec Johnson, a journalist with the Daily Mirror. His book, 'The Battle for Manchester City', documents the process of replacing the late Chairman, Peter Swales with Francis Lee, a former Manchester City player, English international and successful businessman; in short a club folk hero hailing from Bolton in Greater Manchester.

We may provide the background to a successful bid by a Lee consortium to obtain boardroom control by quoting a relevant extract from the book. This portrayal of organisational change by one of the key participants will be followed by interview material obtained from both Francis Lee and the person who became involved in coordinating the campaign for change, a Manchester Licensee, named Alan Tapper. For the moment, let us paraphrase Johnson:

> **"At the end of August 1993, Lee's consortium decided to go for boardroom control at the club. For a week he built alliances before the story about his bid to take control at the club became public.**

At the time many ordinary fans placed their support behind their former star. "A heaven-sent chance we have waited so long for ... a change we simply mustn't miss..." (quote from Derek Partridge).

Partridge, along with two other solid City fans, Tony Meehan and Alan Tapper, formed the 'Forward with Franny' campaign. Over a period of just under four months, the campaign team captured the hearts of the majority of supporters as they mounted a concerted campaign to persuade Swales and Boler, the two majority shareholders, to sell their shares.

Initially, the City board refused to talk, seeming to imagine that those campaigning would soon give up. By the 3rd of February 1994, after disappointments that the deal had not been concluded in January, the takeover was finally completed and Lee's consortium had gained control of the club."

We may now examine from the perspective of a member of the 'Forward with Francis' movement how the idea of organisational change was translated into a reality. The following is a verbatim account of an interview with the City activist, mentioned in the above quotation, who emerged as the coordinator of the movement – Alan Tapper:

Observer: **"Let's start by just establishing your bonafides if you like. How did you come to be a Manchester City supporter?"**

Respondent: **"I've been a Manchester City supporter for something like 45 years now. It all started off with my dad taking me down to Maine Road and watching football in the very early days down there. I've always had a very keen allegiance to Manchester City and I've always been a very keen supporter."**

Observer: **"Have you gone regularly to home games for example?"**

Respondent: "Yes, all my family had season tickets for many, many years. The boys grew up a bit and then wanted to go off on their own in the Kippax and stuff like that. The season ticket side of it lapsed a bit and then we came into the pub game and sometimes Saturdays was a bit difficult so my wife couldn't always go. But I've always gone to games and certainly before I came into the licence trade I used to go to a lot of away games as well. I didn't miss many away games so I've always been very keen on the Blues."

Observer: "Fine. So you can speak with some knowledge about the club and its development over a very long period of time. Can you tell me why you thought change was necessary? Why do you think what is now called, 'The Forward with Francis' movement developed?"

Respondent: "Well basically change was necessary because of the lack of success at Maine Road. They talk about sleeping giants in football, well Manchester City have been in a coma for probably 20 years! It's been a long, long time since there's been any form of success and in any business, management or the leadership must take the brunt of the blame 'cause when you're successful, they take all the plaudits; they get all the pats on the back. When there's lack of success, they of course, must take the brickbats. I feel that in this situation, City has gone for 20 years without having any sort of success. They've been relegated several times and they've had more managers than they should have had. There's been no cohesion, no backing; but there's never been anybody out in the wings prepared to take over because the Chairman had an iron-clad position. Well when you've got the backing of 66% of the shares at Maine Road, I suppose he was very safe."

Observer: "So there was a general feeling of frustration with the performance of the club?"

Respondent: "Yes. Change came about because Francis Lee declared an interest in buying the club. I think you can say that City supporters for 20 years have been a very patient bunch. I can't image any other big club putting up with the sort of inept performances both on and off the field that the Blues have put up with all these years. Then when a major ex-City player like Francis Lee, who's a very successful businessman, presents himself as the man to lead us to better times, this sparks off a great feeling of happiness amongst the City supporters. And they want to get involved then; they want him to be the man in charge."

Observer: "So you had a catalyst – Francis Lee who could mobilise the energies associated with the frustration that was being felt over a long period of time?"

Respondent: "That's right."

Observer: "How then did this take an organisational form? How did it develop?"

Respondent: "Well, when Francis Lee declared an interest in the club and said he wanted to buy the club, there were many little factions all over the place. People wondering what they could do to help in any shape or form. Derek Partridge was a very vociferous man at this time as was Tony Main and I felt I was doing a little bit. There was the Reverend Jim Burns of course, who was very high profile in the Daily Mirror – "Please God, go" he was saying. That more or less started things going and I got to thinking really that this was no good – all these separate factions. So I set about contacting them all. I contacted Derek, Tony and Jim Burns and I said, 'Why don't we all get together and go under one banner and organise as many demonstrations for Francis Lee as possible'. This met with great success. There were people who came in who were a great help – very intelligent people, college lecturers, businessmen in their own right. Not the sort of ..... it's difficult to say ..... not like 'the football yob' variety. They were businessmen, middle-aged businessmen in the main who all got together and decided that this was the way forward for City. My view was that if we could organise people under one heading, we could achieve our goal. We also contacted a lot of ex-players from Francis's era who were very helpful in advising us what we should do. So we organised demonstrations – peaceful demonstrations, I must stress that. We did stress the 'peaceful' and we were congratulated by the police on many occasions. There was not a single arrest at any of our demonstrations; they were conducted properly; very noisily, very vociferously but never any arrests. There was never any public disorder and we went on from there. It grew and grew and grew until many of the official supporters clubs dropped out and formed themselves into an independent branch which is a very strong, thriving branch at the moment."

Observer: "So it was very much a kind of stable, organised, orderly protest movement concerned with changing the management of the club. Please correct me if I'm wrong."

Respondent: "You are wrong. The protests were primarily directed against the past Chairman of the club and his board of directors. We felt that the managers were very much hamstrung by these people and paid the penalty for the board's ineptitude. At this stage we felt that the board was not doing enough financially or otherwise to ensure that the manager could get on with the job of managing. And it appeared people who had been relatively successful were sacked on a whim. This we felt was terrible. We were becoming the laughing stock of football. I mean you couldn't even get a manager of stature to come to City because the job wasn't good for them. I mean, you know nobody'd go there and work under the conditions they were expected to work under.

The club still, despite all this lack of success, was getting 25,000 people there week in, week out. And that to me, in itself, speaks volumes for the support of Manchester City."

Observer: "That's very helpful. So, just very briefly, did you organise things by committees? Did you all meet or was there a steering group?"

Respondent: "We got great backing from Alan Johnson via the Daily Mirror which was very important for us to be able to get the message over to the supporters. The first one was the big demonstration at the home game against Queens Park Rangers. That was the first home game after Francis declared his interest in the club and that was a massive demonstration – really noisy – and Francis turned up and of course it was a great day. And City won. I think the team won because of the warmth of the support. But we organised ourselves as a committee and decided on the name 'Forward with Francis'. We organised via supporters' groups and supporters' branches and as I said, mounted various demonstrations."

Observer: "So you used the existing network to communicate?"

Respondent: "That's correct."

Observer: "Francis Lee is now installed as Chairman. What next?"

Respondent: "At this moment in time, Francis has only been there about three to three and a half months. There's an awful lot of work to do. Certainly he's got the controlling interest with the full backing of the major shareholders, such as Greenhall Whitleys."

Observer: "So if we look to the future now, you have been highly successful. You have brought about a change, a massive change which nobody thought was possible. And you've done this despite all the scare-

mongering and so on, very peacefully because it
seems to me that demonstrations are a double-
edged sword in terms of public order."

Respondent: "We worked as closely as we could with the police
on everything. We had planned various marches and
were told by the police that these wouldn't be
allowed on certain days and we complied completely
with all the police wishes. The demonstrations we
made were confined mainly to outside the ground.
There were a couple of demonstrations during
matches but then again they were peaceful
demonstrations and people, in the main, behaved
themselves impeccably. It speaks volumes, not only
for the organisation, but for the people believing
what we were at and trying to do."

Observer: "How do you see the future now? Your man's
installed, you're still in the Premier League."

Respondent: "Well I think with Francis Lee – he's a very
substantial person in his self. I've met him on a few
occasions and he's a very, very ordinary man and he
would certainly make sure that the future now is
rosy for City. I know if you speak to any Manchester
City supporter, they can't wait for the season to
start. They can't wait to kick off again. He's made a
couple of signings already and he got the German
player, things like that and we're looking forward to
Nial Quinn coming back, looking forward to Gary
Flitcroft coming back. There's a couple of signings
on the pipeline we're led to believe which will make
us a strong squad. And I feel, and having spoken to
Francis, he feels, he wants to instil that sense of
pride back in the players. Proud of the blue shirt.
Not all, perhaps, orchestrated by money which it
seems to be these days but to get some pride back
in the club and get the players playing good
football."

We thus have a first hand account of events which led to the resignation of the Chairman of Manchester City from one of the influential 'change agents'. The other side of the coin is given by a public statement from City's joint major shareholder, Stephen Boler, which confirmed the resignation of Chairman, the late Peter Swales in the following terms:

"As a major shareholder in Manchester City FC I have obviously taken a close interest in the affairs of the club and the speculation surrounding the future of the Chairman, Mr Peter Swales. I own 30 per cent of the shares in the club and Mr Swales also owns 30 per cent.

I am acutely concerned about the effects of the publicity surrounding the proposed takeover of the club by the consortium headed by Mr Francis Lee. Since the start of the campaign by Mr Lee and his consortium, Mr Swales has been the subject of a vicious and violent campaign. I accept that Mr Lee and his consortium would never support the actions of many of their supporters.

However, over the last two months, Mr Swales has been subjected to personal abuse and threats of violence both against him and his family. On one occasion, several thousand leaflets were circulated detailing his private address and he has since been subjected to harassment at his private *home*. His business premises have been attacked and severely damaged on several occasions. All his family have received abuse and threats and recently Mr Swales' eighty-seven year old invalid mother has been threatened. I think it would be impossible for anyone to appreciate the level of stress this placed on Mr Swales when his family has been exposed to such evil and vicious conduct.

Mr Swales now considers that the time has come for a new Chairman to be appointed. Discussions have taken place and the club hopes to appoint a new Chairman within the next few weeks who will be independent by nature and capable of continuing the development of the club with the principle aims of bringing Manchester City into a leading position in

the English Premier League. Mr Swales has, therefore, resigned as Chairman with immediate effect."

Let us now turn our attentions to Francis Lee and his view of the club and the circumstances surrounding the takeover. Prior to the 1993/94 season, Johnson quotes Lee as saying that he wouldn't be prepared to consider the idea of a takeover. Slowly, as City's defeats on the field were exacerbated by what appeared to be somewhat irrational decisions emanating from the boardroom, Lee declared, after consultation with the man who came to be his Chief Executive, Colin Barlow, and a former director, that he would be prepared to lead a bid for control of the club; sustained pressure from fans, who delayed buying season tickets, led to a boardroom capitulation.

An account of the then new Chairman's perspective, recorded in an interview with the author in August 1994, runs as follows:

Observer: "Right, you've got an interest in soccer but your interests are far wider than that; you've an interest also in the commercial sector of our society and in the leisure industry by way of training horses. For present purposes however, lets just focus specifically if we may, on your recent involvement with Manchester City. This was called the 'Forward with Francis' movement. How did you become involved with this?"

Chairman: "Well I obviously became involved with Manchester City when I was a player many years ago and I had eight happy years at Maine Road when the club went through its most successful era. I was lucky enough to get picked for England several times and that again is part of my association with Manchester City, because I was playing with them at the time. Manchester City then transferred me to Derby. I played two years there. Then I left football to concentrate on my business interests which were quite substantial by then. Apart from watching the game on TV, reading about it and obviously following my favourite clubs, which are the clubs I've played for, I've not had a real involvement. But the problems which have been coming to the surface at Maine Road over the last two or three years finally came to a head last year.

There was a body of people who represented the supporters and some shareholders and people who were behind the club asked me would I lead a challenge to actually take over the club and give it a new focus and new direction, which I did. This involved getting some friends, well not friends, for there were people I didn't know who became involved and we formed a consortium to put up the money to eventually gain control of the club and take it over. The team was bottom of the league at this time – they were struggling and it looked like they were going to go out of the Premier League."

Observer: "So would you say your involvement was an altruistic gesture or a commercial judgement, or both?"

Chairman: "Well it couldn't have been a commercial judgement. If I'd had wanted to make it a commercial judgement and do it for profit then my approach would be quite different. Let me explain – if you buy something, you buy it obviously at the lowest possible price and then build it up from there. What I would have done if I'd bought the club purely as a commercial judgement would have been to let the club slide down in to the Second Division. It was virtually bankrupt. It would have been bankrupt then because without the money involved in the Premiership, they would have had to sell all the players to survive and the club would have been there for the taking for nothing really. But I felt that what we were trying to do was for the good of Manchester City. This involved making sure we could get the club on the right footing and making sure we stayed in the Premier League."

Observer: "So what has been achieved since you became Chairman?"

Chairman: "I think the most important thing is to be playing, as I've already said, in the Premiership. It was the most important thing because I don't think that at that time, Manchester City could have stayed in the Premiership. But from there onwards, we started to build a new spirit in the club because it's like any other business, you must have the right spirit; you must have the right motivation coming from the top. And I've never been the sort of person who, through his business career or anything like that, has ruled by fear or threat. I'd rather put my arm round someone and get the best out of them. I've backed a lot of losers ..... but I've had a lot of winners. You know people, who if you'd been too strong with them would have, to speak colloquially, 'turned it in'. I always find that to motivate someone in the way I feel is best pays dividends. So this is what I am trying to do for everybody at the club. It doesn't matter if it's the lady who cleans the stand or the groundsmen, the players – I want everyone pulling in the right direction and wanting to make Manchester City successful. And if we can keep this momentum going, we are going to be successful. I can't say we are going to be successful this season because who knows? It's a sport really – there's a round ball involved; a round ball can take some very cruel bounces at times. However, we're going the right way and the important point is for everybody to feel part of the act."

Observer: "So really your job as you see it, and correct me if I'm wrong, has been really psychological. To offer not so much a particular kind of direction but rather social, emotional support for everybody in the club?"

Chairman: "You're only partly right. You also have got to show a financial direction and develop a strategy. You've got to tell people what you're trying to achieve and explain your difficulties. We've got a problem at the moment because our gates are down this year because of the rebuilding of the Kippax stand. Our income is down almost two million pounds. If your income is down two million pounds, it doesn't take Einstein to work out that you've got to do something about it. You have to cut your costs and we'll have to cut our costs in certain areas. For example we might have too many players and some players are never going to be good enough to play in the first team so you've got to help those players to find a new club and take their cost away from the club and hopefully let them have a new career somewhere else. I know it sounds a bit cruel and a bit like ..... you know, that you have got to get rid of people but that's the name of the game because in the end, to survive in the Premier League, if you want a player, you've got to pay big money for him, so you really have to take the course of action I have suggested. As well as building a new stand, we've got a lot of financial problems but we've got the right strategy in place and we'll have to let it operate."

Observer: "Are there any problems or concerns other than looking to cut costs?"

Chairman: "Yes. The problems arise when a club has been run in a certain way for twenty years; a lot of its employers get into stereotyped ways of doing things, going down the same path they have followed for twenty years. Really they've got to wake them to the realism of the modern world, which is very important. Some people have to leave and some people have to be re-employed. I can't bring this social change on my own; I need good people around me to join in developing group and individual motivation and make it like a team effort. In my commercial career, my staff have always worked together as a team. We've always had tremendous team spirit at Manchester City both on the field and off the field."

Observer: "So what do you think is the most important thing in the long-term for Manchester City? Say you generate this spirit which is obviously a continuing kind of

endeavour – what do you then see as the fairly medium to long-term future for the club?"

Chairman: **"The most important thing is really, and this applies to whatever sport you're in, victory. Victory rewards the fans and it rewards the players and that is what the game is all about. There's an old adage in horseracing, as you know I train a few racehorses, that the winners drink champagne and the rest can please themselves. So it's no good being, as they say in the States, 'nice guys', they do only come second. It's no use having that attitude. We have eventually to reward our spectators with some success and the players themselves have got to put in the endeavour which will result in their success."**

Observer: **"What kind of help do you need to sustain the 'victory' mentality?"**

Chairman: **"If I may answer from a purely personal point of view and take as an analogy my business career, I work at my business career roughly like this; to be a successful businessman, particularly in your own business, is 80% commonsense. In soccer where the result is decided by 11 or 12 people on a Saturday, you need a fair share of luck as well. If it goes the right way for you, the breaks are for you. In normal business you only need a little bit of luck because it's no use bemoaning your bad luck because the good businessman forgets bad luck – he just gets on with the job and makes it happen. In this instance as Chairman of a football club, you can try to make it happen but when it comes down to cups on the sideboard, it's the players who do it."**

Did it happen? Clearly after such a dramatic change in direction with all the social upheaval involved in the 'Forward with Francis' movement, preceded. by the leaflet campaign against the Chairman, it would be churlish to think otherwise. However, normal commercial considerations do not, given the nature of the product apply; as stated by the Chairman at the close of the interview, a round ball is involved. Rationality of organisational procedures and reasonableness of personnel will not alone suffice; a degree of irrationality – call it luck, caprice or superstition pervades the end product – Match Day. While we have talked of luck or caprice in 'making it happen', the influence of Lee's ascendancy to the chairmanship of Manchester City was immediate, charismatic and according to the press, resulted in the irresistible defeat of Ipswich by two goals to one on February 5th, 1994 at Maine Road.

An edited summary of the match provided by the Manchester Evening News may be quoted as follows:

> **"Even in his sixties hey-day, Francis Lee never had a greater influence on a Manchester City match than he had on Saturday. Only hours after winning his battle for control at Maine Road, Lee took his seat in the director's box for the first time as Chairman … and set the whole place alight.**
>
> **Suddenly the old ground was alive again. Thousands of blue and white balloons fluttered up in to the winter sky. A light plane circled the stadium trailing a banner which read, "Welcome Francis!" There was magic in the air. Magic on the terraces. And most importantly of all, magic on the pitch as Manchester City united like a family in a glorious show of support for the ex-England star whose aim is to take the club back to the top of the soccer tree.**
>
> **You could almost feel sorry for poor Ipswich who must have felt like gatecrashers at a welcome-home party. They weren't just playing Manchester City. They were up against a team which would have run through a brick wall to please their new Chairman and in front of 28,000 supporters who just know that a messiah has arrived. The combination was irresistible."**

And the thoughts of Chairman Lee as he surveyed his new kingdom at the close of day, one of his regime?

"Wonderful", he beamed. "The players were great and the fans were great. I'm a racing man and I can tell you this, City won't go down ..... that's a certainty."

However football is a fickle taskmaster; sustained success depends on many factors, not least managerial flair and ability. In this respect and we may note, increasingly, the management of sport, and within that category the management of professional soccer, cannot be understood without reference to the situation, the information available, the people involved, the organisation and the people doing the managing; in short, management is a social process. In this process, the most important ingredient is probably the handling of people. Leadership has been described as a mixture of art, craft and humanity; it is a part of every managerial job. An effective leader is concerned with people and results. Such leaders provide direction (pointing the way), drive (giving motivation) as well as communication and representation to the outside world. The situation is somewhat complicated as we have formal and informal leadership patterns. In addition, there is a time perspective with members of a group performing specific leadership acts such as initiating, regulating, informing, decision-making and maintenance behaviour which may be necessary if group objectives are to be achieved at a given time. How do soccer managers interpret and act in accordance with these parameters?

To shed light on these issues, let us once again turn to our interview data. In the early 90's, City were distinctive in having a dual management structure, namely Peter Reid and Sam Ellis, the latter being assistant manager to Peter Reid; both had responsibility for the team but Sam Ellis had a somewhat detached role in that Peter Reid was a 'player manager' and consequently inseparable from the action on the field of play: at the time, the only player manager in the Premier League. An extract from an interview with Sam Ellis and Peter Reid, conducted at Maine Road, may be given as follows, each responding to a question as they saw fit.

The interview was conducted in the manager's office at Maine Road and each participant played to his particular strengths opting to put a particular point of view, or choosing not to comment as the discussion unfolded.

Observer: "Describe what would be 'an ideal day' from your point of view as a manager of a major league club."

Respondent: "Each day is different. There are training days and there are match days. An ideal combination of this would be to have a good training session, where you think that your players have responded to what you want them to do and where you went out into a match, put it into practice and it came through. It would be difficult to say that a particular day would be an ideal day unless it was just the match day and you went out and won the game."

Observer: "Do you have a routine of training for each week?"

Respondent: "We try to keep away from routines, in that if we believe the players come in and it is predictable what we are going to be doing and how we are going to be doing it, then that does not stimulate their mind and they are getting into habits and habits can be bad ones at times. So, we like to vary it as much as we can."

Observer: "Do the players have a timetable?"

Respondent: "They are told the day before. It is a physical job and it is very difficult to work and train as a normal working man would."

Observer: "Is there a difference between the season and the non-season?"

Respondent: "Sure there is, in that during the season you just keep your fitness ticking over because you get the fitness during the pre-season period."

Observer: "How long does the pre-season period last?"

Respondent: "Ideally between five and six weeks before the season starts."

Observer: "Do the players attend every day at the club?"

Respondent: "They are given their instructions each day they come in and if there was a day off or a day we would not be doing so much, they would be told the day before. Sometimes a rest is as good as work. Professional athletes as well as being physically conditioned also have to be mentally conditioned."

Observer: "Are the physical and mental conditions related?"

Respondent: "Without a doubt, yes. If a player does not think he is as fit as somebody else or he missed a bit of pre-season training, then that might affect his play."

Observer: "How do you see your role as a manger then?"

Respondent: "If you are managing the players, then you must make sure that every time they go out to play, physically and mentally they must be as fit as you can get them to be."

Observer: "Do you have to know the players individually?"

Respondent: "As part of every manager's job, he should know his players, know the mood they come in at in the morning, know the mood they are in, in training."

Observer: "Are there other aspects of a manger's role which are non-player related?"

Respondent: "The manager has his own staff, his own office staff that he needs to be on good terms with to keep the club going well so that everyone works for him. He has a public side; he has the press and media to attend to and he has his boardroom side. So there are a lot of background things besides the match that go into a manager's job. And besides those things, he will also travel around at nights watching games and doing his job that way."

Observer: "How does the job differ from this club (Manchester City) in relation to clubs in lower divisions?"

Respondent: "There is no difference to the fragmentation side. You still have an office staff which may not be quite as big, you still have a media to deal with which may not be quite as heavy and you still have a board (of directors) to deal with that will be just as difficult."

Observer: "Is there a resource difference which makes greater problems in the lower divisions?"

Respondent: "It just depends on the people you work for. I think that a big club and a good club these days is not necessarily the size of it but the people that run the clubs. A good club would be a very small one with a man (Chairman) who is willing to back his managers' judgement and give him the raw materials, the services and the supplies to do well. By that, I mean finance and support. The difference comes in the size of the fragmentations of the manager's job. In a big club he might have seven or eight staff members, in a smaller club he might only have two. That's working on the football side. In the office staff, he might have something around thirteen or fourteen and he has to have a good relationship with all departments within the club; administration, commercial and whatever other departments there are in a football club."

This interview points up some of the comments we have previously made in terms of decision-making and role differentiation in leisure organisations. Let us develop these points further by updating our interview material by presenting the point of view of a subsequent appointment to the managerial position at Manchester City, following on from a brief tenure by Brian Horton, namely Alan Ball. The interview was conducted in mid-summer 1996, after a training session at Manchester Universities Wythenshawe complex and began, as before, by enquiring about an ideal day:

Observer: "First of all, what is 'an ideal day'?"

Respondent: "An ideal day is more or less a typical day. In other words, I leave my home at around half past seven and then I leave an hour to deal with the press, the media – I'm always in my office for that hour at the beginning of the day so that I can be contacted with regard to any problems that may have arisen. Then I see players, deal with any playing problems, perhaps have a training session then after the training session I could be visiting another ground somewhere in the country, watching a match, looking at new players and that would take me up to midnight; back home and then start again the next day, into the office for the hour making sure everything's been sorted out."

Observer: "Is the manager's role essentially one concerned with the playing side?"

Respondent: "Well at Manchester City it does seem to be a dual type of function where I'm concerned with the playing side, involved as you see today in the training and Francis Lee, the Chairman would be involved with the financial side – the checking out of transfer monies and so forth. We work together in that I would first of all speak to a player who might be interested in coming to City and look at his form and would leave the financial side to the Chairman."

Observer: "Is there a difference in managing at different levels in the league structure?"

Respondent: "Basically, no. I don't think there is because we are essentially concerned with dealing with human beings – we're dealing with players so we're responsible for managing people and this occurs regardless of whether you're in the Third Division or the Premier League. However, there's obviously a difference in terms of scale, in terms of the resources that are available at your command. And that's where there is a big difference, the financial side."

Observer: "Were you worried about making the move to Manchester City?"

Respondent: "No, neither anxious nor worried; the reason being my wife is a very stable, accommodating person who supports me in my work and has helped me considerably. And I spoke to Francis Lee, the Chairman and after I had spoken to him again I received the kind of assurances that I needed. In other words, I knew there would be problems at Manchester City but it gave me a bigger stage on which to play."

Observer: "Is managing Manchester City special, and if so, in what way is it special?"

Respondent: "Well yes, it is rather special in the way that it presents a challenge. A challenge in terms of what resources we can have, but also, as I said previously, because it gives me scope and challenge for developing my own philosophy as a soccer club manager."

Observer: "Moving on from that, do you see soccer management being different from management in general?"

Respondent: "Basically, no, I don't because in management you're handling people and here we are handling people, so I don't necessarily see it as being different or separate from say managing a public company; you've got to earn their respect first of all then everything comes from that."

Observer: "Do you need to have been a soccer player to become a successful soccer club manager then?"

Respondent: "No I don't think you do. Basically I think you've got to earn their respect. I mean it helps being in the business for thirty years or so, knowing the inside of dressing rooms and being able to familiarise yourself with the business side, i.e. playing soccer. Obviously all that helps but that's the same in any walk of life. It does help but at the end of the day, it's the management skills, the human resource development that you need which is the main thing."

Such 'human resource skills' have to be developed within a highly competitive environment where success is all important; success in the season 1995-1996 for Manchester City being measured as survival in the Premier League. Gauged by this yardstick, City were unsuccessful in that they were relegated with consequent dislocation of relationships at all levels of the club; morale both individually and collectively plummeted and Alan Ball recalls the relegation effect in the following reported terms:

"Relegation was a shattering experience for myself and everyone connected with City. I have had my share of 'downs' during my years as a manager and a player, but going down has to rank as the biggest disappointment of my career.

Until I came to Maine Road last summer, I had no idea just how big the club is and what magnificent supporters they have. It is the supporters, as much as myself that I feel sorry for. I was desperate to give them something to cheer this season and nobody deserves a Premiership side to watch more than they do.

Looking back over the season as a whole, I have to say that in the end we paid a very heavy price for the start we made. We didn't win a match until November and two points out of a possible thirty three was a shocking return. If there was anything which sent us down, it was those results from the opening eleven matches because it left us with an awful lot to do just to catch up to the team above us.

Our results since November have been reasonable. We collected thirty six points from our final twenty seven Premiership matches which isn't a bad haul by anyone's standards and proves that we got better as a team as the season progressed. If we had only made a reasonable start to the season, we would certainly have ended the campaign in a comfortable mid-table position.

If we had started with a run of victories we could even have been looking at a European spot by the time we met Liverpool in the final match. That shows what a thin line there is in soccer between success and failure. However, despite the fact that we were relegated, it has not been all doom and gloom this season. I was delighted to see the progress made by young players like Michael Brown and Martin Phillips and don't forget that Gio Kinkladze is still only twenty two years of age. I brought Kit Symmons from Portsmouth to give him a chance of Premiership soccer and he has been an outstanding success in his first season at this level.

When I came here the team had been involved in two successive relegation battles and I felt it was obvious that changes had to be made. In terms of personnel and the way their football is played, the team which finished the season is unrecognisable from the one which began it. We couldn't quite make good the damage caused during the first couple of months but to miss out at the death on goal difference shows what a fight the players made of it.

It was a bitter experience for us to end the season with relegation but sometimes you have to take a step backwards before you can move forward again and I can promise our supporters that we will get back where we should be and we will be stronger than ever when we bounce back.

Unfortunately, this prediction turned out to be unfounded with Alan Ball leaving the club in late August 1996 with a new appointment not being made until late October of the same year. This inter-regnum created great controversy and depression among both supporters and staff with 'named' managers turning down the opportunity to come to Maine Road and thus lowering morale even further. It was during this period that it was seriously suggested that the Chairman, Francis Lee should consider adopting the managerial role until such time as an appropriate appointment could be made. The author as psychologist (O) engaged in a radio broadcast interview with Tommy Docherty (R), former manager at Chelsea and Manchester United and a Scottish international during his playing day, about the implications of this initiative; we may quote the exchange in unedited form as follows which reveals some of the deeply held beliefs and values about professional soccer management from those with a long association with the game:

Observer: "Why was Tommy Docherty 'amazed' at learning that Francis Lee was prepared to take on the role of caretaker manager at Manchester City? In my view, he has impeccable qualifications for the job; he was at Manchester City club as a player for eight years during which time he was picked for England. He has been very successful commercially, has a grasp of financial strategy and so on."

Respondent: "The reason he couldn't in my view, take on a managerial role is that with all his business commitments it would make for difficulties. It would also put the players in a funny position – here we have someone who is the Chairman of the club, the coach, the manager telling us what to do on match days and what not. I just don't think it would work."

Observer: "But surely as a successful businessman Lee knows how to prioritise his interests? Also you previously mentioned the need for support from fans – Lee came into the club at the request of the fans and the so called 'Forward with Francis' movement."

Respondent: "Yes, that is true but fans being fans, they are cheering when it is going great and then when it is going badly, they can become aggressive and turn against you and that is the present position."

Observer: "Let us turn to the qualities of the manager – what is the problem with combining the roles of leader of the club, that is Chairman and of the production unit or team, that is manager? - as for example, Barry Fry at Peterborough; there is here a precedent."

Respondent: "I think if Lee became the manager he would be that as well as the Chairman, the coach, the trainer dictating tactics. I just think it would be a disaster and I hope I would be wrong. The reaction of the players wouldn't make this a good move."

Observer: "To particularise then from roles, what qualities do you see are necessary in a Premier League manager?"

Respondent: "It depends on what you are looking for – a tactician, motivator or both; a fellow who is very good at man-management or delegating jobs to his staff. It would also be nice to get a manager of proven experience but they are few and far between; the clubs that have them are holding on to them. The only other possibility would be an outstanding young man waiting to break through into the big time."

Observer: "But you have experienced managers in commercial organisations like ICI and so on."

Respondent: "I'm sorry but I don't think you can recruit from these non-football organisations and bring them into a football environment and make them a manager. Yes, a director maybe. It won't work because the football environment is totally different from a business environment elsewhere."

As events turned out, this transitional arrangement was not undertaken as Stephen Coppell was appointed as manager of Manchester City from October 7th, 1996 and a process of rebuilding morale at all levels of the club was given top priority. A priority which had resulted from the disastrous 1995/96 season in which both caprice and performance combined to doom

Manchester City to non-Premier League football, this being well expressed by a Manchester Evening News columnist in the following terms:

"For Manchester City it was a season which began with a mountain of hopes and ambitions .... and ended in a river of tears.

Alan Ball, the fiery, feisty little red-head who endeared himself to the nation as a World Cup winner in 1966, would not have known what lay in store for him when he arrived in Manchester with his wife Lesley on the eve of the new season to take charge of the Blues as successor to Brian Horton. But what the former England midfield star could not have foreseen, even in his worst nightmare when he walked into Maine Road for the first time in July was that, months later, he would become the third manager in the space of thirteen years to suffer the ignominy of taking Manchester City into a lower division.

New boss, Ball, was given the first inkling that he had taken on a bigger task than he probably realised as he watched his players struggle to string two passes together during a series of disastrous pre-season warm up games. By the time the season started with the opening game against Spurs at Maine Road, Ball had brought at least some order to the chaos and must have been reasonably content to mark his first match in charge with a point – particularly in view of the fact that he had three brand new players in his side in German goalkeeper Eike Immel, Welsh international defender Kit Symmons and the unknown Georgian midfielder Georgi "Gio" Kinkladze ... the last hurdle of all ... the final match against Liverpool at Maine Road which the Blues had to win to have a fighting chance of escaping the drop.

As events proved, if the Blues had taken three points off the Anfield Reds, the Premiership flag would still have been fluttering over Maine Road next season. The 2-2 draw was enough to see Ball's side finish the campaign with the same number of points as Southampton and Coventry only for the

Blues tragically to slip through the relegation trap-door by virtue of an inferior goal difference."

The rebuilding process under Coppell's management was short lived as he resigned from his position on health grounds only weeks after taking up the post. The managerial reins were taken up eventually by Frank Clark who began very promisingly turning City's team results around surpassing Manchester United in an FA Cup run and notching up a number of league successes. Surprisingly, attendance at home games in the old Second Division blossomed with crowds over twenty thousand turning up at Maine Road despite indifferent performances on the field prior to Clark's arrival. However, the beginning of the 1997/98 season was less than auspicious. By October, 1997 seven games into the season, City were fifth bottom of the League, had been knocked out of the Coca Cola Cup by a team a division below them, Blackpool, booed off the Maine Road pitch after a defeat from a lacklustre Norwich side and the media again howling 'crisis' in banner headlines. In an interview in the Official Club magazine about this time, Clark presents his diagnosis and prognosis in the following terms; the convention of observer and respondent is retained for this account, though obviously did not feature in the article:

Observer: **"What's gone wrong?"**

Respondent: **"Well we haven't played well enough (laughs); seriously, no matter how thoroughly you prepare it's very, very difficult to legislate for individual mistakes and that's what's happened recently – we've literally thrown away six points through individual errors…. We've also got to try and get the tension out of our play at Maine Road."**

Observer: **"Is part of that tension communicated from the fans to the players?"**

Respondent: **"It's part of it – of course you can sense the anxiety in the stands, but that's totally understandable. They're paying good money and for that they expect a good game and us to win. You can't expect the fans to set the mood for the players, the players have to**

set the mood for the fans. There is apprehension and frustration from the fans, partly because of the lack of success throughout the years, partly because of the team down the road (Manchester United) from us, but it's no excuse. It works both ways; if things are going well, you get that tremendous support and it's a great bonus; if things aren't going well, it can be a bit of a negative influence. If you take all the benefits of playing for a club like Manchester City, in terms of big contracts and being well looked after, you have to take the down side as well."

Observer: "Being booed off the field after the Norwich game was a 'downside'?"

Respondent: "Yes but I don't like it when individuals, and this is general in football, get the treatment. That doesn't help anybody and there was a bit of it going on against Norwich ... a lot of it is the weight of expectation in playing for a club like this ... While it would be nice to see the supporters come in and cheer the team non-stop regardless, all we can ask them to do is keep faith, pay their money and turn up. The club now has some good young players who are being held back because of the number of seasonal professionals we have got here and that's why I'm trying to thin that out so some of the youngsters can come through. One of the problems we have at this club is giving everybody a game, which shouldn't be the case .... As to the question of what you say to them if they're not playing well enough, they get left out. Simple as that. It doesn't matter how much you paid for them; once they join the club, the transfer fee becomes irrelevant ... This leads to media pressure ... take Gio Kinkladze – if we lose, we're selling him, if he gets a little injury, he's out for four weeks. It's got to the ridiculous extent that if a pass of his goes astray, it's somebody else's fault. Fans say, 'that player (the recipient) is not good enough to read it', which is plain rubbish because even Gio occasionally makes a bad pass.

It's a bit unhealthy, this obsession with a quality player like Gio and it affects club morale... so these are some of the problems but they're problems we have to solve..."

Observer: "This draws attention to the media. Your view?"

Respondent: "There seems to be - and I can't explain it at all - a really destructive edge to how the media look at Manchester City. I don't think I'm paranoid about it. I'm always on my guard to never become paranoid about criticism because in our game, if things don't go well, you get criticised and you expect it. But there seems to be an almost hysterical edge to the reporting of this football team; something I have never experienced before anywhere else in my whole career. There is not a lot we can do about it other than give them the answer on the pitch..... As for it being related to the past 'underachievement' I don't know as I have only been here nine months. Also remember that we have United down the road and they are continually successful – it's obviously easy to contrast them with us and write negative stories based on that. Comparisons lead us to receive the odium! As I said before, the only way we can answer criticism is on the park. Banning journalists is not going to work ... I have faith in my squad to make a promotion challenge."

Such optimism was eventually to be found without foundation and some of the informal pressures effecting club morale, were made explicit only one month after the interview was concluded, at the AGM as reported in the official magazine for November 1997. With City 21st in the First Division, the AGM took place at Manchester's Bridgewater Hall, with Francis Lee chairing his fourth meeting and declaring:

"There will be an open forum session after formal business where shareholders can ask questions to the board or the manager. But I would be grateful if shareholders could

refrain from making comments on personalities, player's wages or anything of that nature."

The flavour of such comments is provided by the lead off provided by a City fan of some fifty years standing. Addressing the meeting, he opened:

"You will have noticed that the deficit on the club's ordinary trading account has gone from half a million to over two million pounds. It doesn't yet indicate, Chairman, that we have turned the corner in the bullish manner you suggest in your annual report. We seem to be a very long way from the promised land which was given to us when you first became Chairman ... However, I do hope that whatever the results this season, we stick with the present manager .... because I do think any manager needs three or four years to establish himself."

The speaker then went on to criticise the PLC's treatment of the youth team coach who had sued the club for wrongful dismissal. Issuing a direct challenge to the Chair, he concluded:

"It reflects very badly on you that you allowed this to happen in the way that it did."

In response, the Chairman reminded the meeting that the case was brought, not by the club, but by the plaintiff and that it would have not been possible for him to personally intervene as he was non-executive Chairman; the decision to relieve personnel of their duties was a management one. To quote:

"There were a lot of problems between youth development and the youth team manager and when Frank Clark came along, he gave them four months to sort things out".

Frank Clark intervened in the debate at this point, in the following terms:

"Listen, both men were offered very generous compensation. But the board of directors have to draw a line somewhere between what is generous compensation and their

responsibility to you as shareholders…. They were dismissed because, in our opinions, they weren't good enough at their jobs for what was required for Manchester City PLC in the future. On the second day of the industrial tribunal, the chairman of the tribunal got each sides' barristers together and said "I think you're all wasting my time here. Can't you all get together and come up with an agreement?" In a nutshell, they did. It wasn't a climb-down by any means. I would rather have left it alone because it won't do me any good – a youth policy takes five years to mature and if you look at the average tenure of a football manager, you have to say it's highly unlikely I'll be here to see the benefit."

A prediction that turned out to be quite accurate! But to stay with the AGM for the present, it was pointed out that some of the £11.5m raised from the share issue at the last AGM had gone on reducing the club's debts and this left little in the way of meeting transfer fees. The manager confirmed that the transfer 'kitty' was now empty and outlined the difficulty in securing players to strengthen his team while needing to reduce the number of professionals on the pay-roll; 53 full time professionals.

The catalyst in removing Frank Clark from office was City's unexpected defeat against Bury on 14th February, 1998 which left the club third from the bottom of the First Division; Clark's reign had lasted little more that thirteen months, well within the five years he had predicted as his maximum. A new chairman and manager were required and David Bernstein and Joe Royle took up the challenge.

Royle's appointment did not stop the drop to the third level for the first time in the club's 104 year history nor Francis Lee's resignation as Chairman on 16th March 1998. A national 'daily' comments:

"Joe Royle, Lee's last manager, did his best to save the club from oblivion in the fifteen games left. But he was fighting against the death wish which has for too long gripped the club."

A death wish characterised by scenes of disorder at the final game of the season against Stoke City, away from home, which City won 5-2. Notwithstanding this victory, the headlines of the troublesome seventies reappeared, 'POLICE BATTLE RAGING FANS'. The Daily Mail storyline for May 4th, 1998 ran as follows:

"Police and stewards engaged in running battles with hundreds of hooligan fans at Stoke City's Britannia Stadium yesterday during Manchester City's meaningless 5-2 win, as both clubs crashed into Division Two. Crowd violence turned the stadium into a frightening football war zone and once again shamed the game as more than 20 people were hurt, 300 ejected and 15 arrested.

Fears of fan trouble became a reality during the game and after, trouble spreading to the wasteland that surrounds the £14.7m stadium.

Two supporters suffered fractured cheekbones as thugs hurled bricks and stones while 200 police and 450 stewards fought to keep both factions apart.

Mounted police charged around 500 rioting supporters as they fought at a footbridge near the stadium. Superintendent John Wood said, 'Three hundred supporters were ejected for having tickets for wrong sections of the ground. Another 20-25 were hurt when fans threw missiles at each other near the coach park where the Manchester City supporters buses were. We made 15 arrests, two before the game, 10 during it and three after. This is the worst fan violence we have seen at this stadium'.

Supporters' groups and club officials from both sides had pleaded for calm before the game after Stoke had allowed tickets to go on open sale.

By the ninth minute, dozens of Manchester supporters forced a minute's stoppage as they fled areas designated for Stoke fans. Throughout the game, fighting broke out in several parts of the ground. Supt. Wood said there were fears that at least 4,000 Maine Road supporters had bought tickets out of

the zone segregated for their club. In the Britannia Ground's main stand where alcohol was on sale at half time, stewards escorting two Manchester fans to safety were ambushed and assaulted. The worst trouble broke out after the game. In the area outside the Manchester supporters' end, rival fans charged a cordon of police and broke down one fence designed to keep them apart. Bricks, stones and bottles were thrown at stewards and police who had to resort to hand-to-hand fighting amid the bombardment.

Supt. Wood confirmed, 'Fans from both clubs were trying to get at each other and throwing bricks and stones. One fence was broken as we tried to contain them'. The worst injuries were two broken cheekbones. John Johnson, the Regional Divisional Officer of the Staffordshire Ambulance Service said, 'The injuries were caused by flying bricks. Both sets of supporters were trying to get at each other and we are lucky there was not more serious damage.'

Hundreds of fans clashed and mounted police charged them to restore order."

Sounds familiar? Yes, we have been here before during the troublesome seventies and this episode shows how difficult it is to 'design out' problems from football stadia – the Britannia is a brand new purpose built facility – where there is a collective 'revolution under the ribs'. Once again it brings to the fore the perennial problem of handling large crowds which are emotionally 'super-charged' with regard to issues like promotion and relegation. We may quote a commentator writing towards the end of the century, who in literary vein, uses the following terms to describe the Peterloo massacres; words which we have already deployed in this books' companion volume, 'Manchester United at the Millennium':

"The meeting of large numbers of disaffected people ... becomes threatening in the aggregate. No-one cares much for a grain of gunpowder, but mass the grains into pounds and the pounds into tons and there is certainly need of precaution in dealing with it".

The Manchester Man: 1876

David Bernstein's accession to 'the throne' of chairmanship, was the antithesis to that we have observed for Francis Lee. Born in St Helens in 1943, Bernstein tends to adopt a low profile and is admirably fitted for this by dint of his background because he is neither a celebrity, former player nor local businessman. He joined the City board in 1994 as financial director at the invitation of Francis Lee. With Lee forced to resign through fan pressure because of failure on the field of play culminating in further relegation, Bernstein became Vice-Chairman and then Chairman in March 1998. As one might expect from one who is a chartered accountant by profession, he is reported to be happy to delegate and relate to people in a positive rather than antagonistic way; relying on tact and diplomacy rather than aggressive street vernacular. As a director of several multi-national companies, his corporate managerial experience is considerable and in short, he was seen as an antidote to the recent past. Mark Hodkinson remarked in The Times at the time of his appointment:

"Some feel he is a bridge between the past and the future, someone reflective and calm; to hold court until he is superseded by someone drawn from the ruthlessly charismatic breed that drive football clubs to absolute glory! 'He will bring an air of respectability about the place and that's been missing from Maine Road recently' an insider said. 'Everyone says how nice he is, but bland people rarely make good football clubs. There is always a point where you have to stop being nice'. He is not the man who has stood shoulder to shoulder on the Kippax, sipping Bovril and shouting abuse ... However, he shows the patience and perseverance long overdue in these parts. They've had a bellyful of bravado."

As Mr Bernstein was not interviewed by the author, we can neither confirm or deny this analysis.

By way of contrast to his Chairman, Joe Royle was no stranger to struggles in the lower divisions or football fans' behaviour in all its manifestations. He joined City shortly after his 49th birthday and had been involved in professional soccer at a variety of levels since joining Everton at the age of 14 as a £7 a week professional apprentice. He was also no stranger to Maine Road having spent three seasons there as a striker joining them in Christmas 1974. Thus in returning as manager at Maine Road, there was a certain psychological affinity in terms of familiarity with the ground and its environs. Physically large, he is known for his smile, generosity of spirit and sense of humour, excelling in 'the one liner'. Testimony to his stable temperament is the fact that he was sent off only once in approximately 500 games. Reared as an only child in Norris Green, Liverpool, his father was traditional skilled working class; a steam engineer by trade. His values and attitudes were thus moulded in a different way from his Chairman and are rooted both in a traditional working class culture and the game of professional football.

As a manager, Royle's most notable achievement was at Oldham Athletic where his team reached the Littlewoods Cup final, the semi-final of the FA Cup in 1990 and then promotion to the Premier Division in 1991. He returned to his former club Everton as manager but eventually left under difficult circumstances. In taking over from Frank Clark at City in February 1998, he inherited a squad of over fifty full-time professional players with little or no money to negotiate in the transfer market and indeed a negative balance sheet; the club carrying a considerable debt. During his first year in office, he almost halved the wage bill by selling or releasing nearly thirty players and obtained some £5m for Gio Kinkladze by transferring him to Ajax. Reviewing his first year in office in an interview with Mark Hodkinson of The Times, he is quoted as saying:

> "It takes time to build a team. We are not going to turn round a tailspin that has been in place for the last 23 years (City's last trophy was the League Cup in 1976), in just ten minutes. Alex Ferguson took four years to get it right at United and that was with a great deal of money to spend and a team he inherited that already contained several internationals."

This plea for patience was largely heeded by the fans during the initial year of transition even though they might not have expected reversals against the likes of Reading and Mansfield Town. The general view being that they would show a clean pair of heels to the cloggers and honest journeymen of the lower division – 'pub team sides'. However the journey away from such malign influences into more elite company, proved more difficult than expected despite the best efforts of Royle, his head coach Willie Donachie and Jim Cassel, City's chief scout and director of the youth academy. The latter cannot be charged with being unmethodical in his approach to interpreting his brief to restructure the clubs youth policy; an area which we have seen caused concern to both shareholders and management. A new plan backed by £500,000 of funds was announced to lay the foundations for success in the future with the 1997-98 season seeing the first intake of students to the club's football academy; the main objective being the developing and nurturing of a small group of adolescents aged from 13-16 years of age. The club pledged support for both their full-time education and football skills development. The initial intake comprised eight youngsters, all from St Thomas Aquinas Comprehensive School in Whalley Range, Manchester, with the students attending full-time education and reporting to the ground for specialist coaching between 3.30 and 5.30pm. In addition to this weekly timetable, there was a Friday afternoon visit to the club's physiotherapist and a competitive game on Sundays with the club's under-13 team.

Success, however, had to be measured more immediately by promotion out of the Second Division; a job for seniors, not juniors but one only to be achieved with great difficulty. Let us lean on Mark Hodkinson's account in The Times to summarise the position at the close of the 1998/99 season and the dilemmas facing the manager:

"Despite City's present league status, Maine Road is still a special place on a Saturday afternoon. It will be even more so today, the last day of the regular Nationwide League season when York City are the visitors. A sell-out crowd of more than 32,000 is expected, which will mirror the attendance of the opening game of the season against Blackpool.

August to May, Blackpool to York City, has been a long nine months. While City have qualified for the promotion play-offs, it has largely been a season of phlegmatic endeavour rather than joyous rejuvenation. Rarely have they looked

anything greater than the solid but inconsistent outfit that – Fulham aside – typifies the division in which they play.

During the first half of the season, City were more than disappointing. Their nadir came just before Christmas when a defeat, away to York City, left them twelfth. They were collecting more sendings-off than points and Joe Royle's after-match habit of lambasting the referee or whining that it was "their cup final" was beginning to grate.

After the York defeat, City embarked on a run that Royle had forecast for some time, though fans had started to mock this assertion. They lost just once in 21 games and propelled themselves into the play-off area. Supporters were pleased to witness this recovery, though a play-off place is more an appeasement than a cause for celebration.

Many observers believe that City's progress through the play-offs is a formality. They feel that the sheer weight of support from the stands will propel them to victory in these death-or-glory matches. History would suggest otherwise for City are not good under pressure.

In fact City did secure promotion but only after a penalty shoot-out as the score finished 2-2 against Gillingham after ninety minutes had elapsed. Kevin Horlock and Paul Dickov saved the *Blues* and secured a 3-1 penalty win in front of 77,000 Wembley fans. Joe Royle is reported in the Manchester Evening News as saying after the match:

"When I took over, I knew there was a unique set of problems to overcome. There was, and is the huge expectations of the supporters and the urgent need to stop the rot and stabilise the club. We have stopped the rot but I cannot get carried away by the fact that we have won what is the equivalent of promotion from the Third Division. A club like this should never have been in that position in the first place…. As always, we had to do it the hard way but I hope that this has gone some way towards curing one of our old traditions of losing on big occasions."

More specifically, we may draw on interview material featured in the official City magazine for August 1999 to describe the meaning of playing in the Second Division from a managerial point of view and the calculations required for survival. Again, we retain the observer/respondent format with Mike Barnett, the editor, being the observer and Joe Royle, the respondent:

Observer: **"Did anything surprise you about our spell in the Second Division?"**

Respondent: **"It was the first time that I had been to a lot of the grounds, except on scouting missions. It didn't surprise me but it was new to me and it took me a while to get used to the teams... Remember I'd spent the previous five and a half years...in the Premiership, watching Premiership players, foreign players, not Second Division players. There was a familiarity thing we all had to go through."**

Observer: **"Looking back now, how would you assess what happened?"**

Respondent: **"The season was in two distinct halves; the first half where we played a different system with different players and the second half where we played the system I wanted and we sorted ourselves out... the high point was against Fulham. At that point, they were running away with it (the League Championship) and were well clear of anyone else in the division. But I looked at us on our best days and I knew there wasn't that much between the sides, no matter how heavily they spent. It was important for us to beat them. (City did)."**

Observer: **"You made it a priority last season to reduce the size of the senior squad. You've made some progress on that score – could you let us know how far away you are from an ideal squad number?"**

Respondent: **"The ideal would be probably a first team squad of 18 to 20 seniors and then 10 young pro's making up**

most of your reserves and then your YTS boys on top of that. We still have too many players here. A number of players are available for transfer."

Observer: "That said, what is the current transfer policy of the club?"

Respondent: "When you can (ideally) it is one in, one out. We need to be Bosman aware, we need to know of players whose contracts are coming up and WHEN they are coming up and we have to spread the net further afield now... our attention is to be aware and ready for players in Scandinavia and Northern Europe, people we know who have got a similar mentality to ourselves and who can adapt. Remember I brought one of the first Norwegians over her, Gunner Halle in 1991. We tightened our belts (after relegation in 1998) all over the show and scouting was one area. We cut it right down to the bone, but now we're going again. (John Hirst being appointed as chief scout during the close season)."

Observer: "Let's talk about this season (1999/2000). Do you get as excited as ordinary fans do when the fixtures come out?"

Respondent: "When I was at Bristol City on Saturday, I saw their fixture list, which we had last year, in their match programme ... I'm not demeaning any of the clubs but that could have been us, it was traumatic ..."

Observer: "'Fear' is the wrong word but looking at the teams for the coming season, which teams do you respect?"

Respondent: "I think there's one or two unknown qualities. You don't know how Forest is going to re-group, how Bolton will react to their play-off final defeat, Wolves might have their star man but they might not, so you don't know what's going to happen there. Huddersfield Town have spent quite heavily so they'll be the Bradford City of this year. But I have a sneaky feeling that Charlton Athletic won't be too far away. So if we are on their tails going into the New Year, I'd be quite happy. Blackburn Rovers are going to have the problem we had last year, in that everybody's waiting for them. Brian Kidd's got the task of raising a team that's been struggling for three years."

Observer: "Finally, you said this time last year promotion was the priority. Can I ask you the same question this time round?"

Respondent: "Same answer. We haven't got time. There's been too much time spent at this club. We've got to think we've got a realistic chance of at least the play-offs. If Watford can go through and Bradford City, there's no reason a club this size shouldn't emulate them."

In fact stability was restored and the season 1999/2000 proved highly successful for the club although it again culminated in a dramatic finish; only just short of the breathless anticipation of the play-offs of the season before. In brief, City managed a ten-match winning run prior to their game with Blackburn Rovers at Ewood Park on Sunday May 7th, 2000. A win would see them back in the Premiership with all that implied in terms of status and financial gain, a loss would lead to a rehearsal of last seasons' climax. In front of a capacity 31,000 crowd containing 7,000 of their own fans, City emerged victors scoring an unambiguous 4-1 route of the home side. They thus gained promotion to the Premier League finishing second behind Charlton with 89 points; two points clear of third placed Ipswich.

Both interviewer and interviewee reconvened one year later to review the progress made through this time; their encounter is related in *City Life* (August 2000) under the headline, 'By Royle Ascent'. Mike Barnett, in his header to the interview, states his own position in unambiguous and forceful fashion taking no literary prisoners in the process!

"Alex Ferguson became Sir Alex Ferguson 15 months ago for winning the European Cup for Manchester United. Joe Royle's achievements across town at Maine Road are a little more modest, but do a compare and contrast. Manchester United are a global phenomenon, reputedly one of the best known brands, if a football club can be referred to in such terms, in the world. City fans will hate to admit it, but wherever you go in the world, everyone knows of Manchester United.

Manchester City on the other hand, have been the laughing stock of English football for 25 years, forever in the shadows of their more illustrious neighbours. When former Chairman, Francis Lee, one of the club's most outstanding players who later became a multi-millionaire businessman famously said a few years ago that, 'if there was a cup for cock-ups, we'd win it every time'. He wasn't joking.

In July 1995, Lee appointed Alan Ball – unquestionably the least gifted manager in English football history – to the Maine Road hot seat. As he followed that 18 months later by giving the job to the almost-as-inadequate Frank Clark, Lee can be said to be something of an expert in the art of the cock-up.

In a forthcoming book promised by Lee, he denies responsibility for City's relegation to the Second Division but even George Carmen QC, would have difficulty getting Lee off that rap. Lee did however appoint Royle as manager but in reality, he had little to do with the appointment. Lee resigned as Chairman within weeks of Royle arriving.

Joe Royle, 51, has never criticised Ball and Clark in public, managers' union and all that, but it is clear that almost his every action since taking over as City boss in February 1998 has been to repair the damage inflicted by Lee's appointees. That he's managed to rectify their errors at the same time as restoring the club to their place in the Premiership is unquestionably, whatever United fans may say, the managerial achievement of the last decade. No more are City a laughing stock".

Joe Royle's response is typically low key merely restating his long held belief, that arriving in the Premiership is not an achievement as such but merely the confirmation of City's 'pre-ordained status' as a Premier League club; that League being the appropriate base from which to actually achieve honours.

Barnett concludes his interview in the following fashion:

> **"Having guided the club back to the Premiership, Joe Royle obviously aims to keep them there. He recently signed a four-year contract giving him the sort of job security most Premiership managers can only dream about. Naturally he expects the club to prosper in the Premiership. He doesn't want the club to be a Leicester City, he wants them to be a Manchester United".**

This sentiment being expressed by the manager in the following terms:

> **"We ceased to be a problem to United four years ago but now we're back in the Premiership we want to be a problem to them. Whether we like it or not, they're where we want to be. They'd had the sort of success story that I want for Manchester City. When we're winning trophies the way that they have, then we'll know we're back".**

But, as Francis Lee remarked early in this chapter, football is a fickle taskmaster and we may ask rhetorically having experienced the triumphs and defeats of promotion and relegation over the last five years, in a sense mirroring the cycle of life for their fans, would the club now be sufficiently strong to maintain its position with the elite of the nation's corporate soccer enterprises? Would the relief and exhilaration of returning to the top flight burn steadily or flicker and fade like a candle flame in the strong slip stream of air left by superior players? Sadly, the latter imagery turned out to be the appropriate one with City finishing in the bottom three of the League. The Manchester Evening News, for Tuesday May 8th, 2001 headlining a special feature entitled **'Shame, How It All Went Wrong For City'**, giving a blow by blow account of results throughout the season. We may quote from interviews conducted with both Chairman David Bernstein and Manager, Joe Royle as reported in that special edition after City's defeat away to Ipswich (2-1) sealed their fate yet again; ironically by a club which had come up with them at the beginning of the season from the First Division. David Bernstein responds as follows:

"After two years of progress, we have taken a step back. To say I am disappointed would be a serious understatement. The defeat at Ipswich was symptomatic of the whole season. Once again we had a good lead and let it go but there was real spirit there. Sometimes you have to take a step back to take another two forward and this might be one of those occasions. We have done and achieved an enormous amount over the past three years. We need a few days to clear our heads and then we will continue the necessary hard work and planning to make sure we will get back to the top quickly. As a club, we are as solid as a rock, we are OK financially and we have some great people and everyone can rest assured that we will go flat out to come back up straightaway…..

Our back- to- back promotions created a great opportunity on which we have been unable to capitalise. Some said we reached the Premiership too quickly. I do not agree with this but with the benefit of hindsight, I admit we have fallen short in some areas. We have been carrying out a complete review of the season and our organisation; lessons have to be learned. Our club has come a long way and we are building an infrastructure to take it confidently and strongly forward. We will strive to make an early return to the Premiership and once we do, we must make sure it is a lengthy one…. I would just like to say again how wonderful the fans have been, not just last night but throughout the season. They are unbelievable and have never once wavered in their backing for the team. We are extremely proud of them."

The Manager, in sombre mood, opines:

"I never thought it would come to this (relegation) but it has and now we have to deal with it. We gave ourselves the chance last night (against Ipswich) with the goal and then switched off. We fell asleep twice and that has happened too

often for us this season. We have conceded more than 60 goals and there you have the main reason – along with our home form – why we have finished in the bottom three. It is no coincidence that the three teams which have been relegated conceded the most goals. Of course everyone is low, they are very low…. We didn't come up too quickly. I feel I have a stronger squad and better team than I had last year. It has been very hard for us at times. I still believe that, realistically, we could have been at the top of the bottom half of this Division…. Once again our fans have been unbelievable and I thank them for their backing, not just last night, but throughout the whole season…. Quite honestly, there really are no others quite like them anywhere. Even people on Merseyside come up to me and say how much they admire the City supporters. There is a genuine warmth to them."**

While the manager's sentiments are clear, how does it feel to be a player buffeted by the realities of relegation after a long season of spectator expectation and support? We need not quote in extended fashion to portray the emotional tone felt by the professional ranks but a few reported comments will provide a description of the essential feelings involved; **Steve Howey** who skipered the side to defeat at Ipswich:

"It is a humble feeling and we never want to endure it again. The hardest thing about it is the fact that we have absolutely magnificent supporters who deserve a lot, lot more than we have given them over the season!"

Shaun Goater, who scored the one City goal during the match:
"I am lost for words and that is not like me…. An awful lot of work has gone into the last couple of years getting to the Premiership and for it all to end so quickly is really upsetting and mind-numbing…. The fans did us proud and they have my condolences."

Carlo Nash, goalkeeper:
"We have fallen flat on our faces and now we must pick ourselves up quickly and get on with improving…. We honestly thought we could pull off the Houdini set but it

wasn't to be. The manager didn't say much after the game but he didn't have to. We are all completely down".

Richard Dunne, Republic of Ireland International defender: "It is not the fault of anyone but the players and there is a determination that we all stick together and put it right next season. Relegation is a new experience for me and it's not one I'd care to repeat ever again. Hopefully, I will see the other side of the coin next May".

Perhaps we should leave the final comment to Paul Hince of the Manchester Evening News who, in an admirable analysis, summary and with a hortative style reviews City's demise in the following terms:

"The last time Manchester City were relegated from the Premiership back in 1996, it wasn't the wind of change which blew through Maine Road – it was more of a tornado. Irrespective of their ability, players were swept through the exit door in a salvage and needless response to a great club's top-flight demise.

There will be no such knee-jerk reaction to this latest sorry chapter in City's chequered history, because the knee of Chairman David Bernstein never jerks. That's not his style. Chairman Bernstein is a calm man. He thinks before he acts. He brought stability to Manchester City when stability was required before any other single commodity.... the last thing on his mind right now will be to demand a cull of manager Joe Royle's senior squad as some sort of sacrificial offering to his club's army of heartbroken fans. But, there are times Mr Chairman, when a little knee-jerking doesn't go amiss. And this could be one of those times.

The question asked most frequently by the Blues supporters as they watched the Premiership life-blood draining out of their team in recent weeks is why Royle didn't invest in a top quality goal scorer and a player with the wit and imagination to pull the strings in midfield. The answer of course is that Royle DID try to bring precisely that type of player top Maine Road, but goal-scorers and midfield generals don't grow on trees. And if they do become available, the asking price is prohibitive. In the wider sense it doesn't matter how many mistakes have been made over the past ten months – or who made them. This isn't the time for blood-letting or for naming and shaming. What's done is done. Of far more importance is how Manchester City handle the latest dip on their graph. Lets hope they use their time under the Nationwide umbrella to regroup. Keep the good. Weed out the not-so-good. Give Joe Royle the time he needs to rebuild his team – providing he's still got the energy and the inclination to continue, that is.

Above all, ensure that the next time Manchester City are a Premiership club – and there will be a next time – they will be represented by a team capable of holding down a place in the top-flight."

This 'heartache', depression 'being down', disbelief and crushing disappointment characterised corporate City at all levels of the organisation. However as we have seen, such frustration can be manifest among certain sections of fans not in passive withdrawal and acceptance but by physical aggression and disorder when certain sets of circumstances prevail; the most salient of these being loss of status. These are 'the constants' of the human condition veneered over by success and organisational systems of control and pacification but ever present to erupt like a sleeping volcano during critical phases of stress and collective anxiety; issues we have already discussed in Chapter One and needn't be rehearsed here.

The summer of 2001 changed the managerial landscape completely at Maine Road – a situation that nobody would have predicted only a short year ago with 'The Royle Ascent' as described previously, being given general acclaim. Kevin Keegan became City's new manager with Joe Royle abruptly leaving the club with a considerable period of his contract still to run and in dispute with his employer. Keegan speaks about his plans for the forthcoming season to City Magazine in August 2001. Again, we will retain our observer/respondent format; the observer being in this case David Clayton and the respondent, Kevin Keegan:

Observer: "Having now met and trained with the squad, how do you feel about the task ahead?"

Respondent: "Well, we've had ten days now and the attitude's been terrific. I couldn't fault that at all. You'd be disappointed if it wasn't because when a new manager comes in, it's a clean piece of paper for everybody. The players who have played well need to continue to impress and the ones who feel they have been overlooked – maybe they didn't suit the system being played or a million other reasons – that's all gone, so everybody thinks they have a chance and they've all worked like they really want to be part of it and trained really well."

Observer: "What early influence can you see Stuart Pierce having on the players? (Stuart Pierce at 39 years of age played in the World Cup, captained his country and was recruited from West Ham by Keegan primarily as a player but also as a coach)."

Respondent: "He's having a tremendous influence... on the field he is a quality player and he brings with him, obviously, a vast experience and you can tell he has the respect of the players. I felt we just needed a leader and this is something I've done at all of my clubs. I've always tried to bring in someone who will help you manage the players, in other words, I can tell Stuart, 'this is what we're thinking, go and see what the lads think about it.' He's formed a committee with Shaun Goater and Steve Howey and they're the three that can represent the rest. If the training's too hard or too easy or the travelling could be better, they can give me feedback."

Observer: "So the communication is good and it doesn't become a case of 'them and us'?"

Respondent: "It isn't 'them and us'. It never can be in football. At the end of the day we will make the final decision, but if we just do what we think is right and don't ask them for feedback, then I think we'll make a lot of mistakes. Yes, Stuart's had a major influence already in that the standard of training's been good; he's a great example to the kids and he's still very fit…"

Observer: "Who do you see as your main rivals for promotion this year?"

Respondent: "I think you've got to put Wolverhampton Wanderers in there; they've got money to spend and a good manager in Dave Jones whom I respect and their stadium is ready for the Premiership. Birmingham City, under Trevor Francis have been knocking at the door for a while… Coventry, West Brom will be up there… there are probably about eight teams that can realistically get into the Premiership and have got a chance of staying there. Nobody is just going to walk out of this division this year.

Observer: "Many City supporters would like to see standing areas for the new stadium. Do you have any views on that?"

Respondent: "I understand why, after the Hillsborough Disaster, they made the grounds all-seater, but I do think a lot of fans prefer to stand. There are times during a match where everybody stands up anyway, so I guess the fans are sending their own message. I think it has to be looked at but I've always said that there should be room in every stadium for fans to stand up because they're telling you every week that's what they want to do. So can we solve that problem so Hillsborough never happens again and fans can stand up again? I think we can. As for the new stadium, I don't know. There is one end that could be a possibility so I don't see why not. I'd be for it personally."

Observer: "Lastly, how would you compare City fans to those of say, Newcastle?"

Respondent: "Manchester City fans are special and have always been very, very loyal... The best thing about coming into Manchester City for me is that we don't have to sign anybody to sell seats. We have to sign players that will do the business for Manchester City and make us a better side and get us back into, first of all the Premiership where we belong which is the top end, not fighting for relegation. It won't happen overnight, but with those fans behind us, the sky's the limit... We have to get players wanting to play football in front of their own fans and other teams fearing coming and if we can do that, then we're on the right track and that has to be our priority really."

By way of conclusion we may endorse the last comment with City, currently, playing attractive football and the new manager commenting after his team's 2-0 defeat of Millwall at Maine Road in late January 2002 with due caution that ...

> "You need 88 points for the title and we've got 61 at present with 16 games to go. But if you set targets, you limit yourself".

We might also add, you may also raise expectations which as we have seen in our account so far, City do not always fulfil for fans or shareholders! However, the omens are good at the time of writing, with the manager being reported in a doctrinal daily in mid-March 2001 as saying:

> "We'd have to do really something drastic, not to get there (Premiership) now. Once we get in the Premiership, we won't be thinking about coming back down again only how high we can get and how far we can go. Time will tell!"

Time will tell but with City beating the Championship contenders Wolverhampton Wanderers 2-0 on Easter Monday, 1st April 2002, their Premier League slot seems assured!

CR

DAVID BERNSTEIN (RIGHT) AND KEVIN KEEGAN: CURRENT CHAIRMAN AND MANAGER

BERNARD HALFORD, CLUB SECRETARY: THE HEART AND SOUL OF MANCHESTER CITY

JOE ROYLE (RIGHT): MANAGER: 1998-2001. ALSO SHOWN WILLIE DONACHIE TO HIS LEFT

FRANK CLARK: MANAGER: 1996-1998

STEVE COPPELL: MANAGER: 1996

ALAN BALL: MANAGER: 1995-1996

BRIAN HORTON (RIGHT): MANAGER: 1993-1995. ALSO SHOWN JOHN BOND TO HIS LEFT

PETER REID (LEFT) AND SAM ELLIS: PLAYER MANAGER AND MANAGER: 1990-1993

HOWARD KENDAL (CENTRE): MANAGER: 1989-1990. ALSO SHOWN TONY BOOK TO HIS LEFT

MEL MACHIN: MANAGER: 1987-1989 WITH SIR ALEX FERGUSON TO HIS RIGHT

JIMMY FRIZZELL: MANAGER: 1986-1987

BILLY McNEIL MBE: MANAGER: 1983-1986

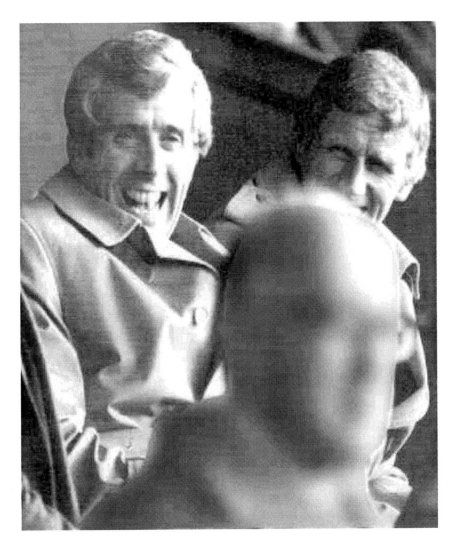

JOHN BENSON: MANAGER: 1983. TO HIS RIGHT TONY BOOK

JOHN BOND: MANAGER: 1980-1983

CHAPTER FOUR

FINANCE, FRANCHISE AND FEES

Manchester City, as a modern soccer PLC is far removed in terms of its financial arrangements from the original organisation that spawned it and which were described in Chapter 1. As we have seen in the previous chapter, 'Managerial Succession', player quality and performance and financial considerations go hand in hand. Likewise, Manchester City is part of a league structure which is continually undergoing change. Such change, as we have seen in previous chapters often carries financial implication but none more so, in fundamental and far reaching terms, than the advent of the Premier League in 1992. An understanding of the club's financial situation cannot be understood without first of all providing an account, albeit, somewhat abbreviated, of how the idea of a 'super league' became a reality rather than another transitory phenomena littering the soccer highway. In order to provide an authentic account of the formation of the league and its development, we may draw on interview material with its first Chief Executive and its Secretary. Both interviews were conducted, by the author, in 1993 shortly after the league's formation and are given in verbatim form as they may be of some interest to future soccer historians.

The Premier League

The transcriptions referred to above, provide an original account of the most fundamental change for over a hundred years in the way soccer is organised in this country: the Chief Executive remained with the organisation until the 1996/97 season and the Secretary still hold that position, at the time of writing, some ten years on. The then Chief Executive recalls:

> **"The idea for the start up of a 'super league' came, somewhat ironically as things turned out, from ITV. They had a very close relationship with the large clubs, the so-called big 5, which stemmed from the 1988 TV deal. In the knowledge that the TV deal was coming up for re-negotiation this year, Greg Dyke of ITV called a number of the bigger**

clubs together and asked them to discuss the formation of a 'super league'. Greg recognised that the best chance of ITV gaining the contract again was if the big clubs were properly in control. A number of clubs in December of 1990, approached the FA with a view to obtaining their perspective on the formation of a break-away league. The FA were in fact quite receptive, not least because they were being bombarded with power sharing proposals from the Football League who produced a document entitled 'One Game, One Team, One Voice', which somewhat naively suggested the Football Association and the Football League should merge. Whatever, at that stage, the FA and the Football League were not getting on together particularly well: this probably made them more receptive to the idea of change, than they would be normally. However, they were very, very wary of throwing their lot in with a number of major clubs because they had to act in an even-handed way and be seen to act in an even-handed way. Also, talks of 'Super Leagues' in years gone by, had foundered because the concept had not been properly developed and the implications not thought through – the practicalities were never considered.

In December 1990, I was working on Manchester's Olympic bid, as a consultant for Earnst & Young. I was approached by Graham Kelly and asked to act as a third party so that the FA could consult with me and obtain feedback from the clubs while remaining at some distance. Running the league isn't one of the most complicated things in the world to do, where it foundered in the past was in obtaining sufficient communality of purpose amongst a critical mass of clubs to make it happen. The problem was therefore, to persuade a sufficient number of clubs that it was in their best interests to form a league.

The FA put out some ideas in a discussion paper called 'The Future of Football' and called all the first division clubs together and informed them that they thought the time was right, to restructure the organisation of the game, with improved unity at the top and better dialogues. The intention was made clear that there would be an FA Premier League run as an integral part of the FA and the twenty two first division clubs at that time were simply asked for an expression of interest in joining it. There was sufficient interest to carry the idea forward and I was the nearest thing in the room at that particular meeting, to somebody who was independent. In this regard, the clubs said that every time we have a meeting, it is normally a complete shambles, because we never agree among ourselves and therefore would you act as an independent chairman, to act as facilitator, for the first meeting? I didn't duck quickly enough and duly took on that task. Knowing some of the characters involved, I decided that there was no way I would chair a meeting without doing a lot of homework, so I did insist on having the opportunity of spending half a day with each of the 22 clubs prior to the meeting, to find out what their concerns and aspirations were. The idea was that arising from this exercise, the first half of the meeting would be based on areas of agreement, rather than disagreement, and the hurling of insults. I spoke to about 16 club chairmen and Graham Kelly covered the remaining 8, focusing on the London clubs.

The main point to emerge was that there was a lot of dissatisfaction with the Football League, considerable anxiety about the financial aspects of implementing the Taylor Report and general dissatisfaction with the management and voting structure of the Football League. The way the management of the league was structured, you had representatives from the various divisions; four from the First Division and four from the rest, so you end up with a body of people who first and foremost, are representing their own clubs, secondly, their divisions – which always tended to lead to deadlock because it was First Division against the rest – and a fairly poor third looking at the best interests of the game as a whole. It was a very inward looking structure without any vision or wider perspective and completely unable to meet the challenges which were being thrown up and which needed to be tackled. This is interesting, because if you go way back and read the Chester Report of 1963 and I think 1972 was his update, then all of his warnings had come to pass. Basically, he said that if the League didn't restructure itself and face the problem of unrealistic income sharing, then there would be major difficulties. Well, now it was clear that among all the First Division clubs, there was a desire for change, stimulated by the Taylor Report and, though it was ambitious, we should really aim at the first meeting to get the basis of a constitution drawn up. Ironically, we have stuck to the constitutional principles of that first meeting. Underlying it all was the idea of a 'League of equal opportunity', not necessarily equal shares, but a league where financial rewards reflected playing success, not past reputation. This was a throwback to the ITV deal, where five clubs were guaranteed 80% of the televised matches regardless of their performance. To illustrate, one of the smaller clubs made the point that they didn't mind finishing the season £2M behind Arsenal if, for example, they came top of the League and they finished say 18th, but it was a real killer to go into a season knowing that whatever they did, they were going to finish up £2M worse off; they couldn't survive on that basis. It was also clear that if it was to be a true Premier League of the top clubs ranked, purely on achievement, then everyone in that league should have an equal voice. In the past, the Football League had often tinkered around with trying to weight voting structures; what we needed was one club, one vote. Also it was clear that the majority of clubs, not all for sure, didn't want the management committee. They were fed up with vested interests running the game and wanted a structure with one club, one vote, but a small executive committee to run things ridding the game, once and for all, of the vested interests. This provided for a non-executive chairman, myself as Chief Executive and two others, thus, providing a team of four though drawing on the services of the FA; we were physically located in FA headquarters at Lancaster Gate and thus, it made matters easy. This streamlined matters as we didn't double up on matters like players registration, referees and so on. The basic principles we drew up at that very first meeting were enshrined in what was called a 'Founder Members Agreement' and involved a two-thirds majority for matters put to a vote. This was to give a degree of stability, because the clubs were notorious for changing their minds every five minutes. This has given us problems in certain instances like the question of sponsorship but it does mean that it is very difficult for people to change their mind unless it is demonstrably right. At that very first meeting we did agree, somewhat remarkably, how we would share TV and sponsorship income.

At the moment, I am very pleased with how it is working because we have come an awful long way quite quickly. Given the timescale – a final ratification from the FA to establish the Premier League only came in February 1992, which gave us six months to get everything up and running – things have gone quite smoothly during our first season. We continually said, 'do not expect too much too soon, judge us in five years'. At our December meeting in 1992, we formed a working party to ensure that we do have quality criteria for improving grounds and started a consultation process with supporters' organisations to find out what they really want from our FA Premier League. Inevitably, that is a long term process but for the first time ever, in professional football, we and other interested bodies are actually sitting down and establishing our own standards. Another strand which is beginning to be woven onto our cloth of many colours and equally a long term development, is that of the whole issue of youth football and schoolboy development.

The thinking there is that if you want a better product on the pitch, you have to go back to basics and start looking at the recruitment system and how we teach our 7, 8 and 9 year olds. Thus, instead of bickering about commercial matters, we are now getting down to really the issues which are fundamental to our game. Thus, our constitution allows us to make changes. For example, I am not saying we will do this, if we wished for each club to invest a minimum of £250,000 in some aspect of Youth Development and soccer with our 22, it is possible; within the old structure of 92 clubs it was never possible because what might be good for Arsenal was not likely to be good for say, Hartlepool. Our new constitution should, in theory, make it possible to bring about positive changes. Remember also, we could not have formed the Premier League without the agreement of all the clubs, because there was the problem of the three-year regulation which required any club leaving the League to give three years notice. They voted this out by an overwhelming majority, I think it was 51½ votes to 9, thus, these and Fourth Division clubs were supportive of the Premier League. The dream factor was still there– a system of promotion and relegation gave every club a chance to become a member. We left enough money 'behind' to ensure that the league clubs outside the Premier League last season, had as much income as they had the previous year, also they were able to negotiate their own TV deal with ITV. Thus, without any doubt at all, in absolute terms, they were significantly better off than they were before!"

Let us continue with this Financial theme by recording the views of the Secretary initially appointed to the League and still in post at the time of writing. First of all he defines his role in late 1993:

"I am the Company Secretary of the Premier League, so have the customary statutory duties associated with any commercial organisation such as looking after the share register, making sure the annual returns to Companies House are made, and so on. You would expect this of any Company Secretary but from a football point of view, I am responsible for production of the fixture list, the registration and transfer of players, the disciplinary aspects, contractual disputes between players and clubs and the appointment of referees and linesmen. I am well used to this, for prior to taking up employment with the Premier League, I worked for the Football League for some 18 years, first joining them when I was in the middle of my 'A' levels and finishing up as Assistant Secretary.

In terms of your expressed interest in the financial aspects, one of the major attractions in breaking away and forming a separate league, was increased revenue. To put it simply, instead of 92 mouths to feed, as under the old system, there was now only 22 mouths to feed. Obviously, the main source of income is from TV and the agreement we have with BSkyB over domestic rights is a joint agreement, which also involved the BBC; that is a five-year arrangement worth £214M all together. The first year, 1992-93, it was worth £40M and this year the figure is £42M. If you cast your mind back to the ITV deal, worth in total £10M, live matches were shown between November and the end of the season and invariably, it would be the same teams featured each week. Consequently, all the money was going to these few clubs and the other clubs thought it unfair. In the new contract with BSkyB, they agree to cover all teams in the Premier League at least once in a season, on a live match transmission basis. In reality, what happened last season, was that every club was covered on at least three occasions. So the money is being much more evenly distributed and to give you a breakdown of its distribution, it is as follows. We take off the top an amount for the PFA, the players union, which this season amounted to £2.6M, a five fold increase on the previous season. The balance of the remainder of the money is put into three categories; 50% of the money – just short of £40M – is distributed between all Premier League clubs on an equal basis. So each club this season gets £743,500 as a right. The next tranche of 25% is paid in facility fees which reflects payment for each live match which is televised – just over £73,000 per club, per game. The final 25% is paid out at the end of the season on a merit basis; the higher the final finishing position of a club, the higher the payment. Thus, the bottom club will receive £39,000 while the champions will receive £856,000; thus, there is a reward for success."

We may build on this last point by tabulating the schedule of TV payments for the first season of the Premier League in the following table.

These payments are of course for domestic fixtures only and considerably enhanced revenue can be earned by individual clubs, if they are successful in entering European competitions. Hence, the 'ticket into Europe' is much sought after, not only because of the 'honours' it can bring and greater exposure for the brand image of the club, but also in terms of the hard currency generated by TV fee income and associated marketing opportunities. Television income from European Cup competitions is distributed by the Football Association and is usually classified in club accounts as being of United Kingdom origin and destination.

TABLE 4: FA PREMIER LEAGUE – DOMESTIC TELEVISION PAYMENTS (SEASON 1992/93)

CLUB	TV APPEARANCES		MERIT AWARD	FACILITY FEE	EQUAL SHARE	TOTAL
	BSkyB	BBC				
Arsenal	6	7	481,715	470,295	750,000	1,702,010
Aston Villa	9	15	778,155	740,340	750,000	2,268,495
Blackburn Rovers	7.5	8	704,045	582,053	750,000	2,036,098
Chelsea	6	5	444,660	454,785	750,000	1,649,445
Coventry City	4	4	296,440	308,360	750,000	1,354,800
Crystal Palace	4	4	111,165	308,260	750,000	1,169,525
Everton	4	5	370,550	316,115	750,000	1,436,665
Ipswich Town	4	3	259,385	300,605	750,000	1,309,990
Leeds United	6.5	6	222,330	497,207	750,000	1,469,537
Liverpool	8	8	629,935	616,720	750,000	1,996,655
Manchester City	6.5	4	518,770	481,698	750,000	1,750,468
Manchester United	10	20	815,210	848,450	750,000	2,413,660
Middlesbrough	3	5	74,110	239,025	750,000	1,063,135
Norwich City	7	5	741,100	524,120	750,000	2,015,220
Nottingham Forest	4	7	37,055	331,625	750,000	1,118,680
Oldham Athletic	6	2	148,220	431,520	750,000	1,329,740
Queens Park Rangers	5	3	666,990	369,940	750,000	1,786,930
Sheffield United	4.5	4	333,495	343,028	750,000	1,426,523
Sheffield Wednesday	3	6	592,880	254,535	750,000	1,597,415
Southampton	4	5	185,275	316,115	750,000	1,251,390
Tottenham Hotspur	6	7	555,825	400,960	750,000	1,706,785
Wimbledon	3	4	407,605	239,025	750,000	1,396,630
			9,374,915	9,374,881	16,500,000	35,249,796
Luton Town			0	0	750,000	750,000
Notts County			0	0	750,000	750,000
West Ham United			0	0	750,000	750,000
			9,374,915	9,374,881	18,750,000	37,499,796

It will be seen that during this first season, the most successful club, Manchester United, earned £2.4 million and that four clubs earned in excess of £2 million while the least successful earned £1.6 million: Manchester City earned £1.75 million. We may chart the revenue earned by both Manchester clubs from the Premier League TV payments since its inception to the millennium in the following table:

TABLE 5: FA PREMIER LEAGUE 1992/93 TO 1999/2000: SCHEDULE OF TV PAYMENTS TO UNITED AND CITY

| | MANCHESTER UNITED | | | |
	M	F	E	T
1992/93	815,210	848,450	750,000	2,413,660
1993/94	856,240	1,011,375	743,500	2,611,115
1994/95	856,800	1,221,160	860,500	2,938,460
1995/96	983,300	1,128,395	878,725	2,990,420
1996/97	2,114,300	2,246,295	1,930,450	6,291,045
1997/98	3,087,500	3,393,673	3,040,278	9,523,451
1998/99	3,707,820	3,630,064	3,544,349	10,882,233
1999/00	3,952,380	4,127,370	3,650,362	11,730,112

| | MANCHESTER CITY | | | |
	M	F	E	T
1992/93	518,770	481,698	750,000	1,750,468
1993/94	272,440	463,035	743,500	1,478,975
1994/95	244,800	432,805	860,500	1,538,105
1995/96	147,489	293,805	878,725	1,320,025
1996/97	·	·	965,225	965,225
1997/98	·	·	1,488,888	1,488,888
1998/99	·	·	·	·
1999/00	·	·	·	·

M=MERIT; F=FACILITY; E=EQUAL; T=TOTAL

It will be seen from this table, that playing in the Premier League and being successful, has a dramatic effect on income. Over the eight year period, Manchester United have received over £39.5M from domestic TV rights alone and that the corresponding figure for City, who were relegated after the 1995/96 season, is approximately £8.5M, just under a fifth of this sum. The overall increase in domestic TV payments has improved by a factor of 4.5 from the league's inception to the millennium – from £37.5 million to £167 million. This is shown in the following table and can be compared to Table 4. Currently, UK Premier League TV income is distributed to members and relegated clubs in accordance with League Rules C25-287, Finance. What happens is that the total of TV income for live and broadcasted highlight matches, is pooled and after deducting £17.5M for the PFA and for youth and stadia development, the balance is divided so that 50% constitutes the Basic Award Fund and 50% is split equally between the Facility Fees and the Merit Payment Funds. The Basic Award Fund is paid by way of fees to clubs representing the League's cost of sales, so that each club receives two shares and each relegated club receives one share. The facility fees are paid according to appearances on live and recorded highlights in television programmes. The Merit Payments are paid proportionally to clubs, dependent on their final position on the league ladder.

Such an increase reflects the success of the Premier League Brand both in terms of direct and vicarious 'attendance'. In terms of the attendances noted in the following table, it is of interest to note that the Premier League published its third and most comprehensive fan survey in November 1996, which highlighted the following:

- About one in eight fans are female;
- More than three quarters of fans with school aged children take them to football 'sometimes';
- Eight out of ten fans believe that football hooliganism has decreased over the last five years;
- Three quarters of fans believe that TV coverage of football has 'improved' since the introduction of Sky TV.

The Premier League concluded with some justification that they are getting a number of things right!

TABLE 6: PREMIER LEAGUE – DOMESTIC TELEVISION PAYMENTS (SEASON 1999/2000)

CLUB	TV APPEARANCES BSkyB	TV APPEARANCES BBC	MERIT AWARD	FACILITY FEE	EQUAL SHARE	TOTAL
Arsenal	7	9	3,754,761	2,431,190	3,650,362	9,836,313
Aston Villa	4	8	2,964,285	1,470,020	3,650,362	8,084,667
Bradford City	5	9	790,476	1,809,256	3,650,362	6,250,094
Chelsea	6	11	3,161,904	2,176,761	3,650,362	8,989,027
Coventry City	5	4	1,383,333	1,667,911	3,650,362	6,701,606
Derby County	4	7	988,095	1,441,751	3,650,362	6,080,208
Everton	7	5	1,580,952	2,318,114	3,650,362	7,549,428
Leeds United	10	10	3,557,142	3,392,360	3,650,362	10,599,864
Leicester City	5	6	2,569,047	1,724,449	3,650,362	7,943,858
Liverpool	10	11	3,359,523	3,420,629	3,650,362	10,430,514
Manchester United	12	14	3,952,380	4,127,370	3,650,362	11,730,112
Middlesbrough	6	3	1,778,571	1,950,609	3,650,362	7,379,542
Newcastle United	5	6	1,976,190	1,724,449	3,650,362	7,351,001
Sheffield Wednesday	4	4	395,238	1,356,944	3,650,362	5,402,544
Southampton	5	8	1,185,714	1,780,987	3,650,362	6,617,063
Sunderland	5	9	2,766,666	1,809,256	3,650,362	8,226,284
Tottenham Hotspur	6	7	2,173,809	2,063,685	3,650,362	7,887,856
Watford	4	4	197,619	1,356,944	3,650,362	5,204,925
West Ham United	5	6	2,371,428	1,724,449	3,650,362	7,746,239
Wimbledon	5	7	592,857	1,752,718	3,650,362	5,995,937
			41,499,990	41,499,852	73,007,246	156,007,088
Barnsley					1,665,459	1,665,459
Blackburn Rovers					1,665,459	1,665,459
Bolton Wanderers					1,665,459	1,665,459
Charlton Athletic					1,665,459	1,665,459
Crystal Palace					1,665,459	1,665,459
Nottingham Forest					1,665,459	1,665,459
			41,499,990	41,499,852	83,000,000	165,999,842

Increases in attendance since the league's start up in 1992 may be presented in table form as follows:

TABLE 7: FA PREMIER LEAGUE: AVERAGE ATTENDANCE FIGURES 1992-2000 (in thousands)

Season	Average Attendance
1992/93	21,125
1993/94	23,040
1994/95	24,271
1995/96	27,550
1996/97	28,434
1997/98	29,084
1998/99	30,631
1999/00	30,707

It is apparent that there has been an overall increase of some 40% since the League's inception, even though the initial 1992/93 figure was somewhat depressed by ground improvements restricting attendance. In it's inaugural season, total attendances were some 9.7 million in the aggregate, 2.3% below the level of the last First Division total aggregate. However, Arsenal and Manchester United both suffered from ground restructuring and in fact, eleven out of the twenty two clubs showed a rise in attendance with a steady increase being shown across the season. Total attendances during the second season topped 10.6 million, this being the first time in twelve years that attendances in the top division exceeded the 10 million benchmark. The following season, the total aggregate attendance of 11.2 million for the first time exceeded the total for all Football League matches and was only previously matched some twenty years previously, in 1981. Even with the reduction of the number of clubs to 20, attendances topped 11 million in the season 1997/98, representing 94% of total capacity across the premiership. The Annual Report of the Premier League for the 1998/99 season showed:

- **Total attendance for season 1998/99 at 11,620,766 a 4.8% increase on the previous season total.**

- **The average Premiership gate up 30,681 from 29,190 the previous season.**

- **Average attendance up 45% from 21,125 at the start of the Premiership in 1992/93.**

Commenting on the figures, the Secretary of the League said:

> **"It has been a fantastic season, full of quality football with an exciting Championship finale to match. A 45% increase in attendances over the last seven seasons bears testament to the unprecedented level of interest in football, which has been generated by the Premiership. Everyone involved in football, and most particularly the fans, should take pride in these attendance figures. Of course there is no room for complacency and we will continue working with our various partners throughout football, to maintain and enhance the quality and appeal of the Premier League to the people who matter most – the fans."**

Such buoyant gate receipts were matched by a massive increase in broadcasting revenue. A deal was successfully concluded amounting to £1.11 billion with BSkyB, for the right to broadcast 66 live games. In addition, a new deal with ITV was secured for £183 million for a highlights package. These agreements were to run for three years from 2001. In fact ITV Digital was made bankrupt in 2002 and reneged on its arrangement leaving clubs in difficulty.

To switch back in time and focus once again on Manchester City, the dilemma facing the club financially is well illustrated by a more or less verbatim transcript of a TV programme, shown the day after

City were defeated by Oxford United, 3-2 at Maine Road (13th Nov 1996), where there was a violent protest by the fans against the Chairman (Francis Lee) and the Board, who were perceived as bringing the club into 'dire financial straits'.

Manchester City: A continuing debate

The participants in the programme were well qualified to offer opinions about Finance, Fees and Management and may be listed as follows:

(PS)   **Peter Stevenson** ~ BBC Presenter

(JF)   **Jimmy Frizzell** ~
Chief scout and former City Manager

(SR)   **Sidney Rose** ~
President and former Director of City

(PP)   **Paul Power** ~ Ex-City Captain

(PH)   **Paul Hearst** ~ Sports journalist
covering Manchester City matches for
the Manchester Evening News

(DW)   **Debbie Walls** ~ Football Supporters
Association and lifelong City fan

The record of their discussion runs as follows:

PS: **"Angry scenes outside the ground last night. Same as those which ousted Peter Swales?"**

JF: **"Well, everyone expects results but unfortunately not everyone gets results."**

PS: **"What about the debt which has been incurred; figures of £14M and £26M have been mentioned."**

SR: "I think nearer £12.3M, which for a club in our position is not overmuch."

PH: "My concern is the way the club is going as a football club – the club has deteriorated drastically over the last 12 months. The team has been relegated, they have lost 9 of the 16 matches this season, we have had four managers this season which is a scandal in itself, it just seems to be going from bad to worse. The luck has got to stop at somebody's door – all of us wouldn't mind if 'Jack the Ripper' was the chairman so long as the club was successful. The buck has got to stop at Francis Lee's door."

DW: "I think the majority of the fans have been very patient and good humoured – the average fan is not interested in executive boxes or fantastic restaurants; we never go into those places. In the seven years I have had a season ticket, it has increased in price three times but my wages have not gone up that much. If the fans could see that finances were being used to bring in players to replace those which have been sold, then we might be happy. Last season, for example, we got rid of the backbone of the team – Quinn, Flitcroft, Kerr, Caton, and who did we replace then with? The fans don't see those players being replaced by better ones."

PH: "I do take objection to the fact that the Chairman of the club says that the quality of the squad has been improved over the last twelve months."

PP: "The two things go hand in hand, that is the poor financial situation of the club and the impoverished level of playing ability. It is a dilemma. Do we carry on and buy top quality players and make the financial situation much worse or do we try and rectify the financial problem and cut our coat according to our cloth? I am sure the thinking of everybody who is working hard to get the club on the correct footing is to sort out the finances first."

SR: "We keep reading in the press that approaches have been made from potential investors. Francis Lee has taken every serious approach into consideration; the problem so far is that the approaches have not come up to expectation, for example, they will not tell us who the consortium is or they want to know details of our finances before they put down any money. But we can't do that, it is out of the question."

JF: "I think the stresses of the managerial position have got worse – particularly the pressure from fans. This coupled with the fact that City have not won anything for a long time, makes it more difficult. I have worked under both Chairmen, Swales and Lee, now neither one of them ever denied me buying a player. It was down to my judgement as manager whether to buy. Now, contrary to the view expressed here by RH, Francis Lee never stuck his nose in (interfered). The Chairman didn't sign players. What happened was that he was told of a potential transfer, went to look at the player and then referred the matter to me and Colin Bell for action. We thought the player in question should be signed and he was signed: the player in question was Gio Kinkladze. Now with respect to Perola, we brought him to Maine Road, he had a game, didn't play very well, so we got him on loan. Then he proved his worth and was signed. It was down to the manager, who was Brian Horton at that time, to sign him which he did. Both players were successful so Francis Lee cannot be blamed for interfering or making poor administrative decisions."

PS: "Was Coppell a victim of stress or finances?"

PH: "I cannot believe that managing Manchester City could destroy the health of a person, which was claimed for Steve Coppell, after 33 days in the job."

PP: "Stress is brought on by situations that are out of your control. I cannot imagine that anything Steve Coppell has encountered at Manchester City, would be anything different from what he encountered in eight years at

Crystal Palace. He worked under Ron Nodes who is a difficult chairman to say the least – any problems thrown up at City would have been seen before. I think in this case, he didn't have control of the situation at City, for one reason or another. He may have felt that he couldn't improve the performance of the team and this goes back again to the unfortunate financial situation we are in at the moment. Both are related."

SR: "It is not stress that does the damage, it is people's reactions to the stress and in Steve Coppell, there was probably this seed of being depressed easily. Now we examine players when they come to the club, everybody is examined rigorously before they are signed. We never examine managers – maybe we should! However, I don't know of any other club who examine the manager before he is appointed."

DW: "I think most City fans felt that Steve Coppell had problems outside of Manchester City, which caused him extra stress. Everybody was totally amazed and distressed when he handed in his resignation, after so short a time. But I am concerned about the long term situation, for example, at one time City's interest in a top player would be considered legitimate and publishable now to express an interest, in say someone like Alan Shearer, would lead to derision and accusations of fantasy. The loss of financial status of corporate Manchester City is unbelievable."

PS: "Alright, given fantasy type money – no limits – which manager would each of you pick and which four players, assuming unlimited availability, would you sign? In short a 'Dream Team'. We leave out SR as he is directly associated with the club."

DW: "Manager - Alex Ferguson, Robbie Fowler, Teddy Sheringham in the forwards; midfield - Paul Gascoigne and defender - Tony Adams."

PH: "Manager - Joe Royle, Stuart Pierce as defender, Les

Ferdinand as forward, David Ginola and mid-field, Vinnie Jones."

PP: "Manager - Terry Venables, players - Gary Pallister in defence and Gary McAllister, forwards Alan Shearer and Palo Maldini."

PS: (Rhetorically) "There is a shopping list. SR, are you going to go back to the boardroom and tell the chairman, 'get after these guys'?"

PS: "Round the panel, what is the top priority now?"

DW: "To get money into the club, to get serious investors in there, otherwise they are not going to be playing even in the First Division next season."

PH: "I agree with that – very much so. Stop shopping at the Army & Navy Stores, start shopping at Harrod's once more. Let's get some quality players into the club."

PP: "The priority is continuity whichever way we get it. We have talked about the number of managers we have had and the financial mess when you have a new manager, they get rid of players or bring in new players which expands the squad. Then you have financial problems and the situation becomes continually problematic."

SR: "We have been to the financial abyss before and we have come back many times since then. I think the priority is to be patient."

JF: "To get results. This would solve the problems. Good press and media coverage would give us a break – the coverage we have been getting has been diabolical."

Unlike other service organisations, in soccer, the natural termination of an employees contract, can cost a club literally millions of pounds and lead to widespread publicity. In addition, the pending completion of a players' services can be a powerful financial lever in re-negotiating levels of remuneration, for any reengagement. If new contract demands are not met, then the player can assume the role of a free agent on termination of his period of employment, at a cost of millions of pounds of lost revenue to the club in terms of transfer fees. To illustrate, Roy Keane of City's neighbours Manchester United became the clubs first £1M waged player and during the summer of 1999, negotiated a further increase on the back of the organisation's realisation that if a deal was not agreed by January 1st 2000, he would be free to sign a FIFA pre-contract with any interested European club. If this scenario were to materialise, then United would lose at least £15M in transfer fees. On the other hand, to continually accede to increased wage demands for one player leads to a 'knock on' effect, with other players using the agreement as a benchmark for their own demands; this process racks up the overall wage bill for the club. A continuing dilemma for management is thus, to ensure that wage increases are funded through revenue growth across all business activities. Smaller top flight clubs such as Manchester City are faced with similar problems of wage cost inflation and, from the reverse point of view to that described above, super heated transfer fee costs for players who might make an immediate difference to team performance. The strands of a financial dilemma facing a manager such as Joe Royle are placed into stark relief by an interview conducted with him in the national press shortly after City's relegation from the Premier Division in May 2001. Signings which can influence the configuration of the team, are important but also financial considerations weigh heavy in developing a strategy to ensure promotion to the elite League. In the former manager's words at that time:

"There are financial implications to be taken into consideration but we haven't bust ourselves this season. I could not have asked for more support than I received from the board during the season. Never at any stage was there a time when we couldn't spend or bring in extra players. It was not a matter of cash but that the players we wanted were not available.

With the possibility of relegation, I didn't want to bring in new players who could have proved a burden to us unless they were going to dramatically improve us. I know what fans are saying, 'why didn't we buy so and so and why didn't we

buy so and so?' – and we would have if they had been available but like I have said many, many times, this is not fantasy football. You cannot just pick up a paper and say we will take Vieira and Bergkamp and while we are at it we will have Zola. It is not that simple. You have to realise that the years out of the Premiership have probably cost the club a little bit in prestige. When getting that kind of player it is not just the financial burden to consider. There is also the London factor; foreign players are invariably keen to play in the capital. At the moment we are nowhere near to anyone coming in or going out. We are monitoring people as we always do, but it is not that easy to get players in.

We are obviously aware of the best talent that exists both inside and outside the Premiership but so are lots of other teams and selling clubs know that. That is why prices these days tend to start at around £3M for unproven players who are just prospects. We cannot pay ridiculously high money for someone who is not going to go straight into the first team."

On the other hand, as we have seen in the previous chapter, a 'youth policy' while saving millions in the transfer market takes time to mature, in short, it is laying the foundation for future growth and development not immediate 'fire fighting'. However, because of City's erratic league form over the last five years, there has not even been time to actually build for the future. This situation is exacerbated by the high rate of managerial succession noted in Chapter Three; for City the present has always been the priority! There has been no opportunity to age the new wine in the reserve casks, to forcibly extend the metaphor somewhat, before reaping the harvest. In brief, City have been short of a period when young players could be brought on and placed in the reserve team to mature, or as the coaches say 'brought along'. The immediate has to be catered for with the present need being one for players who can make an instant impact and result in promotion to the Premiership. Establishment in the Premiership allows the luxury of building a youth policy to ensure the future, as the former manager pointed out in a national newspaper interview:

"The first question I have to ask when looking at who I am going to buy is whether they will improve us now. Once you have got 'now' sorted out you can look at grooming a team for the future. The other way and in many aspects, the better way is of course to produce your own talent. I would say the Academy (grooming junior players) does very, very well. Ian Cassell and his staff do a fantastic job and we compete very well with all the top clubs in the country at all levels. Hopefully that will show in the first team sooner rather than later."

It is increasingly apparent that the marketplace for players is no longer the neighbourhood, the City, the region nor even the country; contracts have to be attractive globally to retain and draw the top players from their country of origin. Wage and transfer inflation are endemic with the latter being seen in part as spectator driven. A City Club official comments with some passion during his interview:

"If every supporter decided to watch the team regardless of its success, that club would never need to buy a player. They would turn them out from their own locality and if they got beat, they got beat and the people would come and watch them the following week... they are the ones that come on at you; they are on local radio, they are writing letters to the papers, 'Why didn't Manchester City go and buy ....…?' They think £2.5M is nothing – and that is only for one player; bear in mind season ticket income for the year may be £2M. That is 14,000 people for one season, their money would not buy one player. We have to pay the wages of a full squad, pay all our running costs for the stadium and so on. That shows you the financial difficulty we are in. If you show prudence and don't pay the inflated transfer costs and wages, people somehow think this is poor management. They say, 'why aren't you paying? You should be paying. We should have it'. Thus it is so easy to become forced and pressured into spending money you don't have as a corporation to try and win trophies for the supporters. It is that striving for success which can cause severe financial problems. So in a way the public have a lot to do with the level of transfer fees. The directors are only human beings; they are there to do their

best and in addition, spending money does not of course guarantee 'success'."

As well as the revenue generated from the sale of television rights, a major source of income without substantial capital outlay, is that generated by media innovations such as Pay-per-View introduced in the season 2001 for the first time and web site installations building commercial opportunities between club and supporters around the world. It is becoming increasingly apparent that the ability to communicate across geographical and social boundaries is a key to the financial success of a club such as Manchester City. The club also, however, attracts a consistently high level of support at Maine Road. Such support is also reflected in increased revenue from using the stadium and adjacent training ground as a multipurpose commercial leisure facility. How is this interpreted in the daily life of the club and its employees? Such commercial considerations and their development are revealed in a series of interviews with members of the merchandising and marketing team conducted in the early nineties and updated to the present day.

Marketing Manchester City

Initially, the then Marketing Manager was interviewed in 1992 and this was followed up in 1996 to look at how this aspect of management had diminished, remained the same or expanded. We will present both interviews in chronological sequence to provide insights into the developmental commercial aspects of running a professional soccer club. The 1992 interview with the Marketing Manager ran as follows:

Observer: **"What is your role in running the marketing side of a football club?"**

Respondent: **"Initially, when people look at the commercial role perhaps they see the obvious things, that is, more on the public relations side, but we are also charged with the responsibility of increasing turnover and profitability from commercial activities. The range of activities have expanded since the last decade, broadly into two areas. On** the one hand the lottery side, including the support from the fans in terms of them going to their workplace or to home, family, friends, selling lottery tickets for twenty five pence. On the other end of the scale, there are the hundreds of thousands, even millions of pounds worth of business in deals with official shirt sponsors and other areas which are sponsored."

Observer: "What is a sponsor?"

Respondent: "The word 'sponsor' does not do justice to the sort of packages that we are putting together and basically, what we are here to do is provide facilities for companies to entertain their key clients or perhaps put a staff incentive together for the sales-force, whatever it may be. In the commercial side of football, companies such as Brother, ICL, Umbro, Mars etc, do not spend money on corporate hospitality markets unless they feel they got a very, very valuable return from it. So we are really in the business of selling corporate hospitality even if we still call it 'the match day sponsor'. Basically, what that comprises is a package for entertaining up to forty five people in an exclusive suite. They come here at twelve noon for a reception, then a tour of the ground behind the scenes, champagne reception in the sponsors' suite and then a meal. There is also half-time entertainment and then, after the game, 'Man of the Match' award where they usually get the chance to rub shoulders with some of the players and get home by six thirty very happy indeed. That is the flagship package but there are lots of subsidiary areas of sponsorship as well."

Observer: "How much would the sponsor pay for that kind of support?"

Respondent: "It would vary depending on the game and on how many people they will bring because sometimes the sponsors may be split into two or into four. But for a full match sponsorship package you will be looking at an average figure of between six and seven thousand pounds.''

Observer: "How do you get in touch with the sponsor?''

Respondent: "I actively go out into the business community and talk to companies which are probably not aware of the facilities here. You have got different grades of potential customers. The ones that have never done work in football before and have no idea of what facilities we have and therefore have not considered it. That is probably the hardest nut to crack because you are trying not just to get them to come to Manchester City but you are actually trying to sell them the concept of corporate hospitality at football in general. So that is the hardest, but they do come in. Secondly, there are companies that are already engaged, but maybe they are interested in other sports like cricket and rugby and have not considered coming into football. Then, we convince them that really it is the customer that matters and if you ask what the customer wants to do, the majority, even now will still say that it is football we believe in, in the North West particularly and Manchester City being one of the top teams in that area. Then, there are the ones that are already in football but in other clubs and never come into Manchester City and in that case we pose the question why didn't you come to Maine Road? Once we have got the company here, they will come back because we do a good job.''

Observer: "What do they expect to gain from this?''

Respondent: Again that will vary depending on how a company will use it. On our behalf, we will sit down with a company, discuss what their marketing objectives are and then try to sell a package to them. It may be they are asking for a match sponsorship and end up by doing something totally different because there are so many commercial opportunities within the club. What normally happens is that companies like to take their biggest or their key customers to the match as a gesture of thanks for their business; also as a way of getting to know them better and basically do what they cannot do in the buying and selling relationship; ask about how many kids you have, what team you support etc. It is a way of fostering closer and better relations with companies and with individuals."

This interview was played back to a relatively new entrant to the commercial management team, in 1996, to elicit a reaction to provide an indication of change and stability in this aspect of organisational activity. His response is as follows:

Observer: "What is your assessment of what was said in 1992?"

Respondent: "The department has expanded a lot since then and corporate hospitality is now a major source of investment for a club and I would imagine, after season tickets, is the biggest financial input. Obviously it is important to have a range of facilities; not only the very expensive ones, say the match sponsorship of six to seven thousand pounds but it needs to be something for every pocket that not only the super rich but the normal fan can come along and can enjoy the facilities. That is what we are trying to do; we are trying not to create an elite but have as many people as possible enjoying watching the football. It seems that the ideal thing to do is to increase corporate hospitality. A sales executive will be employed in the near future whose job will be to go out and physically sell the facilities. At the moment, we bring people in through contacts but a lot of the time the people who come in have come in previously, so it is important that when you get a new customer you look after him so that there is a bigger chance that they will come back again which is basically what we want ... at the moment, the department is a bit stretched and the new Kippax stand now opening, more people come in ... we are now looking at new markets. Only recently we have taken back the club shops. Previously it was all franchised out. There is another store which opened up in town and there is one in the Kippax stand. We have done also individual designs like T-shirts for people to wear. I would imagine merchandising is the new area to look at for this club."

Indeed the statement at the end of the above quotation was prophetic with the appointment of merchandising staff in late 1996. The following is a largely unedited version of an interview with the new merchandising manager, which we may present as follows. It is rather a full account but represents the psychological processes in conveying 'a brand' and hence makes a distinctive contribution to our understanding of 'Attitude Blue':

Observer: "First of all, lets look at the problems and prospects of merchandising Manchester City."

Respondent: "Well obviously, working with a football club is not like working within any of the other sports or leisure industry organisations, whereby your success is truly based on how well you can organise your business and arrange your job, your time, your buying and your selling; you have total control over that. When you work within the sports industry, certainly when you work within football, your success is also wholly tied in with the success on the park; if you've got a team that's successful and winning then obviously you've got more chance of increasing your turnover in all areas, both on the merchandising side and in your sales as well."

Observer: "So really, in a way your job hinges on the success of the team – or does it?"

Respondent: "It does, but not totally. I mean obviously it's also to do with <u>levels</u> of success; you could say that a team in the Second or Third Division could have pushed for promotion, attained success, won most of their games and got promotion and that could be a successful team but they wouldn't be turning over the same amount of merchandise that Manchester City can, even in a relegation season. So it's not wholly based on that, it's also based on the fan and supporter base; some clubs, certainly clubs in large cities, have got a stronger alliance, a stronger fan base that they can call on but then your actual success can fluctuate according to the success on the park."

Observer: "Right, so the problem in merchandising this club is the success of the team?"

Respondent: "Yes."

Observer: "What about the prospects?"

Respondent: "Well, what you've got within football, certainly football but then obviously in other areas of sport where people are closely linked to one specific team, you've got a brand loyalty which is unique in any industry; McDonald's have not got the same brand loyalty that Manchester City or Manchester United have got because at the end of the day, if you want a hamburger and there isn't a McDonald's on that corner, you will go into BurgerKing or to Wimpey, whereas if you were a supporter of Manchester City, irrespective of the success of the team, if you don't like their new shirt or you don't like any of the new products, you're not going to say, 'Well great, I'll go to Old Trafford and buy theirs because theirs are more attractive'. So that brand loyalty is unique and certainly most industries, for example, Nike and Adidas would kill for that kind of brand loyalty if they could get it. I mean some people will tend to stick to certain brands or someone might like Fords or you might tend to stick with things you know but it's very rare that people would never change to a different brand given the right economic reasons for doing so or just logistic reasons because it's available when something else isn't. Within football you've got a brand loyalty that is unique."

Observer: "So do you think there is a brand loyalty for Manchester City?"

Respondent: "Oh definitely. I mean it's been proved by the fact that despite relegation and despite the recent problems, when we went for five weeks without a manager we were still pulling in 27,000 people who weren't guaranteed entertainment and as much as you might hate to admit to being a fan of the club, you know, you turn up week in, week out irrespective. Now over an extended period of time that could go wrong but I think City are very lucky because some teams, for example Newcastle, when they were in our position were looking at gates of eight to nine thousand. Blackburn, before Jack Walker's money, were struggling on gates of that amount."

Observer: "So how do you see the prospects for the club then? I mean, presumably you see this is a basic core group who could be with you through bad times and good times?"

Respondent: "Well we like to think so but obviously you've also got to remember that it's an ongoing process. With most people, their loyalty to a football club is tied in for two reasons, either for the family or because of their location. Now some people will grow up in Manchester and support either Manchester City or

Manchester United for that reason or because their parents have. Some people might move to the city, as I did and follow the fortunes of one of the teams but you have to look to the future because as people grow older and can't attend, you've got a new generation of supporters coming though so you have to look to the future and you have to keep that fan base; if you can't rely on success as Manchester United have been fortunate enough to have, you've got to look to make sure that what you're supplying – whether it's through the Junior Supporters' Club like with the Junior Blues, or through any other areas, you can market the club to make it attractive to younger supporters so you can perpetuate that because if you let them slip away at a young age, it doesn't matter whether the parents have supported the team or you live in that town, you could lose them forever."

Observer: "Just looking at the second question now, if we look at the psychology of selling, what motivates people to buy a product? You're selling Manchester City as a product – what's your view on that?"

Respondent: "Well obviously, again this relates quite strongly to the success on the park because if the team is winning, people are more motivated to come to the matches, to buy products; businesses are more likely to want to take boxes and at the same time, if the team are under-achieving – if they're not winning – it's to do with what we call the 'feel good factor'. If people feel good, they're going to want to keep buying into the dream. But it's not as cut and dried as that as we've proved by saying that despite relegation we are still pulling in big crowds. I don't know whether it's that Manchester City are unique – I don't think we're totally unique but I do think there's a certain aspect of the nature of the City supporter whereby you're prepared to take the bad with the bad! It's like they keep going in the hope that one day things will come better and you can say you were there, you were there when we were at Lincoln and got beat 4-1 and at the lowest point with no money and then now here we are. But also as well for Manchester City, it is a team that has got a history; who have won League titles, who have won FA Cups and so there is a history there that has led to this support and although, as our friends across town like to point out, we've not won anything for twenty years, there are a lot of teams surviving that have never won anything. So you know, you can't just look to the past but it's there in the back of peoples' minds that one day it will turn around. There were times when Manchester United were relegated and their fans had to live through that and now they're on top and you look and you say, 'well, in ten years' time – fifteen years' time, let's hope we're there'. We will be there. It's almost like a kind of blind loyalty but that is, to a certain extent, the motivating factor for the supporters because it's what could happen and to be there when it does happen. It's like anything you know – in the last two weeks when Manchester United have had two heavy losses in a row, it's almost like their fans can't believe it. They're so used to seeing the team win and it's almost like complacency has developed. It's like when you've been away on a wet, windy night and you've seen the team defeated – if you've seen the lows, the highs are so much more positive and so much stronger and that's what I think keeps the fans going."

Observer: "Is there anything else you want to add abut the psychology of selling? We've talked about the fans' motivation, what is your philosophy of selling?"

Respondent: "Well, I came in to work for Manchester City from the situation of actually being a season ticket holder – a regular season ticket holder. I'd stood on the Kippax and then with the all-seater stadium, I took up my seat there. So I've actually come in from that background; you know I've kept my same seat, I still travel to the away matches with my friends and because of that I like to feel that perhaps I've got an insight into what the fans would want – what I would want, I mean, that's how I ended up being offered the job. Because from my previous job with a graphic design company, I'd supplied the club with some merchandise graphics that proved to be very, very successful and the people at the club who were involved in setting up the merchandising department at the time, thought that I'd had the background in the industry but also from being a fan I could appreciate what people really liked. So in developing the merchandise, it's been done from the point of view of truly understanding the product; I'm not some whiz-kid who's been brought in from another club who says, 'I've done this for Tottenham and I've made it a success therefore I can do it for Manchester City'. I sit down with manufacturers and they show me their products, I like to think that I would immediately know what would turn a City fan onto a product, which products they would like and which ones they wouldn't touch with a bargepole."

Observer: "The marketing 'mix' now – product, price, place and promotion; is there anything we need to say about that?"

Respondent: "Well, Manchester United, because of the way that they've marketed their club and marketed their merchandise, a lot of people seem to think that every club can do the same; a lot of people seem to think that, you know we have suppliers coming in saying, 'we've supplied Manchester United with 10,000 of these bubble bath kits or something' and we say, 'yeah, so what?' – it doesn't mean that we could sell them to our supporters. They've got a larger fan base than most people; they've got people who will be sat at home in Bristol or Basingstoke you know and watch their matches on the television and go to the local Tesco store and buy these products. So their brand has been built up from a different perspective to that of most football clubs. There are some clubs, maybe like Glasgow Rangers or if you go abroad to Barcelona and visit Barcelona's museum and club shop, they are very similar to Manchester United's. In these cases, you're talking about armchair fans; you're talking about fans who don't go to the matches. The amount of times that you meet people and they say, 'yeah, I support Manchester United' and they don't even know where Old Trafford is and you say to them, 'well, I've got a season ticket in the Kippax and they don't even know what the Kippax is! Whereas if you meet a City fan, they'll know Maine Road because they've been there when they can get a ticket; they'll know other grounds and that is the difference. So therefore, when you're choosing the products that will be of interest, it requires a knowledge of your fan base and their orientation.

It's also to do with the fact that I couldn't open a club shop and not stock scarves; you couldn't open a club shop and not stock caps because these are products that people expect to see and the club shirts and various things, so it's only when we get away from what we term the 'core items' that you can judge – it's sometimes like taking a gamble. But at Manchester City, we've moved our products more away from perhaps what we would term the technical sportswear which is like the team shirts, the tracksuits and the things that the players actually wear to the non-technical which is fashion; sweatshirts and T-shirts and we've gone quite heavily into pushing what we'd term the trendy side of Manchester City and this is being reflected both in sales and in some of the press we've received.

The Face magazine recently did a feature on our merchandise and said that we were leaders amongst football in trendy merchandise which is partly due to myself coming in from my background in graphic design; working with the sports industry. I also worked in Manchester on Take That's fan-club product so I had an understanding of pop and sports and was able therefore, to pick up on the back of the Oasis collection and push that which the fans have appreciated and also because at Manchester City you didn't have the success on the park to sell on, we had to sell onto something else which is what we call our 'Blue Attitude' – the attitude of being a City fan and being proud to be a Blue irrespective of the performances on the pitch and that's what we have pushed."

Observer: "I think that phrase, 'Blue Attitude' summarises everything that we've talked about. Do you want to add a word about planning?"

Respondent: "Obviously the merchandise side of the club is definitely a potentially very large area of growth for the club – an income stream. I know that from board level, they're looking for this area to grow quite considerably over the next few years and there's no reason why it shouldn't if we can attain a certain level of success on the park. On the back of the promotion season our turnover will obviously be far greater than if we don't get promotion this season but at the same time by targeting or identifying our market and targeting our product to that market, it's a case of maximising our sales so it's about supplying customers with what they want, giving the City fans the products that they want and not, as in the case at Old Trafford, filling up a big warehouse full of products and saying, 'there, go on, just buy it!' It's actually a case of giving people products that they think are worth the money, irrespective of whether it's a City product or not; 'I like that clock ... I like that T-shirt ... it's an attractive T-shirt. It's nice to be associated with Manchester City as well. Given this approach, I think everyone's a winner."

It can be deduced from these three interviews covering the early nineties, that expansion of commercial aspects are perennials in the running of a professional soccer club but that different philosophies may be involved, depending on the nature of perceived 'fan need', which in turn represents a particular psychological and historical context and the experience and attributes of the person occupying a commercial role. To bring matters up to date, a new Marketing Manager, appointed in the middle of 2000, was recruited from Orient Express and his terms of reference are to oversee print production and design work, merchandising, sales, football in the community and the various membership schemes which are in operation. He also develops relationships with outside agencies whether it be through direct mail, web sites, newsletters or other forms of communication; in fact all avenues of communication deployed by the club to market their brand. His perception of the marketing role is revealed in an interview conducted in early 2002 at Maine Road:

Observer: "How is your role at City similar to, or different from marketing in non-soccer commercial situations?"

Respondent: "The principles are still the same. You have a message you wish to communicate to a target audience but in the soccer industry, there is a much higher profile and the impact is immediate. To illustrate this last point, you may have an insertion in a match day programme with a potential audience of 30,000 plus people and if the message is unclear, then the feedback is instantaneous. Come into the club Monday morning and you soon know about it. By comparison, in a different commercial environment, messages do not end up in the public domain so readily or quickly. The travel industry, which was my previous experience, turns things around pretty quickly anyway, but in football, things tend to be wanted to be done today or even 'yesterday'; there is a lot of pressure to turn things round very quickly."

Observer: "Why do you think this is peculiar to the soccer industry?"

Respondent: "It's just the immediacy. You are dealing with a very high profile activity, there are fixtures around every corner. In many respects, for certain personnel, it can be a twenty four hour a day job; not for me but for the directors and executive officers. I do not think that my previous Chief Executive in the travel industry would work to such a demanding and tight specification."

Observer: "How do you see your role at Manchester City?"

Respondent: "My first job is to produce a clear and persuasive message in line with corporate guidelines. I liaise with the retail sales manager, the ticket store and so on to find out what they have to say and then we can discuss the best way of saying it. Thus, my day-to-day activities might well bring me into contact with the Director of Sales, including corporate hospitality, retail management and business development; the latter relating to the acquisition and negotiation with affinity partners and sponsors. All of these co-join to promote Manchester City as an ideal vehicle for communicating a message."

Observer: "It sounds far more differentiated than it was at the time of my earlier interviews in the mid-90s."

Respondent: "Yes. My job is liaison with the various commercial parts of the organisation so as to avoid duplication and confusion. Each component has it's own needs and the various components feed off each other, for example, if merchandise is

mailing out a catalogue to their database and I
know that there are a couple of fixtures coming up
with spare corporate hospitality, I can advise
them to put a flyer in the mail indicating this. My
job is to see that these departments fully realise
the opportunities that are open to them. In
general, soccer clubs are becoming increasingly
commercialised and adopting business models.
Manchester City has grown and diversified like my
last company, Orient Express, which has several
departments to cover its commercial operations.
Thus, instead of having one 'commercial
manager', you have a range of properly structured
departments coming into place – Sales, Retailing,
Business Development, Accounts, Football in the
community, Supporters' Clubs. With the new
stadium due to come on stream in 2003, all our
activities are geared to making it a commercially
smooth transaction and marketing plays an
increasingly important part in that because
people have to be made aware what is on offer.
They need to be reassured that they can gain
access to the stadium quickly and easily, can
make purchases for refreshments and souvenirs
when convenient and have an uninterrupted view
of the game in a convivial atmosphere. The new
stadium provides me and colleagues, with a
unique opportunity to deploy our skills to the
advantage of the club. It is obviously easier if you
have a successful product, that is, a winning side
playing attractive football. Always remember, you
cannot persuade people on a continual basis, to
buy something they don't want."

As the new stadium looms large in the club's marketing ideology,
perhaps we should devote some space here to its description while
realising that it is currently being fitted out as an athletics stadium!
Again, we may resort to interview and observation conducted both
at Maine Road and on site at Eastlands, the site of City's new
home.

The New Stadium

In a sense, City's move to the East of Manchester, more specifically to the Bradford and Beswick areas of the City is a return to its roots. The site is only some one mile from the original ground in Bennett St, Ardwick, which we described in Chapter One. At this new site, somewhat uniquely, the club can enjoy facilities which have been built to a far higher specification than that normally associated with the construction of soccer stadia. This arises because of the location of the 17th Commonwealth Games there, from 25th July to 4th August 2002, with seventy two nations scheduled to take part, competing in seventeen sports. We may draw on interview material with the Facilities Controller for the club to provide the reader with an understanding of how the Commonwealth 'once in a lifetime experience', will be translated into the sustained week in, week out involvement we have called 'Attitude Blue'. Interestingly, City's Facilities Manager had been responsible for opening up a similar stadium to that situated in Manchester's Eastlands in South Africa while international projects manager with Wembley International. Rather than present a verbatim account of the interview, the material will be presented in narrative form, thus, maintaining some variety in the text: it was obtained in January 2002, at Maine Road.

In terms of infrastructure, the new stadium occupies a 'brownfield' site, that is, an industrial wasteland which lies in the heart of the whole East Manchester regeneration scheme. It will be the central part of a Sports City and adjacent to the English Institute of Sport. The latter comprises two buildings; one containing a 200 metre track and performance/training areas for elite athletes, the other, a National Sports Centre joined to it and geared up to stage major championship events. There is also an outdoor 400 metre track and nearby a tennis and squash centre; the whole venture being supported by a leisure based retail complex and a hotel. Just across the main feed road, Alan Touring Way, lies the Velodrome, that houses the National Cycling Centre. This whole development constitutes a truly magnificent hinterland for Manchester City's match days and is further enhanced by the proposed development of the canal and waterway system, which runs through it, and the extension of the tram system eastwards; shades of 1923 with respect to the tram system and Maine Road! Unlike 1923, however, a traffic impact survey, carried out by the architects, shows that 22,000 off-road car parking spaces will be provided within one mile of the stadium with City having on-site parking for some 3,000 pre-sold spaces.

Perhaps it is stating the obvious to make the point, that an athletics stadium does not generate revenue and consequently, its owner, Manchester City Council, had to find a tenant once the Commonwealth Games had finished: Manchester City was that tenant. Thus, from its inception, it was designed with its long-term use in mind while being complete in itself as an athletics arena. Thus, the offices for the club are built into the stadium as a permanent feature while those for the administration of the Games, are temporary, located at a lower level on the concourse.

With regard to design, it is essentially 'state of the art' reflecting building technology in the year 2000 and is bowl shaped with external ramps, providing access to its various levels. The architects, Ove Arup, are the design arm of one of the biggest engineering companies in the world and have produced a bowl shaped stadium with an inverted saddle roof accessed by external ramps. Such ramps are now 'best practice' features of stadium design and allow the paying spectator to gain access to his or her seat, directly from outside the stadium. Consequently, rather than entering the stadium at ground floor level as at Maine Road, and once inside finding your level and seat by stairs or lift, such levels can be accessed at the point of entry. The savings, in terms of crowding and congestion are obvious.

Access to such ramps is gained through electronically operated turnstiles, which are unmanned and activated by a card issued by the club, to the spectator. No more will we see the friendly turnstile operator garnering the gate money from the fumbling fingers of over excited fans! Given the design of the Millennium Stadium in Cardiff, with its retractable roof giving complete protection from the elements, the architects have decided against this type of provision, much to the relief of the Facilities Manager who opines:

"Such an arrangement, retractable roof covering the playing area, is a waste of time. This reflects my somewhat 'purist' sports, as well as professional values. I firmly believe that facility wise, if you are catering for an outside sport such as football or rugby, then the players should be able to play in all weathers and adapt accordingly; thus, taking a ball on the run in driving rain with gusts of wind up to 50 mph, requires different competencies from those exercised in a sterile, fully enclosed arena. Climate factors are written into the skills repertoire of the game and indeed, are inseparable from the training and preparation for it."

This latter point is of course, illustrated most clearly with regard to 'altitude training' and acclimatisation procedures undertaken by sports competitors, prior to major sporting events situated way above sea level. An important point, quite apart from the 'moral integrity' of the sport, is that from a practical point of view, the actual playing surface in the converted stadium, is very difficult to effectively manage with a closing roof system: to summarise the problem in a nutshell and in a non-technical manner, the grass won't grow properly. While water can be readily provided, this is not so easily managed with regard to the other two necessary ingredients, light and air. Full consideration has been given to the 'tone' of the playing surface which will replace the athletics field. A new system of under-soil heating will be provided but which also incorporates a sub-air system, which allows for optimum management of the playing surface. This system will push air into the soil, while at the same time, being capable of extracting poisonous gases and irrigating/extracting water from the playing area. This interactive system is a major advance on drainage systems which rely on, what may be termed, 'passive pipes', to remove water or heat the soil. Thus, Manchester City's playing surface will in reality, rather than the imagination, be 'a field of dreams' from both a maintenance and playing point of view. Given the bowl shaped design, this aspect is very important, because, without such a system, considerable pitch problems may have ensued arising from the circulation of air and availability of light. In terms of the latter, the leading edge of the roof around the grandstands is polycarbonate which allows for 95% UV penetration, thus maximising light exposure.

Huge louvres have also been designed into the stands at two different levels in the corners, which can be opened up, thus assisting in the passage of air and deflecting it onto the playing surface. The computer models suggesting this scenario have been borne out by practical tests. Finally, to ensure optimum playing conditions, the pitch will be seeded rather than turfed and fibre sand in composition, thus providing a robust product. This form of construction installed at Maine Road for the 2000/01 season is more stable than conventional pitches in that polypropylene fibres are fed into a sand mix and the roots of the grass seedlings bind themselves around the fibres, thus keeping everything tight. The end result is a true playing surface marked by an absence of large divots.

In terms of structural alterations to the stadium, to bring about the metamorphosis from athletics to soccer, a whole tier of seating will be installed at a lower level. This will result in a finished configuration of three levels on the East and West sides and two levels on the North and South sides. This aesthetically pleasing shape will be topped by a cantilever roof supported by pillars anchored outside the stadium, providing uninterrupted views of the playing area. The stands do not recede in a straight angular trajectory, they overlap again producing a pleasing symmetry but which are also again highly functional, in that this design provided the spectator with maximum proximity to the playing arena, even if seated in the uppermost tier. Rather neatly, this confers a corporate benefit of increased capacity without conspicuously distancing the spectator from the event. To illustrate, the capacity of the East stand is some 15,000 seated spectators as compared to the current Kippax's 10,000, but the upper tier of the East stand will be closer to the pitch than that upper tier. Overall, the capacity of the 'Athletics' stadium will be increased from 40,000 to 48,000 for Manchester City FC. The Northern Stand erected for the Games will be demolished. The track and encircled field will be removed and earth extracted from the central core to some 6 metres or twenty feet; some 90,000 cubic tonnes of earth will be taken away. A whole new lower tier of terraces and seats will be installed and the Northern end rebuilt.

The paying spectators' refreshment needs are well catered for. Manchester City have contracted with a company to provide both public and private catering. Plans are afoot to issue cards with a contact micro-chip embedded in them to allow for flexible purchase and transferability of funds. For example, a credit card can be inserted into what is commonly termed a 'hole in the wall' machine and then an amount can be downloaded onto the contact chip City card, perhaps, for say fifty pounds. The City card is then credited with this amount and the spectator, so financially provisioned, can then use the card to buy goods and refreshments up to the maximum encoded on it. While there will still be cash sales, this form of financing, from a corporate point of view, reduces cash handling and thus, the potential for fraud and theft. Its usage can also be extended to vending machines with Dutch experience seeming to suggest that this form of system is three times faster than a conventional one.

The stadium will be leased from the City Council by the club for a 250 year period, though its 'life' as a structure is some 60-70 years and will result in a high quality facility as reflected in its build cost, as expressed in a price per seat. Let us quote from City's Facilities Manager, by way of conclusion:

> **"The quality of a stadium in reflected in the price of building a seat. At Sunderland, the cost of their stadium was £30M for 30,000 seats, thus giving £1,000 per seat. Now the cost of our stadium, including everything in, will be approximately £120M; the capacity is 48,000, so that gives a figure of £2,500 per seat. Such a price is reflected in wider concourses, a better standard of finishing, more corporate hospitality areas and public services. In addition, concourse areas are free of external unsightly protuberances such as pipes and beams. Quite simply put, Manchester City will not only have the best stadium in the country but the best stadium by a factor of two or three; certainly, if I dare make the observation, far superior to our neighbours at Old Trafford."**

While the stadium Facilities Manager for City has an overall responsibility for building related matters in relation to a number of sites and complexes, we may ask what specific perspective is brought to bear by those responsible for bringing the new stadium on line and then reconfiguring it from athletics to soccer? While a number of viewpoints could be expressed with regard to the question – from civil engineers, architects, builders and so on, let us focus on the design side and present interview material interspersed with personal commentary from a member of the Ove Arup Associates team which has been associated with the project from its original formulation as Manchester's bid for the Olympic Games.

Arup's philosophy as a company stems from its founder, Ove Arup, who somewhat unusually for the times, made a key speech in 1970 laying out in literary, it might be said even philosophical form, his vision for the firm. This remains the 'Mission Statement' for the company to this day. Central to this philosophy, is the idea of contributing to sustainable societies by involving environmental, economic and social factors in design and build projects; the projects undertaken are choreographed to create an improved environment, both for the clients and their users, but also in terms of their beneficial impacts on local communities and surroundings. This key issue of 'sustainability' may be graphically expressed in its component forms, in the illustrations at the end of this chapter and is particularly pertinent to regeneration projects like Eastlands, which is designed in its totality to express this concept. In particular, the stadium as the hub, illustrates what Ove Arup wrote some 30 years ago, 'If we ..... can show how our environment can be improved, this is likely to have a much greater effect than mere propaganda'. Both physical representations, as in the City of Manchester Stadium and ideas, as represented by the Arup Journal – published continually since 1966, combine to harmonise with an event like the Commonwealth Games which is underpinned by the ideas of community, friendship and individual excellence; with individual athletic flair and imagination adding that extra ingredient of 'delight' to the equation.

Observer: "**Is there an inherent conflict in the role of the architect in terms of the aesthetic v pragmatic between presenting a building which is pleasing to view but limited in usage and vice versa: the design idiom v utilitarian functionalism?**"

Respondent: "**Well, that's what an architect has been trained for over seven or eight years – the synthesis of both**

emerges in the finished product, that is, the professional demeanour of the architect. Some architects may start from a conceptual standpoint for them, their creation is a piece of sculpture, others are more concerned with the functional pragmatic edifice as an end product. The system of training tries to lift the pragmatists to an ideational level while trimming the conceptualists sails to fall in with the reality of negotiating the shoals and currents of actual construction. As a professional architect, you have to know why you are designing a particular building in a particular way. Why you have designed a roof for the City of Manchester stadium with a saddle roof rather than a flat one and so on. Not merely because of the visual impact, but because there are also certain practical advantages. Now normally a client will not start from a neutral position, he may either like the style and approach of the architectural team, as evidenced in their completed projects, or he may have seen a similar building, not knowing who designed it, and say to himself that he wants one similar. Also remember that most public works have been awarded on the basis of a competition entry, although such an entry may be limited to three or four firms, and that in addition to an exciting image there is also the question of costs. Sometimes a design may be selected solely on the latter criterion, that is, fee rather than idea. A high profile project, like the City of Manchester stadium involves the impact of the design and this decided the outcome, not merely cost. Arup won this stadium project on the basis of competition."

Observer: "Could you elaborate?"

Respondent: "Yes. This site was the one originally chosen for the Olympic bid way back in the late eighties, early nineties, but which was eventually lost to Sydney, Australia. At that time, Arup Associates, a special division within Ove Arup as a whole developed the concept design in association with Arup Manchester who handle structures, mechanical and electrical matters; we won the scheme design. When the Olympic bid did not materialise then, there was a proposal that the brief could form the basis of a national stadium but that eventually went to Wembley.

The next stage was a bid by Manchester for the Commonwealth Games and it turned out to be successful. Once this was decided, then certain design features fell into place; it was not going to be as large, it would not be used subsequently solely for athletics and consequently, the building had to be of some future use, not what is termed a 'white elephant'. The design, thus, began as one concept – an Olympic Stadium and finished up as another – an athletics stadium converted to permanent use as a major soccer venue for Manchester City. At each stage, Arup had to bid and prove that we were the best people to design and implement the wishes of the City Council."

Perhaps this is a good point to conclude this part of the interview, and review the specifics of the Commonwealth Stadium. To order our thoughts, we will use the following heads*:

- **Its location in Sports City and the Brief**
- **Design Concepts**
- **Phasing**
- **Configuration and Re-configuration**
- **Site Progress**

In describing this development, both secondary sources, such as the architects' design and implementation documents, as well as interviews and observations conducted while work was in progress, are drawn on.

Thanks to Arup Associates for providing a summary of their 'power pack presentation', from which this structure is derived.

• Sports City, the Stadium and the Brief:

The first point to make, is that it is the City of Manchester Stadium, though no doubt over the decades to come, it will be labelled by different groups in different ways. This is aptly named because it is solely owned by Manchester City Council and will be leased to Manchester City Football Club as their permanent home for 250 years! During the construction phase, Manchester 2002, are the Limited Liability Company established to organise the Commonwealth Games. As we have noted, Arup Associates and Arup Manchester, who are part of the Arup Group worked on the design from its architectural, mechanical, civil structural and electrical aspects. Laing, were chosen as the contractors to transfer their design into reality. All parties have to work within an urban regeneration scheme known as Sports City, which is the show site of Eastlands. This covers the inner urban areas of Manchester – Ancoats, Beswick, Bradford and Clayton – and is 146 acres in extent representing the biggest multi-sport investment in the UK, is expected to attract some 4.5 million visitors every year.

The stadium is, thus, not a stand-alone facility but obviously is the catalyst for the whole idea of regeneration. As the site of the Commonwealth Games, it will bring global attention to Manchester with an expected one billion TV viewers; as an athletic Centre of Excellence, it will attract elite athletes which will hopefully boost Britain's international performance, as the Velodrome has done for our cyclists. As a football stadium, it will draw thousands of people here on a regular basis and this will drive forward all the other developments. The key dates are Phase 1, Commonwealth Games: opening ceremony 25th July 2002, closing ceremony, 4th August 2002. Phase 2, Football Stadium: target practical completion by July 2003.

The brief involved having 38,000 seats ready for the Games and 47,500 seats ready for the start of the 2003/04 football season. The gross capacity is approximately 50,000 seats, that is, without the seat deductions taken for camera positions, press areas, disabled facilities, access ramps and so on. The brief reflects the use of guides and memoranda, which have been issued over the years, particularly since the Hillsborough Disaster. The brief is also informed from meetings held with those who have a legitimate point of view to represent. This can be difficult, because perception can vary so much between different interest groups. Most of the concerns expressed were about traffic management, access to the stadium and crowd turbulence on match days. All of this is fed into the brief, as well as the architect's experience of other stadia and grounds, and the attitudes and views of prospective spectators. Account has also been taken of all those other agencies who are going to be involved; police, fire, ambulance, Manchester City FC, and so on. Thus, the brief becomes more and more detailed as consultations proceed and feed into it. From an original brief of one page, Arup Associates, as lead designers, have developed a voluminous brief culminating in a Design and Development Report* which in essence, represents the building they are going to hand over. This is what the team have designed, this is what the clients, Manchester City Council are signing up for; in short, it is the principle of the building which contains a notional cost, but exists before tenders have been made, contracts signed and so on. The contract is essentially a design-build/construction-management one; this means the contractor, Laing, is running the project on behalf of the client, the City Council with Arup's being independently employed by the Council to advise them and to audit the construction process. At the end of the day, Laing, are responsible for making it all happen – to translate the idea, philosophy, dream if you like, of the planners, into a reality: in short, for realising the bid in tangible form. This is no mean task given the different phases of the project. However, Arup have had considerable experience in designing successful sports stadia and recent examples are given in an Appendix; these are listed chronologically and cover a variety of geographical locations and varying types of provision. It must be noted however that the full original articles are written for architects rather than the general public.

- **Design Concepts:**

The Manchester City stadium Facilities Manager, has already described how the builders are going to manage the 'athletics to football' transition, in terms of creating a lower level tier to enlarge

* *Amounting to three A3 volumes.*

the seating configuration. This, however, will not adversely effect the architectural expression, which will remain, in brief, a stadium in a landscape. To expand on this, the location is on a flat plateau, the Pennine Hill to the East, the urban skyline of Manchester to the West, to the South, the Cheshire Plain and to the North, the gradually ascending moorlands of Bolton and beyond. Given this location, the stadium is a visual statement; the architects have achieved their objectives of clarity of the entrances and consequent circulation of people. The huge ramps and the attendant masts serve this purpose admirably. They draw the spectator, visibly symbolising and becoming beckoning entranceways. These become architectural areas of excitement, similar to the dreaming spires of Oxford or the marching, sometimes flying buttresses of cathedrals. On entering the building, the spectator or participant becomes one with the structure, spectators and 'spires', ramps and masts, becoming integrated and fused as bees are when entering their honeycomb. A far cry from the location as a 19th Century Centre of Heavy Industry, with its local population literally coloured by the industries which commanded their labour; skin colour 'black' for Bradford Collieries, 'yellow' for the Anchor Chemical Works, 'red' for Clayton Analine; the pigments with which they worked, actually discolouring the colour of the workers' skin, not to mention the stench impregnated into pores by Dean & Wood's slaughterhouse*. All of these firms were located within one mile from the Centre Circle of Manchester City's new ground. In it's place, an edifice of the 21st Century, a Sports City in stark contrast to its satanic situation in the 19th Century City of Manchester, where heavy industry and health diminishing occupations prevailed. An area of regeneration where the visitor will be embraced by promenades, boulevards, concourses and a revitalised and upgraded park and waterway system, it is not a 'fenced off – keep out' scheme; the stadium dominates a site, which is calling out to be enjoyed and used. While it is true that, for the Games itself, the whole area will be fenced off becoming a completely self-contained security zone, thus, is only temporary with the buildings 'repossessed' by the community on cessation of the one-off spectacle.

* *The author can testify personally to this as he was born some 400 metres from the stadium in 1940 and lived there until being married in 1964!*

For the first time, the Manchester Games are integrated with both elite athletes and the disabled, competing within their own formats alongside each other and the design readily accommodates this. The stadium is in a place and has been given a generous concourse, internally and externally; it has a very wide tree-lined circular concourse around it. This means on arrival, spectators are not brought straight up against a building. They can 'experience' it close to, but are not over shadowed by it. A 'meeting place' atmosphere pervades it, with plenty of room to enter or leave the building and to engage in social discourse.

From the soccer point of view, the pitch orientation is very important; generally, a North/South alignment is preferable for a winter afternoon event and in fact, the actual alignment is just off a North/South track. For athletes, the situation of the stadium relative to a warm-up track is important. In this regard, it is right next door and will become the athletics track for the Centre of Excellence with its attendant buildings and facilities, when the Games finish.

- **Phasing:**

This aspect is very interesting. Originally there were to be permanent East and West Stands with the North and South Stands being temporary and coming in as Phase 1. At ground level, an 'in field' with a running track was planned to run symmetrically around it. The building of North and South Stands on a permanent basis and an excavated bowl was to be Phase 2.

Having planned this, the contractors found they had to save money and reduce the programme time for the second phase, and in the light of this, the original idea of building temporary North and South Stands looked increasingly problematic. Instead, it was decided to build three stands and then move the track to the North, having only one temporary stand, the North Stand, built out of proprietary scaffolding. This meant that the contractors could build much more of the stadium in one phase: in addition, they only had to buy one scaffolding system. In plan, they thus reconciled themselves to an asymmetrical layout. The centre of the track and eventually of the soccer pitch, has thus, been moved slightly North from the bulk of the main building. From the main Ashton New Road, the stadium gives a finished stadium perspective; however, viewed from one end, the observer obtains a sectional cut: it looks as though someone has sliced the building and this provides a dramatic effect with the tiers going up and the roof swooping down. This perspective will only exist for six months; after that, the stadium will be all closed in. One of the best views at the time of writing, is from the temporary North Stand looking back South at the main building.

- **Configuration and Re-Configuration:**

In terms of access, hospitality and VIP car parking will be quite close to the stadium and its facilities. In the soccer situation, away fans attending the City ground will find their coach park is very close to the South entrances. This will make segmental crowd control relatively easy to manage in terms of ease of access to, and departure from the stadium within the one very generous concourse. For home supporters, there is easy pedestrian access from the North car park and when the Metro Link is established, running to the East of the City, the station will be adjacent to the stadium. With regard to structure, in finale mode as a football stadium, it will have a lower tier or Level 1, a middle tier or Level 2, and an upper tier or Level 3. The four stands, directionally denoted as at Old Trafford, North, South, East and West, are all interconnected apart from Level 3, East and West which are self contained: it is not possible to walk round them. The reason for that is that the design theme have maximised the seating to the Centre line of the stadium and therefore, have created a swooping roof which gives an inverted saddle effect. The North and South stands, which are less saleable, have less seats. The South and North Stands each contain 7,500 net seats, the East and West stands 16,250 net seats. As previously stated, these seats are reached by outer ramps which have gradients of 1:20 so they are easily accessible even by people in wheelchairs. The main internal concourse – what will become the back of the lower tier when it is finished – is accessed from the corners at ground level. This is a quite brilliant innovation because spectators with mobility problems do not have to ascend to their seats and yet, can still obtain an elevated view of the pitch, from the back of the bowl. It is an optimum design concept allowing spectators entry to the ground at the first level and yet, not have to go up steps to obtain a good view of the pitch.

Fire and safety considerations are very important in soccer stadia, post Bradford and Hillsborough and as a design team, Arup's dominant perspective has been that of speed of exiting from, rather than entering the stadium. The computer model of a potential stadium disaster, calling for the complete evacuation of the stadium, actually simulates people as dots. It indicates flows as patterns of dots and within eight minutes, everybody is out of the stadium, which meets a global first class safety standard. Generally, with a few exceptions, spectators can move all around the building via the internal concourse, which houses all the toilet and refreshment concessions. In terms of safety, the concourse was designed so that if there is a panic, it can take the total width or capacity of all the exit routes; like a river where tributaries disgorge into it, so the crowd flow increases until the final exit width equals the total width of all the gangways and vomitories situated all round the stadium. In addition, if one corner is blocked off, everybody can safely exit from the other three. To make the concourse safe, the design team have put a lot of effort into the layout of the concession units. In the event of a fire, they are sealed off with roller shutters and air is sucked out from this area creating a draught which dispels the smoke and lowers the temperature thus, protecting spectators in the vicinity. It means that they can dispense with elaborate sprinkler systems. This is revolutionary in terms of safety design and has never been tried before. Tests have proved very successful. The analogy is that of a domestic chip pan fryer, by putting a lid on it, the fire is extinguished that way. Safety is also written into the design of gangways and vomatories*; on entry, the spectator will note recess steps with as few trip hazards as possible. Paying attention to such detail means that the architects have tried their utmost to produce as safe an environment as possible. In this regard sightlines and seating are

* This peculiar word is derived from the Latin verb 'vomito', literally meaning 'to be sick'. However, in classical literature, it has been used in a metaphorical sense to describe entrances and exits from theatres and amphitheatres. In other words, the stadia are described as 'disgorging' people!

of utmost importance to the spectator and again, if carefully thought through, can remove frustration which may lead to crowd problems. If groups of spectators cannot see what they have come to see and there is not the right 'atmosphere' – using that word in the sense deployed by JB Priestly, not those at the segregation point of the Kippax at Maine Road! – then problems ensue.

There are two main design points Arup have brought to the fore, with respect to making the soccer stadium of Manchester City an experiential and exciting place for their fans and that of their visiting guests. The very first consideration is to make sure that there were no straight seating lines in any of the stand configurations. So the East Stand has got a slight bow in it. Psychologically, what that means is that the spectators feel part of a group; he or she is not in a row looking past someone. Being 'bowled round' physically gives a sense of bonding and community as well as the practical advantage of not having to stand up to obtain a more complete view. The second point incorporated into the design, concerns what the architects call 'C values'. The 'C value' being vertical distance between eye lines of people sat one behind the other: C60 is the minimum. It means that the spectator can just see the head of the person in the seat in front but it is not a problem in terms of observing sight of the spectacle. C100 means a view, well clear of the head of the person in front and there is no obstruction at all. These values are all worked out on average heights and adjusted to the worst sight line of the stadium, which in the City stadium's case, is the closest part of the seating to the touchline, in the corner spot. As the stadium bowls out, the seated spectator is gradually further away from the pitch but sight line or 'C value' is improved. So in the centre of the stadium, 'C values' of 120 and above are recorded where the spectator could still see the game even with a policeman sat in front with a helmet on! Also, the overlaying of the levels and the cantilever design of the stands, mean that the boxes are in a very sheltered area in terms of the weather, but also that no seat is further than 100 metres from the centre spot of the pitch. This arrangement provides a heightened feeling of crowd solidarity and spectator intimacy. Normally, the maximum viewing distance allowed in a modern stadium is 190 metres, measured from the furthest corner of the pitch to the furthest seat on the other side of the ground. At the City stadium, this measure is 160 metres, well within the official parameter. Translated into human terms, the bowl environment and its structures provide both a compact design and a high degree of community expressed in the JB Priestly collective sense. This 'colosseum feeling', with one edifice shared by many with a collective purpose, is also highly practical and environmentally appropriate; the perforated corners, expressed in the huge manually operated louvers we have mentioned before, providing air and light for the grass to establish itself and grow in the natural medium which has nurtured it from seed: transplanted turf may represent, as the poet says, 'the beautifully uncut hair of graves', but is less than optimum for Manchester City's playing field.

The disabled have been fully considered in terms of the configuration and re-configuration of the stadium. It is clear from interviews and observation, that this often neglected aspect of provision has always been taken seriously by Arup Associates and partners, in formulating designs and implementing them. So often, our less that fortunate colleagues are considered late in the day with facilities often treated as an 'add on' or appendage to the central structural systems which are put into place. In addition to the functionality of the ramps, which we have already considered, there are wheelchair positions at every level in the stadium; thus enhancing integration of the handicapped within the collectivity and at the same time, their dignity. In addition, there are induction loops at every grade for the hard of hearing and the visually impaired. With regard to the latter condition, individuals who cannot see the spectacle, can plug into audio transmissions for a commentary. For the hard of hearing, such commentary zones are provided at an enhanced level and provide details of substitutions, emergency announcements and so on. Individual hearing aids can be amplified. Thus, from the point of view of the disabled, the stadium is very user-friendly and has actually been designed with them in mind as well as the general public. With regard to media facilities, in the football mode, there are 50-100 press seats; there is also a gantry for 24 TV commentary positions and 6-10 radio commentary posts. A working area in the basement is dedicated to about 50 journalists with an attendant lounge facility; conference rooms, mixed media zones and so on, are also provided. These facilities have their own private access to the stadium. In football mode, the basement is the functional king. It contains two levels accommodating players' changing rooms, the 'tunnel' access to the pitch, the warm-up facilities with high ceilings, police area, first-aid areas and a huge kitchen to service all the hospitality outlets. The basement is thus, the main hub of the building, where everything happens.*

As the basement is not yet fully operational at the time of writing, it would be premature to describe it in any detail, however, it is best envisaged by being a space entered by a service tunnel which gives vehicular access to the pitch. This space being divided up into discrete areas for players and officials, the media, police, first aid and of course, the essential kitchen facilities.

- **Site Progress:**

Taking the stance of an imaginary observer, we can log site progress in that by November 1999, he would see the first piles driven in. By June 2000, he could see the footprint and first impression of a stadium; into the autumn of that year, a skeleton emerges; the bones being the huge beams that hold the terraces, called the raker beams with their steppings to hold the seats. He sees in ghost form the layout of the stadium. By Christmas, the upper tier, Level 3 has been added, again in skeletal form and by February/March 2001, he can stand on the upper tier and actually begin to emotionally sense the 'presence' of the building and experience its movements. To achieve this progress and in terms of practicalities, in February 2001, the contractors built a temporary wall all the way around the bowl and on this, they rested the front of all the roof trusses. The back of the trusses actually rested on the outer columns; the whole of the supporting fabric of the roof was built like this and at the same time, the twelve major masts were erected with the cables being attached from the top of the mast down to the roof trusses and then all components were tensioned up. The crude analogy is that of putting a tent up by pulling on the guy ropes and anchoring the pegs around to support it. In the case of our stadium, all the support wall was knocked out

For the Games, there is no basement of course and there will be 700 press seats to accommodate the world's media set up on a temporary basis.

in about two weeks and the roof hung there on its masts and cable nets. To stop the wind lifting it up, there are four corner guys, again, just like the tent, which are at the low point and anchor the whole edifice. Even with such high winds recorded* at the time of writing, the whole structure has remained stable and sound; a great compliment to Laing's the builders and Arup's, the originators: a fitting and happy note on which to conclude this chapter and the book. The stadium now awaits the carriers of 'attitude blue' to bring it into life and turn it from a 'house into a home'.

CR

*February 2002 with gusts of 125 m.p.h. recorded in the Cairngorms

M.C.F.C City of Manchester Stadium

A BLUE HEAVEN: NEW STYLE

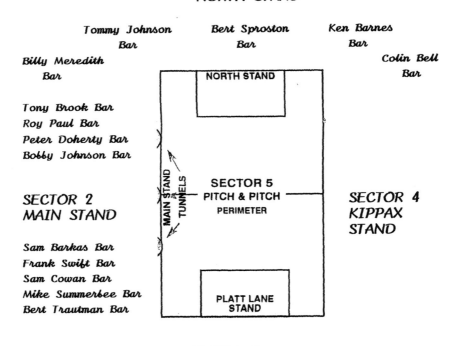

SECTOR 1
NORTH STAND

Tommy Johnson Bar

Bert Sproston Bar

Ken Barnes Bar

Billy Meredith Bar

Colin Bell Bar

NORTH STAND

Tony Brook Bar
Roy Paul Bar
Peter Doherty Bar
Bobby Johnson Bar

SECTOR 5
PITCH & PITCH
PERIMETER

SECTOR 2
MAIN STAND

SECTOR 4
KIPPAX
STAND

Sam Barkas Bar
Frank Swift Bar
Sam Cowan Bar
Mike Summerbee Bar
Bert Trautman Bar

MAIN STAND
TUNNELS

PLATT LANE
STAND

SECTOR 3
PLATT LANE
STAND

Dennis Tueart Bar   Fred Tilson Bar   Don Revie Bar   Eric Brook Bar
Roy Clarke Bar   Peter Barnes Bar   Mike Summerbee Bar

DISPOSITION OF BARS: MAINE ROAD IN 2000

ENVIRONMENT

AIR QUALITY
LAND USE
WATER
ECOLOGY
BUILDINGS
TRANSPORT

SOCIETAL

INCLUSION
AMENITY
ACCESS
FORM & SPACE

NATURAL RESOURCES

MINERALS
WATER
ENERGY
LAND UTILISATION
RE-USE

ECONOMIC

VIABILITY
COMPETITIVE EFFECTS
EMPLOYMENT/SKILLS ETC
SOCIAL BENEFITS/COSTS
TRANSPORT

GRAPHICAL REPRESENTATION OF THE ARUP PHILOSPHY

THE NEW MANAGER EAGER TO START WORK IN THE NEW STADIUM: ONLY 18 MONTHS TO GO

A FULLY FITTED OUT FAN EAGER FOR HIS FIRST MATCH: ONLY 18 MONTHS TO GO

THE STADUIM IN ATHLETICS MODE

MAIN INTERNAL CONCOURSE OF THE NEW STADIUM BEFORE CONCESSIONARY FIT OUT

TURNSTILES BACKED BY LOUVERED FITTINGS AT THE NEW STADIUM

REACHING FOR THE SKY! MASTS AND CABLES HOLDING UP THE ROOF OF THE NEW STADIUM

A FUTURISTIC ROOF WITH NO GUTTERS! WHERE DOES THE RAINWATER GO?

APPENDICES

APPENDIX 1

The Popplewell Report on the Heysel disaster also incorporated findings from an enquiry into a fire at Bradford City's ground in the same year, which resulted in 56 deaths. A brief chronology of nine major crowd problems since the turn of the century with their attendant reports, may be summarised from Popplewell as follows:

1. The Short Report: arose from a disaster which occurred at Wembley Stadium at the first cup final on 28th April 1922. Reported in 1924.

2. The Meolwyn Hughes report arose out of the disaster at Bolton Wanderer's Football ground on 9th March 1946.

3. The Chester Report: an enquiry into the state of association football. 1966.

4. The Harrington Report: a report to the Minister of Sport on the topic of football hooliganism. 1968.

5. The Lang Report: examined the problems of football crowd behaviour. 1969.

6. The Wheatley Report: inquired into the disaster at Ibrox Park. 1972.

7. The McElane Report: considered hooligan behaviour among Scottish soccer supporters. 1976.

8. Department of Environment working group; dealt with problems arising from international football. 1984.

9. The Popplewell Report: Interim and Final Report; dealt with the fire at Bradford City and Heysel Disaster. 1985.

10. The Taylor Report: Interim 1989 and Full Reports 1990; inquired into the Hillsborough disaster.

11. Football (Offences and Disorder Act) 1999: Brings together previous and present legislation in a coherent fashion.

APPENDIX 2

Not all major sports stadia present problems or are associated with 'disasters'. Listed below, by Journal number, are eight recent sports projects successfully completed by Arup's with a brief account of each. A fuller description from the design point of view, may be obtained from the Arup Journal listed for each project. More general information can be obtained through:

DAVID J BROWN PUBLICATIONS, MANAGER & EDITOR
David-j.brown@arup.com Tele: +44 (0)207755 3828

1. 1/1995
   The Hong Kong Stadium: Cheung, Cole & Sneth.

   Provides international-standard sports facilities for
   Hong Kong; nearly 6 million people in 1,000km^2.
   Football and rugby catered for.

2. 1/1996
   The Nynex Arena, Manchester: Burrows, Kay, Paine & Waite.

   A 20,000 seat arena over the Victoria Station rail
   interchange. A permanent international ice-hockey sized
   ice floor was installed: basketball and major concerts
   catered for.

3. 2/1996
   Johannesburg Athletics Stadium: Burland, Jones & Lamb.

   Main use is for international athletics but it also caters for
   soccer, concerts and spectaculars. Great care shown in
   choosing local materials and resources for building.

4. 3/1996
    The Swatch Olympic Pavillion: Chamber

    Located in downtown Atlanta, Georgia. Offered a presence
    for sales, promotion and interactive exhibits during the
    1996 Olympic Games.

5. 1/1997
    International Aquatic Centres, Sydney to Bangkok: Stevenson

    Aquatic Centre caters for elite competition and
    community swimming facilities. The Head of the IAC
    called it 'The best swimming pool he had ever seen! The
    rest is history!'

6. 1/2001
    Manchester Aquatics Centre: Mangall, Waite & Woodhouse

    World class elite and community use swimming and
    training complex built with the 17th Commonwealth
    Games in mind.

7. 2/2001
    International Tennis Centre, Sydney:
    Bardsley-Smith, Herman, McClure and Pugh

    Awarded the 2000 Royal Australian Institute of Architects
    Sr John Sulman Award for Excellence in Public Buildings.
    Contributing to Sydney's new Olympic facilities.

8. 2/2002
    Irish Racecourse Projects: Mulherin

    Arup has either been involved in, or has acted as advisor
    to the Irish Horseracing Authority principally for the
    development of its eight key courses.

APPENDIX 3

INITIAL BRIEF: CITY OF MANCHESTER STADIUM

The Initial Brief stated that:

➤ The completed Football Stadium shall have a minimum gross capacity of 45,000 seats, with optimised sightlines from all seats in both configurations.

➤ The design shall comply with the Building Regulations and licensing requirements of the local and public licensing authority and the technical, functional and safety requirements of the Football Association (FA), Football League (FL), Union of European Football Association (UEFA), Federation Internationale de Football Association (FIFA), International Amateur Athletics Federation (IAFF) and the Heads of Terms agreement with Manchester City Football Club (MCFC).

➤ The design shall pay attention to spectator safety and convenience inside and outside the Stadium, in particular the issues of major crowd movement in respect of;

~ access to the site and use of the transport infrastructure,
~ arrival/departure,
~ ingress/egress,
~ internal and external circulation,
~ spectator access to toilets and concessions.

➤ The design shall address the process of management and the operational safety aspects of the stadium

➤ The stadium shall be developed in two phases. Phase I shall be in an athletics configuration incorporating an athletics track of international standard with permanent main stands and demountable/temporary end stands with a gross capacity of 38,000 seats. Phase I shall be completed in the spring of 2002. Phase II shall comprise the construction of two permanent end stands with associated roofs and an excavated lower seating tier to create a football stadium with a minimum gross capacity of 45,000 seats. Phase II shall be completed by June 2003.

➤ The design shall include a warm-up track and facilities for use during The Commonwealth Games.

➤ The Stadium development shall be the centrepiece of a larger development, named 'Sportcity', incorporating commercial developments, car parking and road and rail transportation infrastructure.

APPENDIX 4

MISSION STATEMENT OF THE GREATER MANCHESTER POLICE

Our purpose is to uphold the law fairly and firmly by preventing crime, bringing lawbreakers to justice and keeping the peace; protecting, helping and reassuring the community. We must be seen to do this with integrity, common sense and sound judgment. We are committed to the highest quality of service to the public, other agencies and our own staff. We constantly seek to improve our standards and encourage our staff to do their best. We should be polite, sympathetic, tactful and understanding. We must act without fear while respecting others' rights, treating everyone equally irrespective of race or gender. We need to be professional, calm and restrained in violent situations, particularly when provoked. When force must be used it should be no more than required to carry out our lawful duty.

We must work hard to reduce public fears about crime and, as much as we can, take action that meets their wishes. We must be prepared to change in response to reasonable criticism. We cannot work without the help and involvement of the community, so we talk regularly to the public about their views. When it is in their best interest, we take action with other organisations. We encourage police and support staff at every level to identify problems and find solutions.

To find new ways of running efficiently, we have a major research programme. We continually monitor the performance of all our departments and divisions to make sure we meet the standards the community expects. The Greater Manchester Police will employ the best staff possible. We train and assess staff to develop their abilities for the benefit of the Service and the community. We expect them all to act with professionalism and in return, we will give appropriate support to those staff who make errors of judgment while acting in good faith on the best information available.

Our philosophy recognises that an effective, accountable Police Service is essential for a healthy community believing in equality under the law.

APPENDIX 5

Recommendations of The Taylor Report with respect to the seating of spectators.

1. The Secretary of State should ensure that spectators are admitted only to seated accommodation at matches played at sports grounds designated under the Safety of Sport Ground Act 1975, in accordance with the timing set out in recommendations 2-4 below.

2. Recommendation 1 should apply with effect from the start of the 1993/94 season at high risk matches as defined under the U.E.F.A. regulations.

3. Subject to recommendation 2 above, recommendation 1 above should apply with effect from the start of the 1994/95 season to all matches at grounds in the Premier division of the Scottish Football League and at national stadia. Standing accommodation should be reduced annually at the grounds by 20% deduction, being effective from August 1990 so as to eliminate standing by August 1994.

4. Subject to recommendation 2 above, recommendation 1 should apply with effect from the start of the 1999/2000 season to all matches at all grounds designated under the Safety of Sports Ground Act 1975.

(Recommendation 4 was subsequently modified by the government to include only Premier league and First Division clubs)

APPENDIX 6

ENGLISH THROUGH IMAGES

"A book unread is a life unlived".

English Noticeboard, St Peter's High School, (Upper School) Manchester.

This book may be used to explore some of the fundamental aspects of language for students on courses in both English language and literature. Particularly it is designed to encourage imaginative writing. In this regard we may remark that images involve comparisons or pictures in words. They rely heavily on:

- Similes
- Metaphors

What are similes and metaphors?

SIMILES AND METAPHORS

A simile is an image which uses the word 'like' or 'as'; a metaphor means a description of one thing in terms of something else. There are many examples in the text. (See in particular Chapter Two). To summarise then, an image is a word picture; it may be a simile, that is a straightforward comparison, or a metaphor, a hidden comparison. We again emphasise that meaning is conveyed through a word picture. By way of illustration let us take two contrasting views of the 'meaning' of the soccer crowd as expressed in literary terms by other authors. George Orwell's views, while being deliberately argumentative, provide a complete contrast to those expressed and rehearsed in near poetic vein by Priestly in _The Good Companions_.

We may quote from Orwell's collected essays:

"People want to see one side on top and the other humiliated and they forget that victory gained through cheating or through the intervention of the crowd is meaningless. Even when the spectators don't intervene physically they try to influence the game by cheering their own side and rattling opposing players with boos and insults. Serious sport has nothing to do with fair play. It is bound up with hatred, jealousy, boastfulness, disregard of all rules and sadistic pleasure in witnessing violence: in other words it is war minus the shooting."

Priestly, on the other hand, sees crowds as 'good companions', viz:

"For a shilling the Buddersford United AFC offered you Conflict and Art; it turned you into a critic, happy in your judgement of fine points, ready in a second to estimate the worth of a well-judged pass, a run down the touch line, a lightening shot, a clearance kick by back or goalkeeper; it turned you into a partisan, holding your breath when the ball came sailing into your own goal mouth, ecstatic when your forwards raced away towards the opposite goal, elated, downcast, bitter, triumphant by turns at the fortunes of your side watching a ball shape Illiads and Odysseys for you; and what is more it turned you into a member of a new community, all brothers together for an hour and a half for not only had you escaped from the clanking machinery of this lesser life, from work, wages, rent, dole, sick pay, insurance cards, nagging wives, ailing children, bad houses, idle workmen, but you had escaped with most of your mates and your neighbours with half the town and there you were cheering together, thumping one another on the shoulders, swapping judgments like lords of the earth, having pushed your way through a turnstile into another and altogether more splendid kind of life, hurtling with conflict and yet passionate and beautiful in its Art. Moreover it offered you more than a

*shilling's worth of material or talk during the rest of the
week. A man who had missed the last home match of 't
United' had to enter social life on tiptoe in Buddersford."*

ENGLISH LANGUAGE EXERCISES USING THIS TEXT

Points for discussion with your teacher and fellow students before
committing yourself to written answers. USE THE TEXT to address
the following points:

- What is the difference between literal and metaphorical
  truth?

- How are feelings conveyed?

- Identify passages describing different areas of _individual_
  experience.

- How are the experiences of <u>group</u> in the text made real to
  the reader.

- What is a 'colloquial expression'? Give examples of how
  colloquial phrases and repetition convey meaning.

- Give examples of how certain words are chosen to
  produce a particular effect.

STYLE

Style is the way something is written or said. A scientific factual
account will differ from an imaginative or narrative one. To help you
understand this distinction, begin by defining the following term:

Scientific:

Preface: Foreword: Appendices: Glossary

Literary:

Threatened: Agitation: Crush: Chant

Why not try now and write a short imaginative essay of about 400
words on 'Watching Football'. Divide your essay into four paragraphs
of about 100 words, each with its own theme. Compare your account

with that which is in the Guardian Newspaper relating to August 25th 1923, the day City's first match was played at Maine Road. In reading this account, it is important to understand that the state of society at any given time reflects the values and opinions in any piece of writing. The time in question, the early 1920's was one of growing economic depression and mass unemployment in England – with 2 million being forecast as the unemployment number for Christmas 1923; bear in mind the population was much lower than at present. Wages were low, even for those in work, profit margins were slim and there was little of the financial cushioning that unemployed people have grown to expect today. Psychologically speaking, there was growing concern about demoralisation among the urban masses associated with prolonged idleness, poverty and despair. These issues being described in an adjacent column in the paper, under the heading 'The Workless Army' to the one given below. With this in mind, we can now read and assess the Guardian piece "Watching Football", as expressed in just under 400 words.

"Another nine months of intensive activity begins today in the professional football world and we sincerely welcome it. Whether so prompt a kick-off (i.e. still summer and hence cricket season) is good for the game may indeed be questioned. But that professional football should flourish through the heart of the winter is a fine thing. Critics may complain that when money flied in at the gate, sportsmanship flied out of the ground. "Fans" whose loyalty is given to other games may talk of the superior virtue of "Rugger" or sigh for the midsummer mildness of cricket

Psychologists and other superior persons may shake their heads at the wild excitement of the Saturday crowds and draw gloomy comparisons between taking part in a game and merely watching it, but all these objectives hurled from different angles do not shatter the strength of football's position. It holds its own firmly entrenched between two main lines of defence. It is, first, one of the fastest and most scientific sports in the world. Secondly – and this defence follows directly from the other – it breaks legitimately into the monotony of many thousands of lives.

When the teams come trotting from their dressing rooms and a splash of colour is added to the great drab arenas, emotion is aroused which would otherwise remain stagnant and unhealthy for lack of exercise. When a sudden hard shot is sent from a struggling group of players and the goalkeeper flings himself across his charge (goal area) one may hear a deep cry go around the stands and cindered ring (track round the pitch). It is a cry of admiration for speed and strength and physical sureness; it expresses the immemorial excitement of the chase.

On such occasions at great professional football matches, many men get their first glimpse of the goodness of simply being alive. The heavy presence of circumstance is for the moment lifted and they live happily and whole-heartedly in the present. Some way of living, thus at regular intervals all men must find. 'Watching football, unlike many other ways, is at once satisfying and without inevitable evil effects. It is a way that will begin to be followed this afternoon by Manchester folk down "Maine Road". Before another summer comes, they will have seen fine things on that new and spacious ground and perhaps they will see again both Manchester[1] teams in the First Division".

The writer is clearly a follower of Priestly, rather than Orwell and in psychological terms sees fans' participation as emotionally healthy through the safety valve of fanship, (Catharsis); there is no mention here of 'soccer hooliganism' or crowd disturbances.

Having completed their own writing, many students will wish to stop at this point. However for others studying the social sciences, a glossary may help them in writing factually, rather than imaginatively and is presented in a short form as an aid to further study; particularly with regards to completing assignments with a psychological focus. A model example of such an assignment follows the glossary.

[1] Manchester United were in the Second Division at the time and finished the league in 14th position behind champions, Leeds United. They would have to wait for promotion until the 1925/26 season.

GLOSSARY OF TERMS FOR THE SOCIAL SCIENCES

This glossary, a dictionary with a specific purpose, is intended to help students on courses in the social sciences 'key into' the processes described in this book. As the emphasis is on the relationships between individuals in groups, let us initially devote some space to definitions of the word 'group' as used by eight distinguished social scientists. We will then follow this by providing a description of terms which will aid in understanding how the material presented here relates to these definitions. If you would like to study psychology in its social aspects still further, then you will find the following book very helpful, Manstead A and Hewstone M (eds) (1995). The Blackwell Encyclopaedia of Social Psychology, Oxford, Blackwell.

GROUPS AS DEFINED FROM VARYING SOCIAL SCIENTIFIC PERSPECTIVES

- A group is an aggregate of individuals standing in certain ... observable relations to each other.

- The sociological concept of a group refers to a number of people who interact with one another in accord with established patterns.

- A group exists when individuals have the same objects as a means of relieving similar internal conflicts.

- A group is a collection of individuals whose existence as a collection is rewarding to the individuals.

- A group is best defined as a dynamic whole based on interdependence rather than similarity.

- A sociological group is made up of members 'pursuing promotively interdependent goals'; psychological group consists of people who 'perceive themselves as pursuing promotively interdependent goals'.

- The distinctive thing about a group is that its members share norms about something.

- A group is a set of people engaged in interaction with one another in a single face to face meeting or series of meetings in which each member receives some impression of each other member, distinctive enough so that he can give some reaction to each of the others as an individual.

Having defined group functioning we may now turn to more specific terms and their meanings.

TERM	BRIEF DEFINITION
Anxiety:	A secondary 'drive' which develops from previous painful experiences; impels people to avoid unpleasant or dangerous situations.
Arousal:	The state of alertness of the individual indicated by a high level of activity in the cerebral cortex (brain).
Behaviourism:	A theoretical approach to psychology based on the objective study of directly observable aspects of behaviour.
Catharsis:	'Cleansing' of emotional fears and anxieties in order to overcome problems associated with them.
Confabulation:	Remembering events inaccurately as a result of expectation, elaboration or because the events fit into well established frameworks of knowledge based on past experience. (Schemas).
Conformity:	The tendency for members of a group to behave in a similar way.
Concept:	Attributes which define an object thus assisting in clarity of meaning.

Correlation Coefficient:	A statistic that describes the degree of relationships between two variables, e.g. the number of arrests at football matches at a given club over a season compared with the number of visiting supporters at each match. A perfect match is expressed as 1; no match is 0. The relationship may be positive or negative.
De-individuation:	A feeling of anonymity which results in individuals not taking responsibility for their behaviour.
Drive:	A motivational force impelling an organism to act in a certain manner. Primary drives are basic to survival; secondary drives are acquired through learning.
Empirical:	Based on factual data.
Ethologist:	A scientist who studies animal behaviour in its natural setting rather than in a laboratory.
Excitation:	A transfer model of aggression. Zillman's theory which states that aggression occurs as a result of transfer of arousal from one context to another.
Extrinsic/Intrinsic Motivation:	Motivation which is not inherent in the task to be performed but directs behaviour towards the achievement of an extrinsic reward as opposed to intrinsic motivation which is inherent in the task.
Feedback:	Knowledge of results. The input from the environment when he or she manipulates it.
Goal:	Can be used at the individual or collective level. A specific end towards which the behaviour under consideration appears to be directed.

In-Groups: Groups of individuals who feel a strong identity with each other and who act in such a way that others (out-groups) are excluded.

Organisation: A social unit deliberately constructed and re-constructed to seek specific goals. Emphasis may be on the actions of individuals (action approach) or the formal structure (structural approach).

Perception: The psychological process whereby the brain organises information coming through the senses.

Reinforcement: Any stimulus which increases or maintains the strength of a given response associated with it. Reinforcement may be positive (carrot) or negative (stick).

Role: The unitary concept of role is an oversimplification. We may distinguish three uses:

1. It may be defined as "Structurally given demands" - norms, expectations, taboos, responsibilities - associated with a given social position.

2. The individual's own conception of his role, his expectations towards himself, constitute the second approach.

3. Thirdly, there is the individual's actual behaviour. The unitary concept of role assumes a high degree of congruence between the three elements, making no assumptions about association between them.

Social Cohesion: Social bonds, norms and structure combine to hold members of a group together, over time.

Social Identity Theory: Draws a distinction between person and social identity. The former refers to aspects of self which are idiosyncratic and peculiar to ourselves. The latter refers to a shared identity with others, e.g. 'a blue' or City supporter. A high degree of social identity promotes social categorisation, e.g. 'a blue', not 'a red'. (United supporter).

Stereotypes: Widely shared generalisations about a group. Often negative, though can be positive. Images are used to stereotype others, e.g. soccer fans as 'animals'.

Sociological View of Adolescence: 'Storm and stress' during the second decade of the life course is caused mainly by external factors such as socialisation, role changes, peer pressure, environmental and social changes and the mass media.

Transitional View of Adolescence: Seen as a time when stress and turmoil are inevitable. Internal factors such as intensity of feeling, sexual changes and associated drives are seen as casual mechanisms.

Trait: An enduring personality characteristic shared with other people and leading to a particular type of perception, over a wide variety of situations, e.g. Neuroticism.

T.O.T.E: Stands for 'Test Operate Test Exit'. The individual 'tests' the environment, e.g. obtaining a ticket for a match via a number of 'contacts'. If unsuccessful, he 'operates' again, e.g. turns up at the stadium and obtains a ticket informally. This behaviour then terminates, i.e. exit, he is ready to see the match.

Having familiarised themselves with these terms, those students pursuing social science courses at sixth form and first year undergraduate level may now want to write a **factual essay**, of about three thousand words, in response to the following question:

Discuss aspects of motivation and management at Manchester City Football Club during the 1990's.

Having made notes to help write this essay follow the guidelines below and structure material under the headings which are given. Ensure that like all good 'stories', the assignment has a: B+M+E !!

Beginning	(B)	Introduction	(I)
Middle	(M)	Theory	(T)
		Application	(A)
End	(E)	Conclusion	(C)

In terms of word count, try and achieve a balance (the figures given are approximate only) e.g:

I	=	500 words
T	=	700 words
A	=	1,300 words
C	=	500 words
Total		3,000 words

Appendices and references are not included in this word count.

The marking scheme is as follows; note the essay provided by a first year BA Leisure Management student (as a model), scores in the 75%+ range.

<u>% of Total Marks</u>

I	=	12%
T	=	20%
A	=	44%
C	=	12%
Refs	=	12%
Total		100%

**Discuss aspects of management at Manchester City FC
during the 1990's**

By

A. SAMPLE STUDENT

℞

CONTENTS

1.0   INTRODUCTION

I decided to focus my assignment on the topic of motivation, as it is an area which I find to be both interesting and particularly relevant to the leisure industry. I have previously touched on this subject during my GCSEs and gone into it in some depths during A-level Psychology course, which I undertook. However, as motivation can be related to such a vast range of situations, I decided to narrow my topic down and focus my attention on motivation related to managerial positions and within that, the problems associated with a major league soccer PLC, Manchester City Football Club.

There are a great number of varying theories on motivation, but I chose to look at just a few of these – the theories of Abraham Maslow, Frederick Herzberg and Douglas McGregor, as I found these to be the most relevant to the world of management. Also, having studied many different theories, I felt that these contained the issues that were most true to life and relevant to my chosen area for a Case Study. Rather than conducting my own interviews, I decided to take advantage of various interviews reported in 'Attitude Blue: Crowd Psychology at Manchester City FC' as a source for this assignment. This data was more than adequate for my needs.

I decided to conclude my assignment by establishing just how useful theories of motivation had been for understanding the daily life of Manchester City Football Club and to put forward suggestions, which could help to improve employee's motivation in the future.

2.0 THEORY

The topic of motivation has been the focus of much research and investigation over the years. As such, many theories have evolved, concerning themselves not only with what motivates individuals, but with why one is motivated and why it is so important to be so, specially in the workplace. There are three theories which were found to be particularly relevant to the topic in question, the first being that of Abraham Maslow.

2.1 Abraham Maslow

During the 1940's, Maslow devised a motivational theory, known as the 'hierarchy of needs'. The diagram below shows the various levels of Maslow's hierarchy and the meanings of these in relation to the work environment:

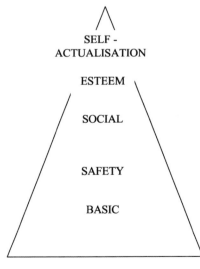

SELF - ACTUALISATION — i.e. personal ambition and self-fulfilment - complete job satisfaction at work.

ESTEEM — i.e. eg needs – at work, this is recognition of a job well done, and promotion.

SOCIAL — i.e. friendship – at work, sports and social events, good relations with other staff.

SAFETY — i.e. protection from danger – at work, this could be health and safety, or job security

BASIC — i.e. physiological needs for survival – at work, food, drink, rest, payment…

(Page 2)

Maslow suggested that in order for an individual to progress on to another level of the hierarchy, they must first have fulfilled the needs of the present level. This process is not as mechanical as it seems, as the higher ranked needs can be achieved before the lower ranked needs.

What Maslow's hierarchy does indicate however, is the importance of work to an individual. Realistically, in the developed world, an adult cannot really fulfil their basic needs without employment, as money is essential to purchase necessities such as food. This employment is a necessary pre-requisite in order to obtain the means to ensure minimum conditions of life whether it can also provide psychological satisfaction, so meeting high order needs is a mute point and one we will return to.

2.2   Frederick Herzberg

Frederick Herzberg believed that human needs fell under two main headings, 'motivators' and 'hygiene factors'. The motivator factors are similar to Maslow's higher ranked needs and include achievement, recognition, responsibility, the work itself and promotion or advancement. He suggested that "Managers must provide motivators in the form of satisfying jobs, e.g. through job rotation and job enrichment schemes". David Floyd (1994, p.122).

Hygiene factors include company policies, supervision, status, security, interpersonal relationships, money and the quality of working conditions. Although these themselves are not responsible for motivating employees, they are very important, as motivation has been shown to decline when they are ignored. Using Herzberg's theory, the organisation must achieve a balance of both 'motivators' and 'hygiene' factors in order to motivate employees successfully.

(Page 3)

2.3 Douglas McGregor

McGregor's theory of motivation involved two bi-polar groups of attitudes, consisting of positive attitudes known as *Theory y* and negative attitudes, *Theory x*. The theories look at the types of management in place and we shall firstly look at *Theory y* management. This has three main beliefs:

1. That 'expending effort at work is as natural as play or rest, and the average person does not dislike work'.
2. That 'employees can exercise their own control and direction, and are rewarded through their efforts made towards achieving the organisation's objectives'.
3. That 'the average person learns to both accept and seek responsibility, its avoidance coming from experience only'.

Supporters of the *Theory y* management believe that the main limiting factors in an organisation are the management's willingness and ability to channel employee potential. Motivation flows on from this, with employees gaining positive motivation as a direct result of their employers' actions.

Theory x management also has three main beliefs:

1. 'People inherently dislike work, and will try to avoid it if possible'.
2. 'They must be coerced, controlled, directed and threatened in order to get sufficient effort towards achieving the organisations' objectives'.
3. 'The average person wants to be controlled and directed, and has little ambition, and seeks to avoid responsibility'.

Theory x assumes that people are solely motivated by money. However, this is clearly not the case with everybody and no doubt, the safe course would be for a manager to use a mixture of both *Theory x* and *Theory y* in order to motivate their staff.

(Page 4)

3.0 APPLICATION

The above are merely a selection and with so many different theories of motivation to look at, it is extremely interesting to examine how these theories are put into action by management staff in the leisure industry, either implicitly or explicitly in their day-to-day activities. It is also worth looking at the effects of attempts to directly motivate staff, and the dangers of what can happen if motivation is not included as a key issue in the working environment.

In this respect, the management situation at Manchester City Football Club is particularly interesting, especially during the 1990's. Not only has there been a change of Chairman during this period, but the team manager has changed no less that seven times! However, let us first look at the effect that the change of Chairman had on the football team.

3.1 The arrival of Francis Lee

During the past twenty years, prior to Francis Lee's arrival, the club had been performing extremely poorly, both on and off the field. This resulted in the 'Forward with Franny' movement which was aimed at Francis Lee, ex-Manchester City player and businessman, taking a majority share of the club, thus removing the then control of Chairman, Peter Swales. In the book, 'The Battle for Manchester City' by Alec Johnson, a founder of the movement, Derek Partridge described the attempted management change as 'a heaven-sent chance we have waited so long for ... a change we simply mustn't miss ...'. Indeed, the chance of change was not missed and in February 1994, Francis Lee became the new major shareholder and Chairman of Manchester City Football Club.

In an interview conducted with Francis Lee in August 1994, by Chris Murray (see text), one can infer that Lee is a firm believer

(Page 5)

in motivating all of his employees, in order to get the best results from them. Lee described how one of his first tasks of taking over Manchester City Football Club, was to start to *'build a new spirit in the club'* and stated that *'it doesn't matter whether it's a lady who cleans the stand, or the groundsmen, the players. I want everybody pulling in the right direction and wanting to make Manchester City successful'*.

So it would seem that in order for a business to be successful, Lee believes that the whole team, the whole workforce, must strive for success and this is seen to be done by motivating all staff, regardless of their position, or abilities. Lee goes on to say, *'you must have the right sort of motivation coming from the top... I've never been the sort of person who through his business career has ruled by fear or threat. I'd rather put my arm around someone and get the best out of them... I always find that to motivate someone in the way I feel is best pays dividends'*.

Francis Lee's appointment as Chairman at Manchester City Football Club was thought to be going to bring about a new success for the club. His recognition of the need for motivation was just the factor which could help to ensure this, but also, the fact that he realised that he could not improve the club single-handed. *'I can't bring this social change on my own – I need good people around me to join in developing group and individual motivation and make it like a team effort'*. However, the club had always had an amazing corporate spirit, largely due to the enormous support of the many loyal fans, and this was to be a great advantage in bringing about the changes that Lee wanted.

The first football match to be held after Lee's appointment as Chairman, showed just how ecstatic everybody was about his new position. Both the crowd and the players were aware that things would now begin to improve with a man such as Lee in charge. His great business sense and desire for the club provoked an

(Page 6)

304

amazing atmosphere in the match against Ipswich, which City won by two goals to one. In the match summary provided by the Manchester Evening News on 6th February 1994, it is noted, 'suddenly the ground was alive again ... there was magic in the air again. Magic on the terraces ... magic on the pitch as Manchester City united like a family in a glorious show of support for the ex-England star whose aim is to take the club back up the soccer tree'. Lee's entrance to the club was described as the 'Messiah' arriving!

3.2   The Arrival of Frank Clark

In spite of all the drive that Lee provided for the club, they were still to encounter more problems with motivation. The quick change of team managers during the 1990's had quite a severe effect on the motivation of the actual players. There became a lack of stability, which Abraham Maslow would have described as their 'safety needs' not being met; there was a certain lack of security about the players' jobs. The club was relegated to Division One at the end of the 1995/96 season and motivation became problematic. The supporters of the club also began to get uneasy and restless and were soon demanding that changes to the management should be made.

The relegation of the club had left morale so low, that by Christmas 1996, the club was fighting further relegation to Division Two. However, after so many managers had tried and failed, Frank Clark arrived and began to change the situation. He brought about a renewed motivation within the player group, which resulted in better performances on the pitch, in fact, during the first three months of play under Frank Clark, Manchester City did not lose a single league game.

(Page 7)

In a statement made by Clark in the official Match Magazine on 5th March 1997, he said, '*I have been delighted with the attitude of my players over the past few weeks and rightly, they have been receiving the rewards for their efforts... it is pleasing that we are now making things happen*' (p.3).

Clark showed a regard for the players that no other team manager had previously shown and as a result, gained the respect of not just the Manchester City staff and players, but of the thousands of loyal supporters as well. If the team did not play to their full potential, or had a bad match, Clark would still remain optimistic and supportive of his team's ability. In the official Match Magazine of Saturday 22nd February 1997, Clark talked of his team's defeat by Middlesbrough which resulted in Manchester City being knocked out of the FA Cup. However, despite the disappointment all round, Clark went on to say that, '*the players were told ... not to be disheartened and my staff have noticed a mood of real determination in training this week*'. (p.3). Clark had achieved Maslow's 'esteem needs' in his players, by giving them recognition for a job well done (even though they lost) and giving them the confidence to go into the next match, believing that they could win. In fact, Clark's motivation of the players was so positive that they went on to win their next match by three goals to nil!

As one can see from the above snapshots, the case study material related to Manchester City Football Club is extremely interesting. After such a long period of poor management, the club now had both an effective Chairman and Team Manager and the club's fortunes certainly began to improve. The role of motivation has been very important in Lee and Clark's aims and both members of staff, players and supporters would agree that it certainly began to pay off after their appointments. However, only the long term will tell whether these patterns will be sustained – clearly beyond the scope of this essay.

(Page 8)

4.0 CONCLUSION

Having now examined the various theories of motivation and fleshed this out with some case study material relating to the management of Manchester City Football Club in the 1990's, it is time to look at both the pros and cons of the theories in relation to the club's management.

Abraham Maslow's theory of motivation, the 'hierarchy of needs', was found to be a particularly useful theory. It had a clear layout and was extremely easy to comprehend. Each level of the hierarchy has been given its own name and just by glancing at these, one can deduce what emotions may be felt by participants if needs are not achieved. For example, if the safety needs are not achieved, then the subject would perhaps feel unsure of the stability of their job, which would lead to anxiety and so on.

Maslow's theory is relatively easy to put into action, once the individuals needs have been established and Francis Lee and Frank Clark seem to have adopted such strategy, no doubt, implicitly rather than explicitly. Some of the needs suggested in the theory are now beginning to be met with regards to the players, which in turn, has lead to better performances during football matches and a lift in the once tense and strained atmosphere at the club.

However, Torkildsen (1992) sounds a note of caution in the following terms:

> *"In a leisure context, many writers see Maslow's self-actualisation as the goal for the leisure delivery service ... But what becomes of these ideals in the practical world of budgets, cut-backs, redundancies ... In the harsh world of recession, the cry from industry is far greater output at less cost"*, (p.263).

(Page 9)

In the light of these increasingly prevalent conditions in the football industry, Maslow, Herzberg and McGregor's theories may have limited application in an organisation which is resource depleted and which, due to the overall league structure of promotion and relegation, is continuously having its goals set by outside influences. Dramatic and sudden management changes are brought about by relegation and failure in that soccer PLCs, as leisure organisations, continue to compete and struggle to survive in an increasingly differentiated environment; differentiated in terms of fans' expectations and the resources made available to meet them, by management.

5.0 REFERENCES

1. Angelsey, S. (1997) CITY: the official magazine of Manchester City FC, Greater Manchester Publications. Manchester.

2. Atkinson, R.L., Atkinson, R.C., Smith, E.E., Bem, D.J., Hilgard, E.R. (1990) Introduction to Psychology, tenth edition. London. Harcourt Brace Jovanovich.

3. Floyd, D. (1994) A-Level Business Studies, West Midlands. WM Print Ltd.

4. Murray, C. (1996) Attitude Blue; Crowd Psychology at Manchester City FC, Manchester. MUS Publications.

5. Torkildsen, G. (1992) Leisure and Recreation Management, London, E & F.N. Spon.

5.1 Further reading

1.   Vroom, V.H. (1964), Work and Motivation.

(Page 10)